A PASSION TO LIBERATE

A PASSION TO LIBERATE: LA GUMA'S SOUTH AFRICA — IMAGES OF DISTRICT SIX

FRITZ H. POINTER

Africa World Press, Inc.

P.O. Box 1892
Trenton, NJ 08607

P.O. Box 48
Asmara, ERITREA

Africa World Press, Inc.

P.O. Box 1892
Trenton, NJ 08607

P.O. Box 48
Asmara, ERITREA

Copyright © 2001 Fritz Pointer

First Printing 2001

Book Design: Wanjiku Ngugi
Cover Design: Debbie Hird

Library of Congress Cataloging-in-Publication Data

A Passion to liberate : La Guma's South Africa-images of District Six / Frit Pointer.
    p. cm.
  Includes bibliographical references and index.
  ISBN 0-86543-817-X -- ISBN 0-86543-818-8 (pbk.)
   1. La Guma, Alex--Knowledge--South Africa. 2. Literature and society South Africa--Cape Town--History--20th century. 3. District Six (Cape Town, South Africa)--Social life and customs. 4. District Six (Cape Town, South Africa)--In Literature. 5. Cape Town (South Africa)--Social life and customs. 6. Cape Town (South Africa)--In literature. 7. South Africa--In literature. I. Title.

PR9369.3.L3 Z84 2000
823--dc21

99-05948

Dedicated to my parents Elton Pointer (1901-1979)
Sarah Silas Pointer and to my partner for life Liziwe
Kunene Pointer

CONTENTS

Acknowledgements ix

Introduction
Alex La Guma: The Apprentice and the Press xi

Chapter 1
A Walk in the Night: Image and Idea 1

Chapter 2
And a Threefold Cord: Image and Idea 45

Chapter 3
The Stone Country: Image and Idea 123

Chapter 4
In the Fog of the Seasons' End: Image and Idea 177

Chapter 5
Time of the Butcherbird: Image and Idea 225

Bibliography 275

Index 291

ACKNOWLEDGEMENTS

First and foremost I wish to express my special thanks to Contra Costa College for supporting my completion of this project, and to my colleagues for their confidence and faith in my promises. I must also express my appreciation to the curators at the Cape Town District Six Museum for the warm hospitality and help my family and I received during our 1996 visit. I am especially grateful for the museum's possession and preservation of oral and photographic history and extant texts on District Six and Alex La Guma. Next, I would like to acknowledge the love and support given by my family: especially my wife, Liziwe, and our children and granddaughter: Shegun, Nandi, Somori, Thiyane and Jadah; my brother, Aaron, and sisters, Ruth, Anita, Bonnie and June, without whose love this work would not have meaning.

I am profoundly grateful to Professor Daniel Kunene of the University of Wisconsin, who planted the seed and encouraged me to do this book. Throughout our protracted afternoon and evening discussions in Madison, in Iowa, in California, and in South Africa, his insightful and invaluable guidance and direction, nurtured this book into fruition. Thanks also go to the editors at Africa World Press for their meticulous and critical reading of the manuscript. Finally, I must thank the La Guma family, in particular Alexander "Alex" La Guma the primary, seminal, resource for the material in this book; and, of course, the ordinary people of South Africa who continue to fortify me with their images of heroism, struggle and resistance to the awful myth of white supremacy.

ALEX LA GUMA:
THE APPRENTICE AND
THE PRESS

*There are years that ask questions and years that
answer.*
—Zora Neale Hurston, *Their Eyes Were Watching God*

Alex La Guma was born 20 February 1925, in Cape Town, South
Africa to James and Wilhelmina (Alexander) La Guma of No.2
Roger Street, District Six. District Six was the Harlem, the South
Side Chicago, the West Oakland of Cape Town. In 1966, in keeping with the illogic of white supremacy in general and the Group
Areas Act in particular, District Six was declared a White group
area. What followed, in the late 1970s, was the destruction of homes
and businesses in which generations of families had lived and
worked. The intent was to erase District Six from the map and
memory of Cape Town if not the world. It is here, on the streets of
District Six, that La Guma learned the language and mannerisms
of the people who became the subject of his journalistic and creative writing. He attended Upper Ashley Primary School and
Trafalgar High School (Abrahams 1991:17). In "The Real Picture," an interview with Cecil Abrahams, La Guma says: "I went
to school up on the hill above Cape Town. Most of my friends
came from among my schoolmates. They all lived in the area of
66th and Upper Constitution Street " (16). Alex and Blanche
Herman were at high school together but showed mutual disinter-

est. A bit later they found themselves in "the same social clubs" (7). Not satisfied with coincidence, Alex arranged for tea, one Sunday, at his home; Blanche reports: "Half an hour after being with him, he proposed marriage, and I accepted" (8). On 13 November 1954, at the age of twenty-nine, Alex married Blanche Valerie Herman, a nurse and midwife, and they have two sons, Eugene born in February 1956 and Bartholomew, "Barto," born in April 1959 (9-10).

Alex's father, James La Guma, was a man of intelligence and power, who influenced his son's life by word and deed. The elder La Guma was a former president of the South African Peoples' Congress and a leading member of the Communist Party of South Africa. Alex himself also joined these organizations as soon as he was old enough to do so: in 1947 the Young Communist League, and the next year he became a member of District 20 of the Communist Party (Odendaal and Field 1993:viii).

James La Guma was a militant fighter for democracy in South Africa, a man of sharp intellect and immense integrity, who remained also a simple, honest, and hard-working family man. Born in Bloemfontein in 1894, Mr. La Guma served his apprenticeship as a leather worker in Cape Town. At the age of eighteen, he went to Namibia as a labor recruit and later organized a branch of the Industrial and Commercial Workers' Union (ICU) in the territory, and led a strike of diamond field workers in Pomona. Subsequently, Jimmy La Guma became administrative secretary at the ICU head office in Cape Town.

In 1924, one year before the birth of Alex, James La Guma joined the Communist Party of South Africa. And in 1927, he was a delegate to the international conference of the League Against Imperialism in the Palais D'Egmont, Brussels. That same year, he went on a lecture tour of Europe and attended the tenth anniversary celebrations of the Soviet Union in Moscow. In 1932, he helped organize the garment workers of The Cape, and served a term of imprisonment as a result of a strike by these workers. This is probably the time about which Alex wrote:

> I remember when I was seven years old, when my father
> was arrested and he was in jail for ten days for leading a
> strike or being involved in a strike. My mother took me up

to the prison to meet him when he came out. By then my
father had grown a beard during his time in prison and I
was wondering who this man was. Only when he shaved
himself did I see it was my father. (Abrahams 1991:16)

In addition, James La Guma was a founding member of The Non-
European United Front in the thirties, and of the National Liberation League in 1936, which led the massive demonstration of
coloured people against the Stuttaford Segregation Bill in 1939.
When the Communist Party was dissolved in 1950, he was a member of its Central Committee ("Jimmy La Guma" [Editorial], *New
Age*,3 August 1961:2).

James(or, as he was commonly known, Jimmy) La Guma died
29 July 1961, passing on to his able son, Alex, an example of courageous struggle for a democratic South Africa. Throughout his
long political career, he was fired with an indomitable passion to
liberate the exploited, White dominated African majority of South
Africa. Alex, happily concedes to the influence of this father on
his formative years:

My father had a great deal to do with moulding my philosophical and political outlook and guiding me towards the
reading of serious works, both political and literary. He
himself was an avid reader, and I suppose this had something to do with my development one way or the other... I
loved reading books. Since early childhood I was always
looking for books. I read first the books that children loved:
Robert Louis Stevenson, Dumas, Victor Hugo, and so on.
Then I read adventure stories, westerns, detective stories,
and gradually began to turn towards the more serious clas-
sics such as Shakespeare, the Russian authors, Tolstoy,
Gorky, and then the American writers, James T. Farrell,
Steinbeck and Hemingway. Whenever I could lay my hands
on a book I took the opportunity. In fact, I used to use my
meagre pocket money to buy books at secondhand book-
stores and sometimes I had saved enough to enjoy the luxury
of buying a book at an expensive bookstore. (Odendaal
and Field 1993:vii)

At the time of this father's death, Alex was in his sixth year as a staff journalist for the Cape Town weekly newspaper *New Age*. His column "Up My Alley" was a regular feature of the paper from 2 May 1957 to 28 June 1962, on which date *New Age* carried the following message:

> As Alex La Guma is banned from attending gatherings, we regret that, in terms of the General Laws Amendment Act, we are no longer permitted to publish any of his writing. ("Prohibited." [Editorial] *New Age*, 28 June 1962:2)

From 1962 to 1966, he was under house arrest and his writings banned, and in 1966 went into exile to Havana Cuba. He never made it back home and was 60 years old when he died of a heart attack in Havana on 11 October 1985. And "as a sign of respect for the man and the movement he represented, La Guma was buried in the family acre of the parents of Jose' Marti, popularly known as the founder of the Cuban nation" (Odendaal and Field 1993: ii-iii).

To Alex, like other South African writers—Hilda Bernstein, Alfred Hutchinson, Ezekiel Mphahlele, Duma Nokwe, Alan Paton, Reg September, Walter Sisulu—the weekly, New Age, was one of the mouthpieces of the intellectual resistance movement against white domination, so-called white supremacy (apartheid). In Mind Your Colour The"Coloured" Stereotype in South African Literature, Vernon February (1981) remarks:

> La Guma is a living testimony of the novelist turned warrior, freedom fighter (154).

La Guma is clearly aware of the historical importance and power of the press in its ability to shape the ideas and opinions of a nation, and its particular vitalness in the cause of South African resistance and liberation. He states, for example, that the significance to literature of the 1913 Land Act was not only that it deprived the African people of the right of ownership of land—restricting the African population, which outnumbers whites four to one, to only 13% of the land area of South Africa—but that, Hitherto the African intelligentsia and others had been able to pawn their lands and buy printing presses and locate them on their land.

Thus, J.L. Dube...first president of the African National Congress was able to establish "Ilanga Lase Natal Press". (Alex La Guma "Writing Under Apartheid" *Afro-Asian Writings*, 23 (1975):14)

Also, in The Cape and Natal a group of intellectuals established an African press. Through these media they were able to actuate and circulate African opinions and expose the most brutal forms of oppression perpetuated by the regime. Resistance was kept alive "through literature produced from African-owned printing presses" (*Afro-Asian Writings* 14).

La Guma, too, used his years as a journalist (1955-62) developing his craft and style as a future writer of short slice-of-life stories, polemical essays and novels; never fearing to use his writings as a political weapon, to inspire resistance to oppression. He holds the view that:

> The dynamic of the South African people will always be represented...by the writings of those who do not fear to reflect real struggle, that is the struggle to overthrow white supremacy, not merely nibble at the fingers, lagging behind the inevitable advance. (La Guma "Culture and Liberation" *Sechaba* 10, 4 [1976]:57)

Such comments, gleaned from La Guma's later work, express in various ways that even as an apprentice-journalist he used his writing talent to clarify the experiences of South Africa's majority and to suggest the inevitable direction their struggle must take and the goals it must achieve. He was aware from the beginning—by the specific example of his father, and countless others—of the danger of his position. His articles and short stories for *New Age*, like his later essays and fiction, are full of contempt for colonialism in all its forms, also for social injustice, poverty, human degradation and racial arrogance. Above all his writings are full of the driving spirit of humanity.

Being a reporter-columnist who does not "fear to reflect real struggle" is in South Africa, a country Mr. Albert Luthuli described as "a museum piece in our time, a hangover from the dark past of mankind, a relic of an age which everywhere else is dead or dying"—a very dangerous assignment. On 10 May 1958, shots were fired at Alex La Guma while he was working in his study at his residence in Athlone. When Mr. La Guma reported this attempted murder at the Athlone police station—where, at the time, he was also reporting every Thursday according to his treason bail conditions—the sergeant at the desk said, "Looks like somebody doesn't like you. Just like Johannesburg, eh?" (*New Age,* 15 May 1958). Later that same month, Mr. Reg September, General Secretary of the South African Coloured Peoples Organization wrote in the New Age:

> If these incidents are attempts to intimidate our members and frighten SACPO out of political activity then I am afraid that the people responsible are wasting their time...SACPO will not be deterred from their task of organizing the Coloured people for the struggle for liberation...
>
> No amount of threats and gangster tactics will prevent us from doing our duty to the Coloured people. The attempts to shoot Mr. La Guma and threaten Mr. Naude are the methods of criminals and will not earn the respect of decent people. (*New Age* 22 May 1958)

La Guma replied that he would not be intimidated either from his work on *New Age* or in SACPO and that, "As far as I'm concerned it's business as usual" (*New Age* 22 May 1958). It is this kind of fearless commitment to the cause of freedom for the majority of South Africans that characterized his writing and activism from his first days as a journalist to his present international reputation as an essayist, short-story writer, and novelist. His commitment could hardly be otherwise. If writers in Africa or elsewhere in the world do not accept the need for social commitment in their writings and daily actions, for the South African writer it is imperative. The imposition of this responsibility by the brutally oppressive South African environment is their specific and unique literary reality. It is, in fact, the only reality in which La Guma grew up (Asien 1974:17). For the people of South Africa, *New Age* was an important vehicle for building organizations and voicing their protests. It is clear by this attempt to assassinate Alex La Guma that freedom of speech is violently opposed, at this time, in South Africa.

One may ask what commitment and liberation have to do with culture, art, literature? Those who usually ask this question wish to separate politics from art or culture. Alex La Guma provides this answer:

> It is perhaps possible, within the environment of developed societies, to create with a certain amount of confidence the impression that art, culture, the level of civilization of a people, have nothing or little to do with socio-economic and political forces within these societies; that culture has nothing to do with politics. In South Africa this is not possible. The proposition of art for the sake of art finds no foothold in the atmosphere of racism, violence and crude exploitation which is the day-to-day experience of the South African people. (La Guma "The Condition of Culture in South Africa" *Presence Africaine* 80 (1971):8)

The condition of culture, in all its manifestations—including journalism—in South Africa precludes the luxury of such a separation. A committed writer, like La Guma, can never divorce him or herself from the life of the people. And the press, as another form of literature can "be important in assisting to determine the specific goals of advancing people" (La Guma "Address by Lotus Award Winner" *Afro-Asian Writings* 10 (1971):196). This conviction, variously expressed, underlies many of La Guma's pronouncements. His allegiance to resistance and revolution, like his hatred for apartheid and racial arrogance, was full-formed, steady, and implacable at the very start of his career.

New Age was, at this time, a spirited, courageous weekly crammed with news of politics, legal actions, anonymous (for good reason) lengthy editorials, analyses of domestic (South African) and international affairs, banishments, forced removals, and many other things in addition to the short stories and essays of the editors. The headlines of 28 October 1954 proclaimed boldly: "Nats Are Sweeping Aside All Freedoms," a reference to the banning of Advance, under the usual pretext of "suppressing Communism," and *New Age* was a clever and effective answer to this attempt by the government (NA 28 October 1954). And a *New Age* "Study Document," 14 April 1955, "The American Grip on South Africa," was a detailed analysis of United States economic penetration in the Union of South Africa by the giants of American finance capital, the Morgan Guaranty, Rockefeller, Du Pont, General Motors, Kennecott, and other multi-national corporations (NA 14 April 1955). Such evidence of international capital's involvement in South Africa La Guma skillfully turns into subtle symbols and images, as in his second novel, *And a Threefold Cord*, when through the mind's-eye view and interior monologue of the protagonist, Charlie Pauls, we see that:

> The shack across the yard was a big motor-car crate...there had not been enough (paint) to cover the whole cabin, so part of the word Detroit emerged where the paint ended. (La Guma 1964:43)

In this and similar ways, we see La Guma using in his "fiction" what the *New Age* is reporting as "fact." A brief perusal of the article written concurrent with La Guma's apprentice years with this newspaper reveals how much the news and topics of that time influenced his later writings and themes. For example, a 16 February 1956 article, "Peoples' Homes Pulled Down," reports the recent demolition of peoples' homes in Kraaifontein, as "one of the most cruel, callous and inhuman deeds ever performed by a local authority" (NA 16 February 1956). This event, the forcible removal and resettlement of whole communities as a necessary part of the oppressive South African system, foreshadows the central theme of La Guma's latest novel, *Time of the Butcherbird* (1979), which is "the inside story, the humanization of the bald facts of perhaps the greatest atrocity of apartheid" (Whitman 1979:111). This book is a microcosmic view of the South African conflict, with the issue of forced removals at its thematic center.

New Age, therefore, was an exhilarating paper to readers who were young, politically minded, and inclined to things artistic. It was informative, analytical and entertaining, and it had found an eager audience. The white nationalist government viewed it with alarm and sometimes-even horror.

Such consternation is clear from the "Suppression of Communism Act" of 1950 and certain promulgation related to the press and how it must function under the strictures of the South African apartheid system. Under this particular law, the government can stop a journalist from writing, banish him (as happened to Alex La Guma in June 1962) and suspend the paper if anything published by him seems to be "revolutionary" or even merely calculated to propagate Communist ideology. In a related essay by La Guma, "South African Writing Under Apartheid" (1975), he comments that:

> Under most banning orders imposed in South Africa to-day—and there are hundreds and hundreds of them—to have even a page of manuscript or a sheet of paper in a type-writer can constitute a criminal offence, punishable by a minimum of one year and up to ten years imprisonment—or even the death penalty if the subject can be construed as encouragement to "sabotage" or "terrorism". Little wonder that in these circum-stances the creative spirit is often crushed.(20)

And South Africa does, in fact, have "hundreds and hundreds" of such banning orders. The Public Safety Act of 1953 allows the South African government to declare a "State of Emergency" in regions where racial riots break out. The press may be censored and papers may even be suspended. Then there is the Riotous Assemblies Act, which makes it possible to prevent papers from reporting racial riots without prior permission from the police. This act also allows the magistrate to prohibit a specific individual from attending a gathering if the magistrate feels that the presence of said individual would engender feelings of hostility between whites and other races; prohibits the dissemination, in any form, of state-ments made by an individual who is prohibited under this Act from attending a public gathering, etc. (*U.S. Congress, Report of Special Study Missions to Africa*, 1972:156). Any ordinary, reason-able, and prudent person realizes that the press is not above the law; but if the laws are too severe (which clearly they are in South Africa) freedom of criticism is impossible. These laws are so drafted that they make a mockery of any discussion of freedom of information or of expression.

The total number of banned publications was estimated in 1971 at 13,000 (*U.S. Congress, Report of Special Study Missions to Africa*, 1972:156). Among them are, of course, hundreds of publications which uphold racial equality, many of them written in the United States or Western Europe. Among the banned authors are Lewis Nkosi, Bloke Modisane, Mazisi Kunene, Daniel Kunene, Dennis Brutus, Ezekiel Mphahlele, Ngugi Wa Thiongo, Kenneth Kaunda, Frantz Fanon, Francoise Sagan, Berthold Brecht, Richard Wright, James Baldwin, Amiri Baraka, Joseph Heller and, of course, Alex La Guma. The list could continue, almost interminably. Specifically concerning banned, predominantly exiled, South African writers, La Guma has written:

> It is a list revealing a talent of which any country would be proud. And, truth be told, the people of South Africa are truly proud of them. But the unrepresentative South African Government, which speaks in the name only of the racist minority, is terrified to let their voice be heard. (La Guma, "South African Writing," 20)

As a result, the works of Alex La Guma and the other banned writers and publications may not be circulated in South Africa, and it is an offense for any journal to publish anything they write or say.

It should also be noted that in South Africa there are no black newspapers as we know them here in the United States; there are black papers, but they are white-owned and subject to white decisions as to editorial policy. The weekly, *New Age*—controlled by liberal left-wing Whites and Coloureds—was an audacious, valiant attempt to fill this void. Newspapers which are directed towards the African market are all written in English; so are most of the books produced by African writers. In fact, "the political and literary lingua franca of Black South Africa is English, which enables all Africans to communicate with one another across the ethnic borders, and also to address Whites in their own country and abroad (La Guma, "South African Writing," 18). For the Africans of South Africa, this has had the dubiously positive effect of overriding cultural differences and the promotion of Westernization. If *New Age* or any other newspaper directed at an African audience were owned by Africans, or perhaps Coloureds, they would probably be even more restricted in their activities by the government. Editors of such papers knew there was much they could report but they did not dare. "These papers were in a position to report the real views and problems of the nonwhite majority, but were not permitted to do so. And the white press, more and more, tended to look the other way" (Hachten 1971:254).

On 30 August 1956, Alex La Guma broke into print inauspiciously as a reporter supplying humorous satiric sketches and biting didactic political squibs for the *New Age*. His first published article, "A Pick and a Shovel" (30 August 1956, p. 3, cols. 2-5), was a mosaic in six pieces; each piece autonomous, possessed of its own power; each piece unique in form and image—like the surface of a cracked mirror that refused to shatter but preserved because of the truth each fragment could reflect.

In the first sketch, La Guma reaches back into the oral traditions of the Coloured people of South Africa and tells the story once told among the old people when he as a child. The story says that:

> One day, many years ago, God summoned White man and Coloured man and placed two boxes before them. One box was very big and the other very small. God then turned to Coloured man and told him to choose one of the boxes. Coloured man immediately chose the bigger and left the other to White man. When he opened his box, Coloured man found a pick and a shovel inside it; White man found gold in his box.

In this very brief sketch, La Guma establishes the historical and literary depths of the South African experience; the Coloured man has the "pick and shovel" and the White man the gold; and, as the tale seems to suggest, this is a result of simple or perhaps "natural" or "voluntary" selection. La Guma, therefore, in this satiric and ironic tale, establishes the folkloristic, superstitious and mythological explanations people have for their lot: explanations indicative of a common consciousness that oppression, suffering and hardships are facts of life. Yet, they have learned to temper hardship with humor, and to soften the blow of oppression with a shield of a satirical philosophy. But always they have been aware of the pain.

The remaining five sketches show a balance of sentimentality and realism. The second narrates the author's casual exposure to

A PASSION TO LIBERATE

an African church service as "The flock was gathered under the pale light of a single bulb," Christ, in his agony, looking down from a "white-washed wall." This second sketch ends with the fledgling Alex La Guma trying his wings, experimenting with style and technique he would one day use in his short stories and novels, as he describes the old preacher:

> ...an old man whose face had known pain and whose hands had grown hard with toil in the country. His collar was frayed and his shoulders stooped. His voice was warm as a mother's touch. His people listened and murmured their Amens when he had finished. They sang and the air was full of their happiness and their agony was lifted from them for that brief time.

At this stage (1956), his style can, perhaps, best be described as imagistic or photographic, in that he is very careful and meticulous in his selection and use of details. His attention to relevant detail creates an atmosphere and brings his characters to life. Still, it should be recognized that La Guma is not as polished and precise as he would become in later years. We do not know, in this second sketch, for example—given the minute observation that the preacher's "collar was frayed"—if he was referring to a coat, a sweater, or a shirt collar. The atmosphere of warmth evoked by the sketch would suggest the latter garment. The recognition of such "oversights," however, is not the criterion for any substantive literary analysis and is mentioned here only to highlight this grooming period of La Guma's career.

The third sketch, a mere 550 words, anticipates an image La Guma would return to in *A Walk in the Night*; that is, the sensuous image of Cape Town's District Six on Saturday night. Universally, it seems, if it were not for Saturday night, Sunday would not mean so much. Saturday night is dancenight. Dance halls are crowded by nine o'clock and the bands are rocking; ecstatic girls are giggling and gay; the boys are sharp in their black hats, red shirts, and green socks; arm and arm, dancing and laughter greet the hard rhythms of the drummer and the screaming shrill of the saxophonist and once again, for a brief time, the agony and pain of an oppressive system is lifted. Just outside the dance-hall doors

the grim, awesome reality of apartheid awaits the temporarily am-
nesic patrons. Here, La Guma observes, "In the slums the people
huddle, sleeping on staircases and in packed rooms. Everywhere
is the smell of stale cooking, sweat and stagnant water."

In a related passage from *A Walk in the Night*, many of the same
items of detail are evident, as those in the above sketch from *New
Age*, with two exceptions: he is using a bigger canvas—the novel—
so he uses more "paint," broader strokes, adding more complex,
accurate inventory of speech and detail: and, at the end of the scene,
he comments, providing the insight that the characters immersed
in the action cannot provide for themselves.

> Those who could not sleep sat by the windows or in the
> doorways and looked out towards the mountain beyond the
> rooftops and searched for the sign of wind. The breeze
> carried the stale smells from passageway to passageway,
> from room to room, along lanes and back alleys, through
> the realms of the poor, until massed smells of stagnant wa-
> ter, cooking, rotting vegetables, oil, fish, damp plaster and
> timber, unwashed curtains, bodies and stairways, cheap
> perfume and incense, spices and half-washed kitchenware,
> urine, animals and dusty corners became one vast, anony-
> mous odor, so widespread and all-embracing as to become
> unidentifiable, hardly noticeable by the initiated nostrils of
> the teeming, cramped world of poverty which it enveloped.
> (La Guma *A Walk in the Night*, 45-46)

The major significance of this third sketch for New Age, as far as
La Guma's personal goals and literary development are concerned,
lay in its greater thematic seriousness. The central, dominating
idea of both this sketch, and *A Walk in the Night* as this excerpt
reveals, is the sordid, wretched, slumlike conditions the Coloured
and African people of South Africa are forced to live under. And
he further twists the knife by commenting that "the initiated" no
longer can identify with and hardly even notice these conditions.

La Guma, willing and ready to see what is happening at the
very depths of South African society, can now offer images of resistance, and fashion bold alternatives by calculated stories and
inspired pictures of heroic action. He does not leave the man of
color in an inextricable malaise; but in the next two sketches he

lifts him to his own shoulders and raises him with a new story of hope. The story is that of a man who owned a plot of ground but had no money to buy building materials. So for a whole year he scavenged amongst the rubble of demolished blocks and in other odd places. He carried bricks and timber and sheet-iron to his site in small loads. He carted sand from the beach and scrounged cement and built a house. (La Guma, "A Pick and a Shovel") La Guma knows, and wants his audience to know, that there is only one solution: to rise above this absurd drama that the white racists have staged around people of color in South Africa. His is not an apocalyptic suggestion, but rather a view that change is inevitable and will come in stages, "in small loads." This short composition is an allegory, packed with the themes of individual commitment, perseverance, methodical progression, and ultimate success.

The fifth sketch gave him a chance to experiment with dialogue; and he took this opportunity to deliver a poignant, serious message (not simply mundane, superfluous, cute, or colorful banalities), while riding third-class carriage on a commuter train:

> I sat opposite a big tough-looking docker and talked to him. His face was streaked with coal-dust and dried sweat and he wore a loading hook in his belt. "The government?..." "What are we going to do about it?" He spat through the window. "Don't worry chummy. We'll give them a go one day. Same as Hitler got." (La Guma, "A Pick and a Shovel")

While an analysis of this fragment of dialogue will not fully answer questions about La Guma's overall achievement with this aspect of his craft—questions other parts of this study will deal with—there are, in this excerpt, implications of an evolving technique and thematic continuity. It reveals a concern for speakability, for example, and credibility, revealing context and character as well as conveying a serious message of Old Testament revenge, even in this early journalistic phase of his artistic development. Comparing the South African government with Hitler's Germany is certainly tenable and most appropriate: a comparison La Guma is wont to use again; for instance, in the collection of essays, Apartheid (1971) where he writes:

I have often been faced by incredulous people who expressed doubts about the shocking truth of racism in South Africa... No doubt people could have expressed similar incredulity about Nazi Germany when told that soap had been manufactured from the fat of victims of concentration camps. South Africa has not sent "inferior" peoples to gas ovens and therefore it is assumed that the concentration camp, the classical institution of fascism, does not exist in our country. Genocide is not necessarily a process of instant mass extermination. On 1 November 1969...*The Rand Daily Mail* stated "...of 22 children who died recently in the area's only general hospital, 13 were suffering from malnutrition. (11)

Once again, a mere sketch, a mere fragment of dialogue anticipates the more penetrating, protracted commentary by La Guma. In both instances, he reveals a willingness to look all the relevant facts of a situation in the face and tell what is—be it creative dialogue or factual narrative reporting.

In the sixth and final sketch, La Guma returns to the technique of the first sketch. And the effect, like that of a painter, brings a marvelous unity to his canvas. His audience is again, specifically, the five million Colored people of South Africa, a significant audience declared by census to be, at least, four million (80%) in the Cape Province alone. Then, from the specific, he immediately raises us to the universal, as he carefully catalogues the criteria of our common humanity, when he continues:

But if you identify a people, not by names and the color of their skin, but by hardship and joy, pleasure and suffering, cherished hopes and broken dreams, the grinding monotony of toil without gain, despair and starvation, illiteracy, tuberculosis and malnutrition, laughter and vice, ignorance, genius, superstition, ageless wisdom and undying confidence, love and hatred, then you will have to give up counting. People are like identical books with only different dust-jackets. The title and the text are the same. And since man is only human, he must rise in the morning, throw off the blanket of night and look at the sun. ("A Pick and a Shovel")

Throughout his essays and fiction, La Guma is, in various ways, affirming the basic humanity of the Colored—as distinct from, but certainly not opposed to African—people. The distinction, however, is important. Anyone who is even moderately acquainted with the history of Dutch and English imperialism in Southern Africa over the past three hundred years, would know that, as a result, there are as many as five million "Coloureds" or "Mulattos" in South Africa. Some want desperately to become "White"; some don't necessarily want to become white, but want desperately to avoid "slipping back"genetically, culturally, socially (Fanon 1967: 54); and then there are the others, like Alex La Guma, who are wholly African in spirit and pride. In South Africa, however, because of institutionalized racism, the Coloureds (because of their Dutch blood) are given special privileges: a higher genetic status, a higher social and economic status than the Africans, and a completely separate society. Education and civil rights denied the Africans are theirs; the best available jobs that whites don't want are theirs. And, above all, given the genetic or ethnic hierarchy of color explicit in racist ideology (e.g., Apartheid), the magic of lighter hue gives immediate and unquestioned genetic, cultural and social superiority over Blacks (Williams 1976:357).

This is very similar to the "three-tiered social system" that evolved in America's lower South of the early 1700s "with mulattos serving as a buffer class between Whites and Blacks"(Russell et al. 1992:15). Even the post-apartheid South Africa my family and I visited over Christmas 1996 and New Year 1997 shows clear evidence and residue of this antiquated and primitive compartmentalization of human beings.

Just as Russell et al.'s research reported of eighteenth century American behavior: "Necessary business transactions between the races could be conducted through mulattos, whose presence reduced racial tensions, especially in areas where Negroes outnumbered Whites" (Russell et al. 1992:15), is true of South Africa today, November 1997. This should by no means imply that American's thinking on this matter has advanced demonstrably over the past two hundred years or so. "Virtually every major urban center across the country has a section where predominantly light-skinned Blacks reside. In Philadelphia, mulattos live in areas unofficially called 'lighty brighty' and 'banana block'" (25). We still think that dark-skinned Black men are more criminally dangerous and libidinous and that light-skinned Black women are more feminine and beautiful (166).

La Guma too wrestles with this universal color problem, this color hierarchy, this problem of the twentieth century, in no fewer than three of his short stories. The first, "A Glass of Wine," is concerned with the courtship of a young Cloured girl by a White boy. The point of this story is to demonstrate, in human terms, the content and ridiculousness of the Immorality Act. This 1927 Act prohibits mixed marriages and casual sexual intercourse among the races of South Africa. The second story, "Out of Darkness," concerns the love of a dark-skinned Coloured school teacher for a "near-white" girl, Cora, that ends in murder when Cora decides to cross the color-line (she either wants to be white, or at least does not want to "slip back"). Then there is "Slipper Satin," another case of a Coloured girl arrested under the Immorality Act for dating a white boy. Her mother, however, wants her to give up the relationship and admonishes her, "What's the matter with your own kind of people?"

In an interview with Robert Serumaga, recorded in London in October 1966, La Guma defends his literary concern with the South African Coloured community when he states:

> I don't think a great deal has been said about the Coloured community or about the Indian community and I think that even within a framework of racial separateness there is a task which writers have to perform. That is at least letting the world know what is happening—even within their compartments. (Pieterse and Duerden 1972:90-93)

If the five novels, *A Walk in the Night, And a Threefold Cord, The Stone Country, In the Fog of the Seasons' End,* and *Time of the Butcherbird* are read in sequence, their political meaning becomes quite clear, and their characters are shown to be drawn largely from a single milieu, the Coloured working class and underworld of Cape Town. This Coloured working class, initially, has little consciousness of how its energies are turned inward on itself by aimless, anarchic criminal revolt of individuals without allies or ideology, as well as the fraternal revolt of men and women who understand

and combat oppression from a posture of socio-political awareness and purposeful, premeditated activism.

Africans, Coloureds, and Whites, like America's three-tiered
social system, are the three main population categories, according
to the Population Registration Act of 1950: and the government
assumes power to proclaim sub-categories within the African and
Coloured categories. By law, therefore, the racial identity of every
person is entered in a population register, and every South African
citizen must possess an identity card stating his racial classification. The effect of these racial classifications is that communication between the various groups becomes extremely difficult. By
law, then, Coloureds are a distinct ethnic group, and under the terms
of the Group Areas Act no person of color can live in an area set
aside for people with no color. This act has meant the displcement
of thousands of Coloured families, forced removals such as from
District Six in Cape Town and form Simonstown. It has also meant
the transfer of control of education for Coloureds to the Minister
of Coloured Affairs. Such rigid separation must inevitably lead to
the Coloureds' consciousness of themselves as a distinct, if not
unique people. There is, for example, the South African Coloured
Peoples Organization (SACPO); the Coloured Labour Party and
the Coloured Development Corporation, all, in various ways, indicative of a growing self-consciousness and political consciousness and nationalism of Coloured people. In other words, one detects the attempt by the white Nationalist Government to define a
policy for the Coloureds with respect to their place in the concept
of "separate development." The National Association for the Advancement of Colored People (NAACP) occupies a similar socio-
political even perhaps-ideological position on the American landscape as, for example, the South African Coloured Peoples Organization occupies in South Africa.

Therefore, one obvious responsibility of a Coloured writer like
La Guma, is to clarify the ethos of a definitive, self-aware, Coloured
population. As Alex La Guma's father, James La Guma, stated in
a *New Age* article (25 July 1957), "the Coloured people are not and
do not in any way feel themselves to be 'step-children' of South
Africa." Rather, they are a people determined to give and see some
account of themselves in what they write and read. One aspect of
this account recognizes that Coloureds in South Africa are ranked,

by law, as a separate ethnic group, below the Afrikaners and English in social and economic status, but far above the Africans. This is reminiscent of the "Free Colored" people of Charleston, South Carolina during the 1840s:

> They were an intermediate class in all the slave states, standing between the whites and the bondmen, known as the free colored; debarred from enjoying the privileges of the one, but superior in condition to the other, more, however, by suffering than by actual law. (Russell et al. 1992:16)

In *The Stone Country*, La Guma describes how, even in prison, the Coloured prisoners are given privileges and opportunities denied the Africans, and by so doing, clearly demonstrates his awareness that when the white man gives them preferential status above the blacks, but always below himself, he does so to maintain the myth of superior "white blood." It may be for this and similar reasons that La Guma concentrates on the fundamental, unconcealed humanity of the Coloured people of South Africa.

> Herded into slums, shivering in shanties, scattered along the hillsides, rocking in buses to housing schemes, living comfortably in bright homes....They toil in thousands in big modern factories and push vegetable barrows, dig up roads, and teach in schools, grow flowers and run shops. They steal and sometimes murder, they beg or carry loads from the markets. They drink, curse, make love and beat their wives or cheat their husbands. Heroes and cowards, villains and gentlemen, saints and sinners, people. ("Pick and Shovel")

Why is such a catalogue, such a thorough list necessary? The obvious and unavoidable answer is that it is because, in the context of racism (apartheid), the Coloureds , like the Africans, are not people. Rather, they are viewed as aberrations or the "missing link" between monkey and man—meaning, of course, white man and woman. And, perhaps, a majority of white South Africans feel an almost physical revulsion against anything that puts an African or Coloured on "their level." La Guma, therefore, in this tedious way reminds us that each and every one of our acts—African, Coloured or European—from the most mundane to the most heroic, reveals us and defines us as human beings (Fanon 1967:89).

We have come full circle; the Coloured is not a man, he is a Coloured man (Fanon 1967: 114) and it is from the particularity, the specificity, and commonality of this historically determined reality that La Guma makes his bid for the Pan-African and the Universal. It is also the particularity of his Coloured context and experience that necessitates critique of his images of African people, generally, and African women in particular. La Guma, in his first sketches for *New Age* and in his later fiction, had to come to terms with this identity as an inherent, irreversible aspect of the South African and Pan-African reality.

It is not surprising or accidental that in the three short stories— "A Glass of Wine," "Out of Darkness," and "Slipper Satin"— the complex social and political problems which are studied, appear against a background of suppressed or tragically resolved interracial love—"illegal" love, "immoral" love. Africans, Coloureds and Europeans: each is victimized by the problem of the twentieth century (DuBois); each is faced with the choice of perpetuating it or of working toward its resolution. La Guma's novels widen his focus in an effort to establish the complex relationship between race as well as color consciousness and class, and the total social, economic, and political situation of the entire South African people.

Alex La Guma's output with *New Age* was immense. For a family man also active in political organizations, the six years he spent with this newspaper was an extraordinary achievement. During his career with New Age, he developed a style notable for its meticulous, photographic attention to detail that proved to be a useful and distinctive characteristic of his style as a novelist. Among the New Age material is "Little Libby" a cartoon character created by La Guma. According to Andre Odendaal and Roger Field's recent (1993) book, *Liberation Chabalala:The World of Alex La Guma*:

> "Liberation Chabalala" provides unique cameos of South African life and politics during a turbulent time in the country's history —the late 1950s and early 1960s, the years just before and after   Sharpeville. (iv)

La Guma's writings are indeed "District Six talking. It is unmistakable—terse, racy, humorous, as convincing as truth," as Odendaal and Field go on to say:

> "Liberation Chabalala" gives us an insight into the making of a novelist, revealing the 'hidden' world of Alex La Guma —material, social, emotional, political and intellectual— at a time when he was developing into a serious writer. Many of the themes in his fiction are first encountered and developed in these early newspaper articles.... (iv)

Thanks to the seminal work of Odendaal and Field, time has brought luster to La Guma's journalistic career, as these early sketches reveal major themes that he would use many times; these sketches also help define the ethical and political values that would reassert themselves in his later work; themes he would expound even more "violently" in his political journalism and fiction after the Treason Trials and Sharpeville.

On 2 May 1957, Alex La Guma's column "Up My Alley" appeared for the first time, and continued weekly, religiously, for the next five years. Prior to this regular column and concomitant with it, readers would find articles by La Guma like: "What Goes on in Roeland Street Jail" (27 September 1956); a lengthy article and gripping story told to La Guma by a prisoner. This article anticipates one of the most important themes in La Guma's writings; a theme to which his novel *The Stone Country* is specifically dedicated, namely the emotional, psychological, human consequences to the daily average of 70,351 prisoners in South African jails in 1964; a theme that is also the center of the short stories "Tattoo Marks and Nails," "Out of Darkness," and "Blankets"; a theme that reveals, in all of its dehumanized reality, a range of convicts from simple permit offenders and loiterers to rapists and murderers.

In the follow-up article of 4 October 1956, "Law of the Jungle Rules in Jail," La Guma reveals some of the specific cruel and unusual aspects of South African prison life, in such a way that we too are made to experience the food, "crawling with cockroaches...thousands of them, rustling, and clicking over the food, gorging themselves"; and the "vermin infested blankets, unwashed for years, in fact never to be washed"; prisoners savagely beaten who do not follow orders; work-gangs forced to work on European farms; cells packed tight with forty or fifty convicts; and the Sundays when "ministers of various denominations arrive to preach the ways of righteousness and repentance." And afterwards, those convicts who leave are "broken in health, cowed by brutality, or hardened with bitterness." Here, then, is another example of the material that would provide the inspiration for much of La Guma's realistic fiction. The quotation, by Eugene Debs, at the beginning of *The Stone Country*, underscores his deep concern with this theme:

> While there is a lower class, I am in it.
> While there is a criminal element, I am of it.
> While there is a soul in jail, I am not free.
> (*The Stone Country*, 9)

La Guma's comments on a long list of South African issues exemplify the same sturdy commitment of his later novels. There are then, in these embryonic years with *New Age*, articles which planted the seed in his consciousness for later, protracted literary treatment; and imagistic blurps containing explicit pictures he could and would enlarge for more detailed and careful study: articles that focused, invariably, on the plight of the common people of South Africa—as opposed to the famous, the elite, the intelligentsia—a voluntary, chosen focus. For example, "A Day in Court" (1 November 1956) deals with the inequities of the South African judicial as experienced by ordinary people; and "Don't Sneeze, the Wall May Fall Down" (8 November 1956), addresses the issue of the Cape Town City Council building cheap and inferior housing and letting them at unreasonably high rents. These "houses," the article informs us, were being built at the rate of twenty per week: "they have three-inch walls, unplastered, cement floors and except for the bathroom, have no door inside. The bathrooms have no baths or showers, and all electric light switches are placed together in one part of the house" (*New Age* 8 November 1956). This particular interest of La Guma foreshadows its more extensive treatment in *And A Threefold Cord*. A variation of the theme of housing, for people of color in South Africa; at the heart of this book is the collective life of shanty-dwellers and their struggle to build houses and a sense of community out of the junk and litter that makes up their physical environment: where the building materials for their homes include: rusty corrugated iron, random planks of wood, pieces of cardboard, flattened fuel cans, rags for stuffing cracks and holes, strips of bailing wire, sides of packing-cases and a pair of railway sleepers(La Guma, *Threefold Cord*, 9). The journalistic account conveys bare documentary information, not elevated by means of art to a created exciting force and emotional effect. Whereas the completed artistic image, which is why we have taken pains to show this development in La Guma, is an emotionally exciting and moving story and not just an affidavit or logical exposition of fact. For example, describing the Pauls' family house in *And A Threefold Cord*, which could have been one of those "built at the rate of twenty per week," La Guma brings the house to life with a simile and personification:

> Finally, the house had held out, warping here and there, groaning like a prisoner on the rack, then settling down in the face of the seasons with the stubbornness of ancient ruins. (41)

And later, in the same book, a similar image recurs:

> A few old brick and plaster houses still stood, or rather tottered, at intervals along the ruined street. Most of their windows had gone, and cardboard, box-wood or stuffed rags gave the impression of rough patches over gaping eye-sockets. Paint and plaster had fallen from the walls, leaving raw wounds of brickwork....(96)

The recurrence of the image and the close similarity in wording—the continuity of theme from the earlier journalistic sketch—ensures that it will be recognized and remembered by the reader. One indication of the serious meaning La Guma intends in this theme-image, is the personification used to heighten its effect; first, the house is "groaning like a prisoner on a rack," and then its windows "gave the impression of rough patches over gaping eye-sockets," while paint and plaster fell, leaving "raw wounds of brickwork."

La Guma owes, perhaps, to his journalistic career the gift of synthesizing social issues and visual experience in a compact and vivid artistic image. Such an image is firmly attached to the themes of the book and play a dynamic part in conveying its meaning and deepening its artistic effect. In fact, one feature of La Guma's language which has received little attention is his use of imagery. For that reason, it is fitting that I devote the next chapters to a study of his use of imagery as an instrument of analysis and communication.

Before doing so, however, it may prove additionally illumination to review some specific elements of content and style observable in his column "Up My Alley." As every important event should be greeted with a fanfare, Alex proves equal to the task, as he sarcastically tells his readers, "Happy reading and may you become a regular frequenter of the Alley. Both bricks and bouquets will be welcome." These opening remarks, in his first column, immediately establish the satiric and sardonic tone that would characterize La Guma's column from beginning to end. A satire that was both genial and witty while simultaneously exposing and denouncing the faults and frailties of mankind in the particular context of Cape Town, South Africa. Another sketch from his first column bears witness to this technique:

> Strolling about the Golden City proves an interesting past time. One of the things which struck yours truly with force was the number of beggars. Because of the general economic condition of the Non-European people one would expect to find beggardom rife among them, but when one sees the number of whites, both men and women, begging for money in the streets of Jo'burg—well, it ought to show a lot of white citizens that apartheid and so-called white supremacy are nothing but a big fraud. Stop going around wearing blinkers, white folks. (*New Age* 2 May 1957)

Such incidents are things La Guma must have seen. And such incidents of profound tragedy and profound irony in a system committed to, so-called, "white supremacy" demand a witness. The satire here is one involving both a moral judgement and a desire to help improve the lot of all the people of South Africa—even white beggars. There is also a blend of humor with a critical attitude when he says, "one would expect to find beggardom rife among them (Non-Europeans), but when one sees the number of whites, both men and women, begging...well." While ridiculing, and exposing the folly and stupidity of the notion of "white supremacy," La Guma also shows that the serious, committed writer does not have to be humorless. We will, in fact, see more of this side of La Guma in the discussion that follows.

To further contextualize the political and social atmosphere within which La Guma's column first appeared, it should be noted that the Treason Trial was, at this time, in its sixth month. This trial was an attempt to silence and outlaw the ideas held by the 156 accused and the thousands whom they represented. It reflected a battle of ideas: on the one side the ideas of equal opportunities and freedom of thought and expression for all; on the other side, those which deny to all but a few the riches of life both material and spiritual.

Alex La Guma, prior to his regular column, was arrested along with the 155 others in 1956 and finally acquitted in 1960. While under house arrest, he interviewed a number of the other defendants for New Age—samples of which appear in his article "Triple Wedding of Treason Accused" (*New Age* 7 February 1957). The "triple wedding" refers to the triple wedding festival of Oliver Tambo and Adelaide Tsukudu, Syd Shall and Joan Anderson, Ronny Press and Miss J.B. Sack, all of whom, in La Guma's words, "have decided to face the future with steadfast confidence and courageous determination to build their new life, come what may" (*New Age* 7 February 1957). In one of the interviews, La Guma talked with a young man, Peter Ntite, who was about to become a father, who though in prison could still smile and say, "We need more recruits for the struggle." And another, Henry Tshabalala, who said that both he and his wife had lost their jobs as a result of the treason arrests; that they had two children and no income. Everywhere, La Guma observes, there was hardship and longing for home, but nowhere was there any regrets for what they had done and what had happened too them in the cause of liberation.

What was on trial was not just the 156 individuals but the ideas which they and thousands of others in South Africa had openly espoused and expressed. The political views of Alex La Guma and the others accused were a matter of public record, and no attempt was ever made to conceal their aims from the world or the manner in which they hope to achieve them.

Yet, even when reporting something as serious as the Treason Trial in which he too was a defendant, thoroughly embroiled, he managed a certain objectivity, a certain aloofness, a certain literariness. For instance, his first interview describes Peter Ntite as "smiling impishly," and Henry Tshabalala, known as "Chubby" to his friends, "is a young man with an elfish face" and "Little Lungile Kepe...strokes his long moustache and always smiles" (*New Age* 7 February 1957). Again, these early writings show the literary and political inclinations of the now thirty-two year old La Guma, harmonizing a morally serious purpose with artistic excellence. He has that rare gift of sensitivity and insight to bring out the humanity in the most dehumanizing of circumstances. Here are people on trial for their lives and La Guma is observing "impish smiles" and "elfish faces," and young men like Mosie Moolla, who at 22 was the youngest of the 156 accused, la guma's cellmate and secretary of the Transvaal Indian Youth Congress, who had "a premature moustache and a perpetual grin on his face," and who "was one of the most enthusiastic singers, but with the worst voice" (*New Age* 24 January 1957). His compassion for the victimized, imprisoned, and brutalized does not lead to a distortion of reality. Even in this dehumanizing environment people manage, somehow, to keep their essential humanity. Though he treats in this sketch some of the precise content of life in a given, specific circumstance, his anecdotal style of journalism manages, in spite of that circumstance, to provide some escape and humorous alleviation now and then from the hackneyed jargon of political controversy; and even that specific circumstance is raised to the level of the universal; he summarizes this aspect of his experiences in the Treason Trial with:

> I tried to find complaints, regrets, tearfulness among the accused, but instead there is only confidence, geniality and high spirits, all combined with indestructible determination. Here is the spirit of man, the will to go forward, the courage to look ahead and submerge personal hardships for the common good. Here are the bricks and mortar, the

muscles and the sinews, the life blood that go into the building of a new life. (*New Age* 24 January 1957)

Such statements convey feelings of common life accessible to everyone sensitive to the human condition. La Guma's interest and
active involvement in the events of the day do not predominate
over interest in details of feeling, of regret, of sorrow, of confidence and determination that also characterized the accused. In a
later column he describes how "the handshakes and back-slapping
and cheerful greetings all added to the confidence which exists
among the treason trial accused," how "since December 1956 a
great love has grown up among the 156; a great family of brothers
and sisters, a marvelous picture of a New South Africa....while the
cops stood looking on, apparently awestruck at the spectacle of
White and Non-White hugging each other, laughing and singing"
(*New Age* 9 May 1975).

Such observations by La Guma must be kept in context and
should not be interpreted as a manifestation of the kind of "liberalism" that obscures all racial and class contradictions or fosters in
the exploited the illusion of the possibility of peaceful settlement
and painless escape from white imperialist violence, or blurs the
contradiction between European imperialist domination and the
African struggle for national liberation—a liberalism, that is, that
rejects ideological struggle and stands for unprincipled peace
(Ngugi 1981:20). "Imagine," La Guma says, "the great imperialist
powers breaking into tears and deciding to end colonial oppression" (*New Age* 9 May 1957). In other words, when we observe
the handshakes and back-slapping, the hugging and laughing and
singing between Blacks and Non-Blacks, we should not generalize
this specific experience to the South African struggle as a whole:
so that we end up thinking that the contradictions between Blacks
and Non-Blacks, between employees and employers can be resolved
by moral persuasion alone. Alex La Guma is most aware that what
"liberalism" really tries to put across in South Africa, under the
disguise of Moral Re-armament, ...is that there is no necessity for
the oppressed people to struggle for their rights; that the class
struggle between capital and labour, the bosses and the workers is
unnecessary. Everybody should look into their hearts and decide
to be good boys. (*New Age* 9 May 1957)

What the liberals and their ilk need, says La Guma "is some mental re-armament" (*New Age* 9 May 1957).

This discussion has seemed to swing away from the strictly literary aspects of La Guma's writings, from Cape Town and District Six; yet, it has actually attempted to deepen the view of his writing career and the setting, for it has shown what might have grown or might not have grown out of his early background. It has shown that La Guma was not above adapting newspaper stories and his own journalistic observations for his fictional use. This background and his statements are in keeping with the logic of his developing personality, his literary themes and technique. It has shown that literature, including journalism, is conditioned by historical social forces and pressures: it cannot choose to stand above or to transcend economics, politics, class, race, color or the burning issues of the day—because those very issues with which it deals take place within an economic, political, class, color and race context.

Though his column "Up My Alley" and other contributions to *New Age* claimed no special literary attention, such writing provided La Guma, the apprentice, the latitude to explore a variety of literary styles and themes that would become noteworthy in his later fiction and essays. La Guma's column was full of his own pert and flippant observations, like:

> ...the bird who said that Communist literature resulted in the disruption of family life must have confused Karl Marx with the Urban Areas Act. (*New Age* 25 December 1958)

and,

> ...the sack line heard at an industrial board meeting: "Gentlemen, we are falling behind our competitors. They fired 300 more workers than we did last month. (*New Age* 12 February 1959)

and this bit of ironic "self" criticism:

> Aha! were those a couple of play-whites I saw dodging into a local white playhouse to see a play about play-whites? (*New Age* 12 February 1959)

As previously noted, however, the column also served a serious purpose by commenting on domestic and international political issues, forced removals, banishments, racism in America, suggested reading, scientific and technological developments, religion, the military, the arts and a plethora of witty by insightful social commentary on the absurdity of life under apartheid—like the white South African lady who was an ardent Nat King Cole fan, then smashed all her records when she discovered he was Black (*New Age* 8 August 1957) and the White school-teacher who found it embarrassing to teach her African pupils history, because they laughed when she defined a democratic government as one in which everyone has a vote, or when she had to tell them all about freedom of speech, impartial justice for all, and such other foreign propaganda (*New Age* 22 March 1962). Even during the heat of the Treason Trial, La Guma was able to remark, with a certain aloofness:

> Okay. I'm on trial for treason. The cops hauled me out at four in the morning, put me on a plane and dropped me in the Fort. I have to sit on a hard chair from nine-thirty a.m. to four every day, trying not to scream with boredom. I can take all this.But I don't like the prosecutor referring to me as EXHIBIT NUMBER 85. (*New Age* 5 September 1957)

Thus, as he fought for freedom, truth, virtue and justice, he invested common sense with the force of inspiration and humor. Writing primarily, it appears, to put his name before some segment of the public, these early sketches—sometimes written from a "superior" and self-consciously "literary" point of view as if to emphasize a certain objectivity and detachment—were designed to entertain and inform in a superficial way. To ridicule the absurdity of social practices under apartheid; to sharpen his technique in the use of detailed imagery, dialogue and character description, along with occasional displays of political satire are the primary ingredients of most of these early sketches. We cannot, however, overlook the very serious intent and involvement of La Guma during the tumultuous five year period 1961-1966. Blanche La Guma, for example, notes:

In 1961 Alex, among others, campaigned against South
Africa becoming a white republic. He went underground
to campaign clandestinely for a national general strike,
called for by Nelson Mandela. I did not know where he
was over this period. Every night I was visited by members of the security police who visited our house and wanted
to know where to find him. I received anonymous tele-
phone calls at midnight telling me that my husband was
dead, or that my children would be kidnapped. After the
successful strike, Alex returned home, and the next day went
to work. (Abrahams 1991:11)

"In 1962," she tells us, "he was the first person to be placed under
twenty-four hour house arrest. He did most of his writing over this
period" (12). In 1963 the La Guma home was again raided "for
banned literature" and both Alex and Blanche arrested. "In 1966
Alex was again arrested under the 180-days solitary confinement
clause" and "On his release from prison he decided to leave South
Africa with us to live in exile in London" (13). From London,
Alex and his family traveled to Cuba where he became the chief
representative of the African National Congress (ANC), to cover
the area of the Caribbean, Central and Latin America. He "super-
vised the education and training of hundreds of young South Africans" contributing significantly to the struggle for freedom in South
Africa. "Sadly, Alex La Guma was one of those exiles who never
made it back home. He was 60 years old when he died of a heart
attack in Havana on 11 October 1985" (Odendaal & Field 1993:ii).

It seems quite sensible to suggest that one of La Guma's fundamental aims is to dramatize in as powerful a manner as possible
the evils of racism. This being so, it is quite legitimate to examine
the manner in which this aim is sustained in his selection and use
of imagery in his novels and short stories.

Chapter 1

A WALK IN THE NIGHT: IMAGE AND IDEA

Perhaps it was a good thing that they were beating the boy;
perhaps the beating would bring to the boy's attention, for
the first time in his life, the secret of his existence, the guilt
that he could never get rid of.
—Richard Wright, "The Man Who Lived Underground"

"It is better to present one image in a lifetime than to produce voluminous works."

—Ezra Pound

Throughout his literary career, Alex La Guma was alive to the value
of imagery as an instrument of analysis and communication: an
instrument capable of resolving, and reducing the complex political, racial and economic reality of South Africa into a sequence of
clear and poignant pictures.

Although the term "Image" suggests a thing seen, when speaking of images in literature we generally mean a word or sequence
of words that refers to any sensory experience. Therefore, in analyzing the imagery in La Guma's short-stories and novels we will
look at the types of images used, for example: sensory experiences
that relate to sight (visual imagery), to sound (auditory imagery),
to touch (tactile imagery, as the perception of smoothness or rough-
ness), as well as those experiences related to smell and taste. Such
an experience may also be an odor or perhaps a bodily sensation

such as pain, the alleviation of hunger or thirst, or the perception of something cold or hot.

Through skillful use of imagery, an abstraction like racism or love—mere ideas when considered apart from a specific context—can be made understandable through the senses. To render the abstract in concrete terms is what La Guma tries to do, and in this attempt, his imagery is most valuable.

An image may occur in a single word, a phrase, a paragraph, or as a conception of a particular literary work as a whole. It is often tempting to think of imagery as mere decoration, but a successful image is not simply an accessory; it evokes setting, mood and theme —the moral message implicit or explicit in a work of art, while it creates vivid impressions of characters, objects and environment. In fact, much of the meaning in the creative fiction of Alex La Guma is in his imagery. Consequently, in addition to specific types of imagery, predicated on some sensory experience, there are four particular purposes to which his imagery corresponds that reveal basic tendencies of his narrative technique; these are: (1) Images that play a vital part in the development of the themes in the stories: man's relationship to man, to environment, to morality. (2) Images that play a role in the portrayal of character: including dialogue, interior monologue and behavior. (3) Imagery as a means of portraying setting, the chronological and the physical environment, and that particularly La Gumian (4) imagery of the desecration of physical bodies (human and non-human, animate and inanimate) as a metaphor for the South African situation.

For La Guma, the main function of imagery appears to be to elucidate certain political and socio-economic themes. One of these themes is the effects of the notion of white supremacy (apartheid/racism) on the people, particularly the people of color, in South Africa. For instance, in La Guma's second novel, *And a Threefold Cord*, shortly after Papa Pauls, patriarch of the Pauls' family has passed, and his son, Charlie Pauls, and other members of the family must get water to wash the corpse, La Guma punctuates the theme of the exploitation inherent in this system of 'white supremacy' with this picture of a local entrepreneur:

> Water is profit. In order to make this profit, the one who
> sells the water must also use it to wash his soul clean of

compassion. He must rinse his heart of pity, and with the
bristles of enterprise, scrub his being sterile of sympathy.
He must have the heart of a stop-cock and the brain of a
cistern, intestines of lead pipes. (114)

Economic and moral issues loom large in his novels, and most of
his similes and metaphors embroider on these themes. Of direct
relevance to the above image, and how La Guma intends for such
accounts to be understood and assessed is his position that:

When I write in a book that somewhere in South Africa
poor people who have no water must buy it by the bucket-
ful from some local exploiter, then I also entertain the secret hope that when somebody reads it he will be moved to
do something about those robbers who have turned my country into a material and cultural wasteland for the majority
of the inhabitants.(La Guma "Literature and Life," *Afro-
Asian Writings* 1 (1970):237)

From this perspective, image, as creation in words, creates ideas
of which a very large proportion are or become ideas for action
(Cary 1958:21). La Guma's images, as well as his elaborate and
subtle analyses of shanty-town and urban-ghetto settings, his meticulous descriptions, would mean nothing to us without his moral
preoccupation which appears in almost every line and every description. We are told that novelists must not preach; this is absurd. All serious artists preach; they are perfectly convinced of
the truth as they see it, and they write to communicate that truth
(109). La Guma selects and uses the images he does because they
are what he sees, what he feels, and the solution, for those trapped
in the cul-de-sacs of their environment, is to channel black rage
into clearly defined political action. We may not agree with La
Guma's political philosophy, but that does not affect the integrity
of his representations or the force of our experience in the books
he has written, any more than it would affect the force of our reaction when we read the lives of men with a different religion. His
ideas, his themes, are clothed in images based on concrete experience; and, as such, are means to an end and not an end in themselves.

This explication, concerned only with the imagery in La Guma's writings, will cover, respectively, the novella *A Walk in the Night*, and the novels: *And a Threefold Cord*, *The Stone Country*, *In the Fog of the Seasons' End*, and, his newest novel, *Time of the Butcherbird*; with reference to particular short stories as appropriate.

In December 1962, Alex La Guma was served with a notice confining him to his house for twenty-four hours a day under the Suppression of Communism Act. The only visitors permitted him for five years duration of the notice were his mother, his parents-in-law, and a doctor and a lawyer who had not been named or banned. Another provision of the law was that nothing Alex La Guma said or wrote could be reproduced in any form in South Africa. The five months he had served in prison during the emergency were not wasted as he "was able to finish the manuscript of *A Walk in the Night*, which he had started in 1959" (Odendaal & Field 1993: xiii).

The immediate consequence of this banning order was that the novella *A Walk in the Night* became forbidden reading for all South Africans. A few copies were smuggled into the country and passed from hand to hand. While outside South Africa, in the Soviet Union, in England, in America this book had achieved recognition as a work of talent and imagination. This, and his other work, has since been translated into twelve languages and is used in schools and universities throughout the world. (Bunting 1988)

A Walk in the Night is a short novel, about 130 pages long. But in its pages teem the variegated types of Cape Town's District Six: the unemployed, the beachcombers, the petty gangsters and criminals, the prostitutes and pimps, the taxi drivers and workers, the police, alcoholics and derelicts who together constitute, without doubt, the most colorful community in the so-called Mother City. In his "Preface" to *And a Threefold Cord*, Brian Bunting writes:

> ...nobody who has ever passed through District Six can ever forget its winding crowded streets, its jostling humanity, its smells, its poverty and wretchedness, its vivacity and infinite variety...(La Guma) knew the people and their problems, their "troubles"...and he wrote of them with intimacy and care. These are not cardboard characters, strutting life-

4

lessly through his pages, but real, live flesh and blood men and women who, though weighed down by the neglect and insult of the world, yet proclaim insistently their determination to survive, to eat, drink and make love, to endure the loneliness and terror and to welcome the cleansing dawn of tomorrow. (vii)

District Six, before being razed was, among other things, a grim, ghastly, ghetto of winding, crowded streets and ramshackle tenement buildings, of violent, jostled humanity, of putrid smells, of poverty and nauseating wretchedness. In fact, in terms of those images that play a vital part in the development of the themes in this story, the image of nausea and wretchedness is, perhaps, the most important—certainly the most repetitious—image in the work.

This image functions both thematically and structurally. By its abundant use, throughout the book, the image of nausea—internal sickness, disgust and inclination to vomit—forms a symbol and analogy through which the dominant theme of the novella pours forth: South Africa, under apartheid, is a sick society: and the images of characters, events and the environment are explicit metaphors of that sickness. A few specimens of the use of the image will give an idea of its importance to La Guma's overall design and theme in this work. It begins when, "Michael Adonis picked up his drink and finished it....He stood against the bar, waiting for the nausea to pass" (*Walk in the Night*, 14). And the man standing next to him, "belched loudly and swallowed" (14); then Greene "hiccoughed and mumbled" (14). And, a little later, Michael "was muzzy and there was a slight feeling of nausea in his stomach" (18).

He ordered another pint, "choking a little on the second, recovering and feeling the nausea replaced by a pleasant heady warmth" (20). As he entered the tenement where he, Michael, lived, a row of garbage cans "exhaled the smell of rotten fruit, stale food, stagnant water and general decay" (20) He "cursed, climbing the stairs and nursing the foetus of hatred inside his belly" (21).

This sickness, this hatred, rotting his insides, is not just the personal hatred of Michael Adonis toward the foreman for firing him, it is a concise metaphor—and must be seen as a metaphor—for the sickness of the apartheid system (white supremacy/capitalism) and for a condition and a struggle that is everyday, universal and common. In *Tasks And Masks*, Lewis Nkosi (1981) says, "La Guma still holds an enviable position in South African literature. With a frequency which few can match he still manages to find the exact metaphor for the cancer which is eating away at the country's entrails" (86). On the physical as on the moral plane, the feeling of nausea and a retching humanity haunts the narrator. And this condition is not exclusive to black humanity. When Michael meets the Irishman, Doughty, on the stairs, "He was partly drunk and smelled of cheap wine, sweat, vomit and bad breath" (*Walk*, 24). And during the parley between him and Doughty, "He (Michael) turned away from the window, anger mixing with headiness of the liquor he had consumed and curdling into a sour knot of smoldering violence inside him" (24). And, a little later:

> The thick, sweet wine nauseated him and he choked and fought to control his stomach, glaring at the wreck (Mr. Doughty) on the bed, until the wine settled.... (24; emphasis added)

The tone of these images describe the relationship between people, in this case Michael Adonis and Mr. Doughty, and they correspond to the nature of the relationship: and in the context of South Africa that relationship is wretched and despicable.

The old man, Doughty, says to Michael, "We're like Hamlet's father's ghost. I played the ghost of Hamlet's father once. London it was." To which Michael replies bitterly, "You look like a blerry ghost, you spook" (25). And then:

> He jerked the bottle from the old man's hand and tipped it to his mouth and took a long swallow, gagging and then belching as he took the neck from his lips. His head spun and he wanted to retch. (25; emphasis added)

Here, we reach a denouement, as Michael in a fit of anger murders Mr. Doughty. Then, staring "at the bluish, waxy face of the old man...with the blank artificial eyes of a doll" he says "Jesus," ...and turned quickly and vomited down the wall behind him, holding himself upright with the palms of his hands and feeling the sourness of liquor and partly digested food in his mouth. He stood like that, shaking, until his stomach was empty. (27) It had to come out. It must come out. And it is not just the liquor. The liquor is simply a vehicle, a device, for dealing with that "foetus of hatred inside his belly," rotting the belly of South African society.

When the scene shifts to Willieboy, the same imagery is picked up again. After his fight with the sailor in the Gipsy's speak-easy:

> Willieboy looked at him (Doughty) for a moment, and then rolled over suddenly to the edge of the stoep and was sick onto the pavement. He lay there, panting for a while, after retching was over. (54) And, when Constable Raalt and the driver, the two detectives investigating the murder of Mr. Doughty, entered the room of the dead man, "The stench of vomit hit him with a sour blow and he stared at the bluish dead face of the old man on the bed" (57). And the driver looked "around with a grimace of nausea" (57).

Finally, when Willieboy is in the back of the police van, dying:

> He did not move his head and did not try to wipe his running nose. The effort was too much for him, and when he moved his head he vomited and his head spun so that he would go into a coma....He tried to sit up, but could not, and the bile receded into his throat so that he retched and the pain lanced him and his body twitched and he screamed and fainted....
>
> He awoke with the faint smell of petrol and carbon-monoxide in his nostrils. It made him retch again and he shook until the retching turned to weeping and he cried, the sobs wrenching at him, jerking the pain through his abdomen....
>
> Then his mouth was suddenly full of bile and blood and he tasted the sourness and the salt for an infinitesimal instant before he was dead. (85-89; emphasis added)

As if to punctuate the idea of abject physical and moral poverty rotting South African society, suggested by these images of nausea, of retching, of internal sickness: La Guma makes an insect, a cockroach—a sort of universal vermin associated with poverty, and another recurrent image, a symbol, structured into the fabric of the work—the creature ultimately appropriate to taste and consume such filth:

> It encountered some stickiness and it tasted the mixture of spilled liquor and vomit on the floor of the room of the slain old man....The cockroach paused over the stickiness and a creaking of boards somewhere startled it, sending it scuttling off with tiny scraping sounds across the floor. After a while the room was silent again and it returned and commenced to gorge itself. (91)

Although there is a plethora of the image of nausea and vomiting, it is not conspicuous—except, perhaps, to the student of imagery; it was a useful motif for La Guma, so tightly woven into the pattern of the story that it does not, unduly, attract attention. The story moves so fast that the reader has little time to pause and consider fine points of style. To this must be added the terseness and simplicity of the images. To the student of imagery, the book is of particular interest because of the exceptionally close integration of the images into the narrative. These images are firmly attached to the dominant themes of the book and play a dynamic part in conveying its meaning and deepening its artistic effect.

The qualities which make *A Walk in the Night*, and La Guma's other fiction, so compellingly true are its fidelity to its own source materials—which is a life of complete and naked brutality under a repressive regime—as well as the quiet exactness of its tone and the adequacy of its moral pressures. The opening image of *A Walk in the Night* bares witness to the precision of La Guma's observation and the "bare-limbed economy" of his prose (Nkosi 1981: 5):

> The young man dropped from the trackless tram just before it stopped at Castle Bridge. He dropped off, ignoring the stream of late-afternoon traffic rolling in from the suburbs, bobbed and ducked the cars and buses, the big, rumbling delivery trucks, deaf to the shouts and curses of the drivers, and reached the pavement.
>
> Standing there, near the green railings around the public convenience, he lighted a cigarette, jostled by the lines of workers going home, the first trickle of a stream that

would soon be flowing towards Hanover Street. He looked
right through them, refusing to see them, nursing a little
growth of anger the way one caresses the beginings of a
toothache with the tip of the tongue. His thoughts concentrated upon the pustule of rage and humiliation that was
continuing to ripen deep down within him. *(Walk,*1)

The effect of this image, taken as a whole, is a transposition: that
is, it immediately transports the reader into a totally different sphere
of experiences. This process, of transposition, of vicarious identification with the experiences awaiting us in *A Walk in the Night*, is
made significantly easier by the anonymity of the protagonist, "the
young man," in this initial image. This technique, of La Guma's,
lends a distinct universality to our introduction to "a young man"
we will walk with through the streets of Cape Town for the next
128 pages. The image is real and truthful, it's the twentieth century, wherever we are, whoever we are, we can know it directly.

A single, recognizable whole image, however, is composed of
its separate elements. A "complete" image is the result of the assimilation of different impressions and perspectives, a sort of chain
of representations. It is, likewise, through the process of incre-
mental and assimilated images that theme is incorporated. For
example, the young man does not simply disembark—as would a
genteel, paying, bus passenger—rather, he "dropped from the track-
less tram": jumped, that is, from a moving truck or van right into
the middle of a busy street. Nor is his presence, quite pedantically
speaking, welcomed with courtesy or respect, but with "shouts and
curses": which tends to indicated that La Guma is also very sensitive to acoustic impressions and verbal abuse and the thematic associations evoked by them. In the simile, "nursing a little growth
of anger the way one caresses the beginnings of a toothache with
the tip of the tongue," we have, in addition to the subtle alliteration
of the letter "t" (the unvoiced labio-dentals), the theme of alienation. It seems, the young man's rather mechanical, thoughtless,
instinctive behavior is combined with the equally important theme
of the powerful versus the powerless. For example, his anger is
like a toothache, sometimes within and sometimes beyond our
power to control or fully comprehend. This relationship between
"power" and "powerlessness" is conveyed through a number of

images in *A Walk in the Night*. The young man is, of course, Michael Adonis: "

> a well-built young man of medium height, and he had dark curly hair, slightly brittle but no quite kinky, and a complexion the color of worn leather.... His eyes were very dark brown, the whites not quite clear, and he had a slightly protuberant upper lip" (2).

A product of his environment, like the other denizens of District Six, Michael appears restricted to the instinctive emotions of frustration, anger, violence and an intuitive, obstinate pride. His actions, spontaneous and impulsive, are rather reactions to internal and external forces (that toothache again), as opposed to premeditated, contemplated and willed choices of behavior. One purpose La Guma may have had, seems to be to enlarge our understanding of some of the possible consequences in that mundane, but infinite, relationship of man and environment; that is, a man of color, in the specific context of virulent white supremacy. And virulent white supremacy in uniform , armed—has got to be a somewhat terrifying confrontation (see Daniel J. Goldhagen, Hitler's *Willing Executioners*), as our protagonist, Michael Adonis bears witness:

> They came down the pavement in their flat caps, khaki shirts and pants, their gun harness shiny with polish, and the holstered pistols heavy at their waists. They had hard, frozen faces as if carved out of pink ice, and hard, dispassionate eyes, hard and bright as pieces of blue glass. They strolled slowly and determinedly side by side, without moving off their course, cutting a path through the stream on the pavement like destroyers at sea. (*Walk*, 10)

Here, La Guma is showing the experience of a character, the protagonist, in such a way that the reader can vicariously and actively participate. Though unpleasant, this image is of great importance in his portrayal of characters: physically, psychology, socio-politically and in terms of color and class. The image is of psychological importance in that it is a measure of the feeling which has temporarily transformed Michael Adonis' personality.

Earlier in the day he had lost his job at the sheet-metal factory because he returned the insult of the white factory boss "told him to go to hell (4). As a consequence, he keeps swearing "I'll get him...White sonofabitch. I'll get him" (4), but deep down he knows he won't, and is angry and frustrated with this awful impotence. Now he is gripped by fear. And this confrontation with the two white policemen and the image of fear, becomes a major factor motivating his subsequent behavior. The police in general, and Constable Raalt in particular, are the incarnation of the fears and complexes that have evolved since Jan Van Riebeck set foot on the Cape in 1652. They represent the dehumanizing instrument of white supremacy and terror, and Michael reacts accordingly:

> "Waar loop jy rond, jong? Where are you walking around, man?" "Going home," Michael Adonis said, looking at the buckle of this policeman's belt. You learned from experience to gaze at some spot on their uniforms, the button of a pocket, or the bright smoothness of their Sam Browne belts, but never into their eyes, for that would be taken as an affront by them. It was only the brave, or the very stupid, who dared look straight into the law's eyes, to challenge them or to question their authority. (10)

This image of authority, to which the "powerless" dare raise their eyes, defines the moral message implied in this work. This and similar images of the South African police provides a motivation and psychological explanation for Michael's later crime and, more importantly, Willieboy's flight and the state of mind of the policeman who shoots and kills him. Concerning the source of the story, La Guma has said:

> *A Walk in the Night* came about when I read in the newspaper, just a short paragraph, that a so-called hooligan had died in the police van after having been shot in District Six. I didn't investigate this at all. I just thought to myself how could this fellow have been shot and could have died in the police van. What happened to him? And so I sort of created the picture, fictitiously, but in relation to what I thought of life in District Six. (Abrahams 1991:23)

In a rather discursive manner, the principal "walkers in the night" have been introduced: Michael Adonis our Colored protagonist, Constable Raalt the White policeman who is on patrol duty in Cape Town's District Six, and Willieboy, "young and dark and wore his kinky hair brushed into a point above his forehead"—an habitual loiterer and petty criminal who is killed by Raalt during the hunt for the murderer of Doughty—the retired Irish actor who is dying of alcoholism and lives in the same derelict tenement as Michael. What is at issue here, however, is the image of the police. As La Guma says, "In South Africa we live with the police, I believe. Black people are continually being harassed by the police" (Abrahams 1991:23).

Granted, La Guma's method of portrayal can easily turn into caricature, since he portrays the police as brutal, dishonest, racists, white supremacists ignorant and without sympathy or pity. Indeed, and this image is most fitting, and an accurate comment on the South African police, and a natural expression of the narrator's emotional and intellectual reaction to them. It is therefore imperative that the experience, the image and confrontation with the police, and its impact on the narrator's mind, should be vividly imprinted on the reader's memory, and that this can best be achieved by a repulsive and almost dramatically debased likeness. At a deeper level of understanding, La Guma's portrayal assumes a certain social significance. It is not enough to take isolated examples of such portrayals. The thematic and structural value of a specific image can only be fully appreciated in the context of the novel as a whole.

Characters, what they say, think and do, are the primary vehicles for meaning in both short stories and novels, so La Guma's characters represent both general and specific human qualities.

He is concerned with a socio-cultural portrait of Cape Town, South Africa; and the value of his portraiture, as revealed in his characters, must be understood both psychologically and sociologically. Since he is dealing with the identity and behavior of individuals and a particular society, his characters have to be both psychological and sociological types. La Guma has chosen to present selected aspects of the personality and observed behavior of South African police that are consistent with the meaning of his story. Such characters are merely, as Robert Scholes and Robert Kellogg point out in *The Nature of Narrative*:

> fragments of the human psyche masquerading as whole human beings. Thus we are not called upon to understand their motivation as if they were whole human beings, but to understand the principles they illustrate through their actions in a narrative framework. (Scholes and Kellogg 1976:88)

There are those who can become better people the more they know about the evil, repulsive side of life. If African Literature from South Africa is the mirror of life in South Africa, it should be expected that the critical response to the literature of Africans in or from South Africa will often reflect the uneasiness, the fears and the feelings of guilt that such exposures normally engender.

Even more to the point are La Guma's own observations on the problems of characterization for the South African writer:

> No writer in South Africa can see life steady and see it whole. Out of his own experience, he can only tell what he has seen and known, and this is inevitable only a part of the total picture. No White writer has yet managed to create a real and convincing Black character, and vice versa. Nor has any writer, White or Black, been able to describe the relations between White and Black which are accurate and valid for both parties...Such creative failures are inevitable in a divided society. (La Guma, "South African Writing")

Critical responses to La Guma reveal as much about the society that produced the critic, as La Guma's work reveals about the society that produced him and his work. Serious interest in African literature generally, and South African literature in particular, goes beyond sophisticated definitions, and embraces moral, political and philosophical evaluation of the writer's imagination at work in the context and circumstances of his time.

What is at stake is not really whether La Guma's images of the White South African police are fully-formed characters, if that be a concern, but whether affected White critics are prepared to make the effort to overcome their ethnocentrism and psychological reluctance to examine themselves and their "kith and kin" on the basis of the evidence they confront in reading La Guma, in order to understand why the hiatus exist between African characterization of Europeans and, conversely, European characterizations of Africans; and, in special and significant ways, Coloured characterizations of Africans; an hiatus observable in both the past and present writings of the respective groups—universally. "Are Africans not routinely caricatured in novels by European writers? Have the Europeans been faulted for doing so? Have they stopped doing so?" (Chinweizu, et. al. *Toward the Decolonization of African Literature* 127). Also, in *Neither White Nor Black: The Mulatto Character in American Fiction,* Dr. Judith Berzon informs us that "The figure of the tragic mulatto...is the most frequently encountered stereotype in mulatto fiction. This figure is usually a product of the white man's imagination...his assumption that the mixed blood [i.e.,Coloured or Mulatto] yearns to be white" (Berzon 1978:99).

A Euro-African Nadine Gordimer, for example, can tell the reader in passionate and precise prose how a European liberal looks at the African or Coloured world, she can even portray accurately how an African appears in the eyes of a European observer: but, she can never get inside the African or Coloured body or the African or Coloured experience and look outwards, and she says so herself (La Guma, "South African Writing"). Such creative "weaknesses" are inevitable under a system of legalized White supremacy, apartheid, which by definition means "the condition of separateness": where the contact between the various color and cultural lines is reduced to the bare minimum. No literature, however comprehensive it is taken or seeks to be, can ever surpass actual life.

La Guma's character portraits serve to strengthen the impact of the story at the literal level.The most striking feature of these portrayals is its appropriateness and how it is perfectly adapted to the distinctive setting of his work: As Lucien Le Grange writes in "The Urbanism of District Six" in Jan Greshoff's *The Last Days of District Six:*

> Despite its typical characterisation by apartheid officials
> and liberal historians as being an inner city slum, District
> Six contained most of the social and physical elements as-
> sociated with urban life...the heterogeneous and dense con-

centration of people, the high degree of social tolerance, the association of different social classes....(8)

And Richard Rive in *Buckingham Palace: District Six*, concludes:

> The children must be reminded of the evils that greed and arrogance can cause. We must tell about the District and the thousands of other districts that they have broken up because they wanted even more then they already had. We knew that District Six was dirty and rotten. Their newspapers told us so often enough. But what they didn't say was that it was also warm and friendly. That it contained humans. That it was never a place—that it was a people. (Rive 1986:197-198)

Still, like Harlem, New York, South Side Chicago, South Central Los Angeles and West Oakland, California, District Six is characterized by an atmosphere of fear, impotence, abject poverty, crime, and the brutalization of man by man: an atmosphere in *A Walk in the Night* best expressed by Michael Adonis and his encounter with two policemen, when, "deep down inside him the feeling of rage, frustration and violence swelled like a boil, knotted with pain" (*Walk*, 11). La Guma offers: "I don't think that the presence of the police (in my work) is intentional, I think it is inevitable" (Abrahams 1991: 23). It is also a characteristic feature of La Guma's imagery, whether related to characterization, the environment, or images of desecration, that, more often than not, he prefers the explicit to the implicit type, simile to metaphor. This is a "natural" tendency, if not a premeditated technique, in a writer aiming at a simple and direct yet imaginative style. In the citation above, for example, he seeks out what to him is the most appropriate comparison to express Michael's emotional reaction to the police, "rage, frustration and violence swelled like a boil"(emphasis added). And in the description of the two Boer (Dutch/Afrikaner) policemen there are a number of graphic similes:

> They had hard, frozen faces as if carved out of pink ice.... ...and hard dispassionate eyes, hard and bright as pieces of blue glass. They strolled slowly...cutting a path through the stream on the pavement like destroyers at sea.

> The voice was hard and flat as the snap of a steel spring.... The question was without humor, deadly serious, the voice topped with hardness like the surface of a file. (Walk, 10-11; emphasis added)

If one is aware of the overall context in which these similes appear, there seems to be intermittent pauses in the narrative as the author searches for the right analogy, the most appropriate simile to convey his idea. These comparisons cause the characters to come into being as genuine living impressions, and are built up over the course of their action in the work, and not simply presented as whole, complete figures identifiable by simply naming them. For this reason, La Guma's use of simile lends, not only freshness and emphasis to his narrative technique, but also enables him to state truths that more literal, denotative, language cannot communicate; it calls attention to such truths; it comments on character by referring to the, perhaps, more knowable physical world.

Most of his images, the explicit as well as the implicit type, in *A Walk in the Night* and the later novels, are quite short and simple in structure. This is probably due to the speed of the narrative, and a direct style that does not allow for elaboration. Throughout the work, images are separated, characters juxtaposed with each other, then reassembled or brought together again to evoke again the initial image. The image of the two policemen, for example, is interrupted by dialogue, and the interior monologue of Michael, before the reader is brought back to a meticulous description of the hands of just one of them:

> The backs of his hands...were broad and white, and the outlines of the veins were pale blue under the skin, the skin covered with a field of tiny, slanting ginger-colored hair. His fingers were thick and the knuckles big and creased and pink, the nails shiny and healthy and carefully kept. (11)

And this image, specifically the last sentence recalls, diametrically, an earlier one that forms part of the first portrait of Michael Adonis:

> The young man wore jeans that had been washed several times and which were now left with a pale-blue color flecked with old grease stains and the newer, darker ones of that day's work in the sheet-metal factory...He also wore an old khaki shirt and over it a rubbed and scuffed and worn leather coat....
>
> He was a well-built young man of medium height, and he had dark curly hair, slightly brittle but not quite kinky, and a complexion the color of worn leather... His eyes were very dark brown, the whites not quite clear, and he had a slightly protuberant upper lip. His hands were muscular, with ridges of vein, the nails broad and thick like shells, and rimmed with black from handling machine oil and grease. (2)

Here, then, are two direct treatments, two evocations of two human beings, both objectively presented as objects of perception and thought, using the third-person omniscient narrator's voice and no words that do not contribute to the presentation. Therefore, our first impression is the external appearance of the characters; and eventually through conversation, self-examination and the action of the characters, spread out over many pages, our knowledge of them grows until, finally, we obtain a complete image. The desired image is not ready made or fixed, but arises—is born. The image planned is concretized by separate representations, juxtaposed with other images, then combined—in first the author's, then in the reader's perception—to evoke a complete image. The complete image is the work of both author and audience. The relationship between Michael Adonis and the two policemen, Constable Raalt and the driver, can be summed up imagistically by taking two concise excerpts from the larger images, respectively:

> His hands were muscular, with ridges of vein, the nails broad and thick like shells, and rimmed with black....(2)

And:

> His fingers were thick and the knuckles big and creased and pink, the nails shiny and healthy and carefully kept. (11)

These images are placed at critical points in the story, and the close similarity in wording ensures that they will be recognized. Also, what at first appears to be a trite or superfluous citation is, in actuality, the major contradiction inherent in class and color. That is, more specifically, black hands, the hands of people of color, "the color of worn leather...the nails...rimmed with black from handling machine oil and grease"; and white hands "the nails shiny and healthy and carefully kept." This kind of imagery is only possible, as Georg Lukacs (1974) suggests, if the writer himself possesses "a firmly established and vital ideology. He must see the world in its contradictory dynamics to be able to choose a hero in whose life the major opposing forces converge" (*Writer & Critic*, 142). Michael Adonis is such a hero. And, it is clear from La Guma's choice and use of such heroic images (and their opposite) along with his preference for the explicit simile, that the author wants to shock readers out of their complacency. It is further evident that even at this still early point in his literary career—maybe an outgrowth of his apprenticeship as a journalist—overt political ideology informs *A Walk in the Night*; though more apparent in the intellectual physiognomy of the protagonists of his later novels, urging readers to join leftist political organizations to combat racial and capitalist injustices. Making the exploited African and other Colored workers of South Africa the conscious choice as the central problem of his fiction, is consistent with his developing political and literary consciousness.

Thus, whenever La Guma dwells upon images indicative of man's inhumanity to man, and the effects of the inhumanity—objectively and subjectively on individuals and their environment—he is directly attacking a political system, as well as man in general for placing his own egotism ahead of the common needs of humanity. Through images of the environment and characters, La Guma's works preach; yet, the messages they are meant to give have been entirely assimilated into the form. *A Walk in the Night*, therefore, is an experience with the insight appropriate to that form.

It is inescapable, in this work and La Guma's later works, that the characters are what they are, think what they think, and do what they do because the environment is what it is, and it is toward the confining, limiting, debilitating social and political structures that La Guma's writings, and the actions of his chosen heroes are aimed.

Life for the people in District Six, Cape Town, is one of violence and where racism and colorism is as normal as breathing; so, the language and imagery, the incidents in the novel and the characters are carefully chosen to give readers a lasting impression of this life. It is a battlefield, with White people on one side and people of color on the other. Thus, after Michael's first encounter with the itinerant beachcomber, Joe, a militant image is used, as La Guma describes him as, "trailing his tattered raincoat behind him like a sword-slashed, bullet-ripped banner just rescued from battle." This image too is well-suited to the thematic and stylistic climate La Guma intends; as it so effectively harmonizes image and idea with artistic embroidery of simile and alliteration.

This explicit, emphatic stylistic climate—using simile and alliteration, as against, say, more complex metaphorical patterns and assonance—is consistent with the rapid, hard-hitting pace of the novella. As such, each episode, each encounter with allies or enemies or the physical environment reveals a new dimension of a character and his, sometimes, predictable yet unique reaction, if not response, to external as well as internal forces. For example, following his initial fear and confusion about the accidental killing of Doughty, Michael, while talking with the beach-comber, Joe, reveals deeper, latent thoughts and feelings about this incident:

> ...He was suddenly pleased and proud of his own predicament. He felt as if he was the only man who had ever killed another and thought himself a curiosity at which people should wonder. He longed to be questioned about it, about the way he had felt when he had done it, about the impulse that had caused him to take the life of another....The rights and wrongs of the matter did not occur to him then.
>
> It was just something that, to himself, placed him above others, like a poor beggar who suddenly found himself the heir to vast riches. (*Walk*, 62)

At this point, it can be admitted that, for Michael Adonis, this individual act of violence is therapeutic; it is, in Fanonian terms, "a cleansing force" (Fanon 1981:94). It frees Michael from his inferiority complex and from his confusion and inaction; "it makes him fearless and restores his self-respect" (Fanon 1981:94). He finds his freedom in and through violence, it "placed him above others." The violence of the apartheid system and, in this instance, the counter-violence of Michael balances each other and responds to each other in a reciprocal unity. On the South African battle-field, the enemy all wear the uniform of color or lack of color, as the case may be—their "Star of David": all are guilty until proven innocent. On the one hand, there are those who are guilty of being "cursed" with blackness, sin, and savagery; and on the other hand, those who are guilty of being "cursed" with whiteness, idolatry, and bestiality. It is understandable that in this atmosphere charac-ters will act and react intuitively, mechanically on the unwarranted assumptions of their innate guilt. In this context, we can better understand the thoughts and behavior of Willieboy.

Willieboy, the innocent suspect for the murder of Doughty, gives subjective evidence of the psychological climate of life in District Six; through interior monologue and the author's, in this case, ob-trusive third person narrative control Willieboy ruminates:

> Well, I had most nothing to do with it. They can't say its me. I found him mos like that. But years of treacherous experience and victimization through suspicion had rusted the armor of confidence, reduced him to the non-descript entity which mad him easy prey to a life which specialized in finding scapegoats for anything that steered it from its dreary course. (*Walk*, 46)

First, concerning La Guma's obtrusive "authorial intervention," or "failure to let the scene speak for itself" we learn from Wayne Booth that any author "intrudes" deliberately and obviously to in-sure that our judgement of the "heroic," "resourceful," "admirable," or "wise" will be sufficiently favorable; and that, "The author's presence will be obvious on every occasion when he moves into or out of a character's mind or when he shifts his point of view" (Booth 1961:17). The basis of this point of view is the authorial choice of showing or telling which is "always to some degree an arbitrary one...the author can to some extent choose his disguises, he can never choose to disappear" (20).

Although this image is confined to the intellectual plane, the thoughts of Willieboy, and the sharper edges of his psyche conditioned by factors he is unable to articulate become the author's responsibility to elucidate. It is an image firmly attached to the dominant themes of the book and plays an important role in delineating the intellectual physiognomy of Williboy. By "intellectual physiognomy" is meant that La Guma "reveals the thinking processes of his characters and develops their varied intellectual positions regarding the same problem." In a general sense, this problem is the effects of racism and colorism, but, in a specific sense, "problem" refers to Willieboy's reaction to being pursued for the murder of Doughty. "Intellectual physiognomy" therefore, is further understood as "the vital factor in their characters and as the most distinctive manifestation of their personalities" (Lukacs 1974:150).

Form a slightly different perspective, this image is important because Willieboy's facile and immature intellectual brilliance is one of the psychological factors motivating his flight. He knows that even though he had "nothing to do with" the death of Doughty, and thinks, "They can't say it's me": we understand perfectly why he runs away from a murder he never committed.

Professor Daniel Kunene puts the matter quite succinctly:

> He (Willieboy) is afraid of white power justice, especially since the murder victim is a white man. The white police constable Raalt who stalks Willieboy over the rough rooftops of the District Six slum, has been itching to "lay my hands on one of those bushman bastards and wring his bloody neck." Now he has got his chance. (Kunene "Ideas Under Arrest" n.d.)

These portrayals of Willieboy, of constable Raalt, of Michael Adonis indicate the verisimilitude and mimetic integrity of La Guma's characterizations. Each portrait expresses the essence of the character in a way that is possible only because the character is who he is, in terms of the author's conception and that character's life as revealed and lived in the novel. La Guma's characters, these three in particular, are distinguishable—let it be said—first by the color of their skin, and in the context of today's world, this fact conditions the content of their thought and the quality of their actions.

Dr. St. Clair Drake provides a cogent exposition of the relevance of the perspective employed here, when he states that Black writers and scholars, would, no doubt, have preferred to deal with problems of mankind as human problems, but Western science insisted upon defining them in terms of 'race'. They have, therefore, reacted in the same terms. There is a Black historical perspective as well as a white one, and it is equally valid as a frame of reference for research. (Henderson 1963:57)

Africans, in South Africa, America, and throughout the Diaspora, confronted with color prejudice, racism, colorism, economic deprivation, and the nightmare that is for them the dream called "democracy" are asked to create, as one critic put it, "A literature of power...to revitalize our common humanity. This erudite professor goes on to say, that what South Africa needs is "less of the miserable rags of realism" (Partridge 1956: 64). How can a writer like La Guma, or any other South African writer know "our common humanity" in a society separated and segregated by color and race, and law enforces this separation? How can anybody, literally anybody, know life in South Africa well enough to describe it adequately, let alone tell the truth about it, the whole truth and nothing but the truth, as expected from the artistic as well as the legal witness? The artistic vision of La Guma is restricted by apartheid barriers, and even the most vivid imagination is no substitute for experience.

The African writer, in Africa and America, burdened with the struggle of his people, finds it disheartening to have to justify the themes of his literature, to "humanize the White South African police," to "revitalize our common humanity." He considers this to be one more futile exercise in his struggle to be free of the conditions of slavery, colonialism, racism (white supremacy), and discriminatory practices which oppress him both in Africa and America. Such critics seem to forget that when white arrived in Africa "they were instructed and repeatedly reminded not to let down the white race by treating Africans on terms of human equality" (Chinweizu 1983:127). To Alex La Guma, the moral authority and political portent of his themes holds out the possibility of a moral and political remedy. Yet, with the proverbial hope that springs eternal and the strength of a drowning man who never learned to swim, one African literary critic—and there are no doubt others—attaches himself to a literary dilettantism suggesting that the 'weakness' of *A Walk in the Night* is the "over-manipulation of events and characters into the service of an 'obsessive' theme of apartheid" (Obuke 1973:16). It is interesting that what one may view as a weakness another may view as strength.

First of all, for La Guma, it should be suggested that, the "excellence" of literary form is not an end itself, nor is the aesthetic process the only or even primary object of his creative writing.

Instead, his works are a vehicle of self-assertion in a world that seeks to deny meaning to his and his compatriots' life. Thus, principles of criticism will in turn have less to do with the arbitrary, if not superfluous, inanity of "over-manipulation of events and characters"—every writer manipulates events and characters—than with the ethical and moral truth of La Guma's vision of life in South Africa recreated and presented through his art.

Secondly, apartheid and its dehumanizing effects is one of La Guma's major themes, and his imagery, organization of events and selection of characters (and the artful means he uses to control them) are based upon this reality. Concentration upon apartheid and racism (white supremacy) as an evil in South Africa, and the world, are essential to him as a writer; not only because he feels strongly about apartheid and the absurd notion of white supremacy, but also because he had to have a center for his plot. One recognizes easily this center of La Guma's subject: that absolutely and indispensably fixed and selected point from which he surveys his environment and experiences and from which his material emanates. It is this idea, the existence and vulgarity of the notion of white supremacy, and its consequences, that unifies and gives form to his literary works. The internal unity of *A Walk in the Night* is achieved by selection of characters, selection and organization of events, choice of narrative voice and dialogue, as well as the imagery used to portray this particular setting and physical environment. This discussion of the role played by imagery in the portrayal of characters is by no means exhausted. It will be elaborated (below) in the discussion of the imagery of desecration of physical bodies (animate and inanimate) as a metaphor for the South African situation (following the explication of imagery as a means of portraying setting or the physical environment).

The mere representation of squalid conditions people are forced to live under in a racist, capitalist environment, even if it is the central theme in a work of art, does not by any means imply a morbidity or lack of objectivity in the author's creative approach. If anything, it gives the reader the vicarious opportunity to experience this environment with the characters, and to form judgements based thereon.

In order to judge, we must see and understand as clearly as possible the external physical environment that chokes and strangles the inner society and the consequences of this reciprocity in terms of the thoughts and actions of the characters. For instance, as Michael Adonis walks despondently towards his inauspicious confrontation with the drunken, incorrigible Irishman, Doughty, He turned down another street, away from the artificial glare of Hanover, between stretches of damp, battered houses with their broken-ribs of front-railings; cracked walls and high tenements that rose like the left-overs of a bombed area in the twilight; vacant lots and weed-grown patches where houses had once stood; and deep doorways resembling the entrances to deserted castles.

There were children playing in the street, darting over the overflowing dustbins and shooting at each other with wooden guns. In some of the doorways people sat or stood, murmuring idly in the fast-fading light like wasted ghosts in a plague-ridden city. (Walk, 19)

There is something harsh and severe in this image, yet the presence of the children and the sensitivity and love they compel softens even that. The fact that there are no details about their appearance—especially their color—raises a "typical" feature (children) of this environment to a "universal" dimension; these could be my children, your children, children anywhere. Except, they are "playing in the street," as opposed to, say, a park, and "darting over...overflowing dustbins," instead of a well-kept manicured lawn or carefully constructed chutes and ladders and jungle-gyms. So, we can infer from the image, and the twentieth-century problem of the color line, that these are African children or children of color. These children are "playing," that is, pursuing the typical plea-

sures of childhood under the most desperate circumstances con-
ceivable:

"battered houses" showing "broken-ribs...cracked walls...like
the left-overs of a bombed area in the twilight." This is the setting,
the physical environment in which the children must live their lives.
Their presence in this picture illustrates how the unfair distribu-
tion of wealth and provision of basic human needs victimize innocent children under South Africa's white supremacist system.

La Guma wrote about his environment the way he saw it,
and not the way he wished it would be. His perspective is from the
ground level observatory of a present-day South African of color
and not from the lofty vista of a well-intentioned and liberal White
South African writer or academician. There is overwhelming justification, from this bottom level observatory, for Africans and other
people of color in South Africa to view themselves as victimized,
oppressed, even subservient to this awesome racist environment.
Consequently, Africans and Coloureds, especially, are disposed to
regard everything from a relative point of view. Any literary work,
in fact, has to be a partial view of things. First, because all views
are partial and personal, and secondly because of the limitations of
the form of the novella or novel. The more comprehensive creative fiction is in scope, in width of scene, the more it loses in
power and significance. "The most important part of truth," Joyce
Cary wrote, "is what humanity is suffering, is feeling and thinking
at any given moment, and this cannot be known, as a totality, to
any person" (Cary 1958:115). Therefore, La Guma's moral message is implied partially through his character portraits and through
his images of the physical environment; and while such portrayals
may offend some, they have great significance as symbols of a
greater South African reality.

Another feature of La Guma's literary technique, noticeable
in *A Walk in the Night*, is that his images, particularly those of the
environment, in addition to forming some of the most interesting
similes and metaphors in the book, create distinct patterns which
recur like leitmotivs, leading motives, themes, images associated
throughout the novella with a particular situation, person, or idea.
An analogy is not merely noted but is enlarged upon and developed in some detail. After his observation of the exterior of "battered houses," La Guma takes us inside the dwelling:

> Michael Adonis turned into the entrance of a tall narrow
> tenement where he lived...The floor of the entrance was
> flagged with white and black slabs in the pattern of a
> draught-board, but the tramp of untold feet and the accu-
> mulation of dust and grease and ash had blurred the squares
> so that now it had taken on the appearance of a kind of
> loathsome skin disease. A row of dustbins lined one side
> of the entrance and exhaled the smell of rotten fruit, stale
> food, stagnant water and general decay. A cat, the color of
> dishwater, was trying to paw the remains of a fishhead from
> one of the bins....The cat pulled it from the bin and it came
> away with a tangle of entrails. The cat began to drag it
> towards the doorway leaving a damp brown trail across the
> floor. (Walk, 20)

"Is it not true," asks Ama Ata Aidoo, "that when an atmosphere is
polluted...nothing escapes the general foulness?" (Aidoo 1986:
xii) Like Ayi Kwe Armah's *The Beautiful Ones Are Not Yet Born*,
with its images of Ghana, Alex La Guma's desire for writing this
novella—as well as his short stories and other novels—seems to
have been to expose, to express with a view to destroying what he
cannot take, cannot accept about the South African environment.
There is no Purina Cat Chow in this segment of South African
society, and if our feline friends want to eat they must satisfy their
hunger with the heads and entrails of fish remains. "Nothing escapes the general foulness," and even harmless, domestic pets—a
luxury under the circumstances—cannot avoid the general pollu-
tion that engulfs this environment. La Guma, in this way, and others about to be noted, develops the initial image and complicates
the metaphorical pattern.

When he is not using similes, he is using other figures of speech,
the most common being metaphor and personification. In fact,
personification is a kind of metaphor: a figure of speech in which
an inanimate object, like a house, is endowed with human form,
character, traits or sensibilities. A metaphor, unlike the simile, is
not limited in the number of resemblance it may indicate, and herein
lies its value as a literary tool to the creative writer.

Houses are not just houses in La Guma's novella, they are part
of his metaphorical themes, part of the metaphorical patterns, again

leitmotivs, of the work. A battered house whose exterior reveals "broken-ribs," whose floor has "the appearance of a kind of loathsome skin disease," are metaphors for the human body and the ill use and abuse to which human beings in South Africa are subjected; La Guma's unique vision of the desecration of physical bodies as a metaphor for the South African, if not the whole Pan-African situation.

This image of the exterior and interior of the tenement also shows how acutely sensitive the author is to every kind of sense impression, not merely that of sight. Smells, in particular, had for him a strong evocative power, and they too are an elaboration fo the metaphorical pattern. The row of dustbins, for example, "exhaled the smell of rotten fruit, stale food, stagnant water and general decay." And, this rotten, stale, stagnant, decaying atmosphere is an appropriate metaphor for the South African situation.

Langston Hughes once asked, "What happens to a dream deferred...does it stink like rotten meat? Or crust and sugar over—like a syrupy sweet?" Then La Guma complicates the metaphorical pattern, as smell and visual imagery is juxtaposed with that of audio-imagery: and later images are dependent on earlier ones:

> Somewhere upstairs a radio was playing Latin-American music, bongos and maracas throbbing softly through the smells of ancient cooking, urine, damp-rot and stale tobacco. A baby wailed with the tortured sound of gripe and malnutrition and a man's voice rose in hysterical laughter. Footsteps thudded and water rushed down a pipe in a muted roar. (*Walk*, 22)

Without the earlier portrait of the white policeman, his "nails shiny and healthy and carefully kept," or the very first image of "late-afternoon traffic rolling in from the suburbs"—both images depicting a picture of affluence and prosperity—these later pictures would be weightless and without antecedents.

These kinds of selective, realistic images are not incidental or superfluous, but are intended to influence social behavior; to make us take certain kinds of social and political action—in art, in religion, in our families and personal values—or, at least, to see the social situation depicted in ways which had not previously been apparent. The visual, audio and intellectual aspects of the images function as a form of protest, anger, ridicule and social description. In other words, such imagery can influence the behavior of people, affecting the way they think or feel and sometimes the way they act. When, La Guma—and we—can observe, concomitantly "a baby wail with the tortured sound of gripe and malnutrition," as "a man's voice rose in hysterical laughter," we know again the terrifying dialectical essence of the human condition that Dickens captured in the phrase "the worst of times...the best of times." At the same time, La Guma makes all humanity responsible for the need to do something about the "22 children who died recently in the areas (Cape Town, South Africa) only general hospital, thirteen suffering from malnutrition or starvation" (La Guma, *Apartheid*, 11).

Some persons, including artists, regard art which influences social behavior as impure, as mere propaganda, as applied sociology, as diseased art, even as an abuse of power: and postulate certain assumptions about the "appropriate" function of art; who want to censor and control art, literary or otherwise. Nevertheless, artists, especially literary artists, have always sought to influence collective behavior; hopefully, in the direction of more critical thinking, reflection and contemplation more than emulation. It's not just a matter of the world we have, but the world we want...of peace, for example. Hence, a complete portrait of La Guma's literary career could not be presented if we ignore the social functions of his corpus in relationship to his themes and imagery; and the socio-political context he wrote to expose. As long as there are political wrongs to be righted and unjust, smelly and ugly social conditions requiring change, such images must participate through visual, audio and olfactory education and persuasion in the development of popular attitudes that can lead eventually to a better society.

La Guma uses a pictorial description to express the idea of poverty and deprivation. These are dominant themes of his work and the frequency and consistency of their use add intensity and a unifying strength to the work that mere decorative imagery could never accomplish. These images of the environment, though unpleasant and not particularly unique, are of great importance in the psychological development and subsequent behavior of Michael Adonis.

The sequence of images that punctuate these themes—of the effects of poverty and deprivation—helps to give the reader a sense of continuity and, of course, being there in District Six. Even after the accidental killing of Doughty, Michael emerges into the same monotonous environment, where:

> ...in the dampness deadly life formed in decay and bacteria and mold, and in the heat and airlessness the rot appeared, too, so that things which once were whole or new withered or putrefied and the smells of their decay and putrefaction pervaded the tenements of the poor. (*Walk*, 32)

This outward, material poverty is a direct reflection of the sense of frustration felt by the African and Coloured characters, particularly Michael Adonis who has just lost his job. This intense reciprocity of external (material) and internal (spiritual and emotional) chaos and adversity traps Michael in a maelstrom of cause and effect, reducing his desires and actions to fundamentally instinctive, mechanical proportions. The meaning of his personality and actions, however, can only be understood by linking together the otherwise isolated fragments of his character as it develops in relation to the plot and setting. And it is because the sequence of images that creates the completed portrait of Michael Adonis is consistent, faithful to the existing, knowable, objective South African reality that we can trust La Guma's subjective literary motivations for Michael's actions.

An environment, of course, is always more than just the physical world, more than the interrelations of objective historical conditions, but also human attitudes—hate, fear, courage, and love—towards these conditions. Willieboy's and Michael's attitude of inferiority, fear and impotence is correlative to the policemen's (and white South Africa's) attitude of superiority and power. The sequence of images describing the police creates a psychological climate that develops concomitant with and parallel to the evolution of characters and pattern of events (plot) as these—character, event, and climate—converge and diverge with a progressively heightened intensity of anticipation and action. The two policemen, for instance, long after we first encounter them, still have their same attitude. They are "fed up with riding around looking at

these effing hotnot bastards" (29) and exhibit the same mannerisms, the same mechanicalness, the same vacuousness—wearing
their guns "like appendages of their bodies and whose faces had
the hard metallic look, and whose hearts and guts were merely
valves and wires which operated robots" (55). Even though Constable Raalt and the driver are not the same two policemen who
accost Michael Adonis earlier in the novella, the point is perhaps
more emphatically made because, the generic image of the police
remains consistent to the end, to the final convergence when Raalt
mercilessly shoots Willieboy and the driver asks:

> "What did you want to shoot for? We had him.
> I could have got him from behind."
> Constable Raalt told him, "What's the matter with you,
> Andries? Aren't you a policeman?" (83)

From the time Michael first encounters them on the street, "cutting
a path through the stream on the pavement like destroyers at sea,"
their faces hard, frozen, "as if carved out of pink ice, and hard
dispassionate eyes, hard and bright as pieces of blue glass," their
fateful role is brilliantly foreshadowed. Such a sequence, and pattern of images, no matter how insignificant it may appear, is part of
the very fabric of the novella. The technique of image-sequence is
particularly effective when it helps to unify the work by providing
consistency in the portrayal of character and environment and as it
embellishes the major themes of the work.

Images of insensitive, intimidating police: of children playing
around garbage bins: of a child crying because of malnutrition: of
the spiritual emptiness and frustration of a young man of color out
of work while surrounded by white affluence and prosperity: together with the squalid, deserted wasteland that is the physical
environment, tend to generalize and extend the theme of these images to the entire human family trapped within this environment.
And, in South Africa the pain of poverty is particularly acute when
we read in Steven Biko that in precolonial times "Poverty was a
foreign concept. This could only be really brought about to the
entire community.... "(Biko 46).

The hunger and pain of children suffering unnecessarily is a
universal symbol. The emotional strategy of such an image is to

arouse our common feelings of shock and empathy. We are forced to confront unpleasant social and material reality. Although such images have no specific or overt political content, they do seize the imagination and enlist our feelings in favor of some kind of action which can relieve suffering.

Alex La Guma views Michael Adonis' loss of his job as a theater for the performance of a psychological drama, as a revelation of the motivation and anxiety of a person who is out of work. Unemployment translates itself, for Michael, into the feeling of being victimized by, and expendable to , the world he must live in: and this is one of the most profound spiritual experiences of the modern era. As an artist, La Guma offers no economic solution, but deals rather with the objective and subjective qualities of the experience itself, and some of the possible consequences this has for a few individuals. His choice of a proletarian protagonist, in itself, represents an act of rebellion against the white supremacist, capitalist system, but the pattern of imagery and related themes reveal broad human sympathy rather than the espousal of a political doctrine.

La Guma's selection of images fashions a picture which simultaneously expresses multiple perceptions, and consequences of a single event—Michael Adonis was fired from his job because he went to the bathroom without his foreman's permission:

> Every time a man goes to the piss-house he start moaning. Jesus Christ, the way he went on you'd think a man had to wet his pants rather than take a minute off. Well, he picked on me for going for a leak and I told him to go to hell.
> (*Walk*, 4)

The very act of selecting specific portions of our ordinary existence for artistic treatment helps to focus our attention on the quality of this existence, and the inevitable symbiosis of condition and consciousness. Usually, it requires some dramatic event to draw our attention to conventional places and events. Only when the artist gives a particular structure and pattern to his images, images of daily life, do we begin to discover their distinctive quality, or specialness, or meaning.

The effect of such presentation is that it can heighten our insight into daily existence; it allows us to compare the quality of contemporary material and social life with that of other places; it can cause decisions to change, correct, or improve the material, visual environment; it can lead to a new perception of ourselves as part of, and also apart from, contemporary physical and social reality. The environment men build influences their builders as well as their inhabitants, since they reflect human choices and limitations. La Guma's images of the Cape Town, District Six environment describes not only what is objectively seen but also what is subjectively felt by the people who have to live there; and those who are there, by law "have to" be there, by the accident of birth and color "have to" be there. And, if freedom means anything it means the ability and the right to choose. The image of Michael Adonis' confrontation with the foreman is a clear example of lack of choice, in the most basic, fundamental areas of one's life, to urinate.

Such humiliation is a desecration of the human body, and serves as a metaphor for the South African situation. To desecrate is "to take away its sacred character from; to treat as not sacred; to profane" (*Oxford* 489). The sacred character is taken from a human being when he or she is reduced to property: when a human being is viewed as a commodity to be bought or sold. Yet, private ownership of property, and people as property, is the prism through which the light of Western man's vision has been reflected. John Locke had argued that the very reason men enter into society in the first place is the preservation of their property. And Locke's theory of property was one of the most distinctive features of the colonial system of politics in the eighteenth century affecting both slavery in America and colonialism in Africa. It must be understood, that for the millions of Black and Coloured South Africans, it is the laws character, and intelligence of the White South African community which keeps the African in the status of property (Patterson-Mudavanha 1978:302). Daniel Kunene, South African scholar and poet, puts the matter this way:

> I do not propose to define the term "slave" and all its de-
> rivatives for this is something that easily becomes an aca-
> demic exercise little related to the drama of life....Slavery,

the basest thing that one man can perpetuate on another,
can have no other justification but the superprofit motive.
(Kunene 1971:68)

The youthful protagonist, Michael Adonis, is not aware of the
superprofit motive or the multi-national corporate structure ensur-
ing his enslavement: he says to a taxi-driver in a local District Six
restaurant, "Ya. Wish I could get a job on a boat...Go to the States,
maybe." "Must be smart over there. You can go into any nightclub
and dance with white geese. There's mos no color bar." (Walk,
15)

    And when told that an African-American was "hanged up...in
the street in America," Michael Adonis retorts, "Well, they Negroes isn't like us," and a moment later adds, "I don't give a damn
for a bastard white arse." During this exchange, Michael's consciousness has been developing from personal rage to abstract racial hatred and, as the dialogue progresses to some acquaintance
with that "superprofit motive":

> "It's the capitalis' system, " the taxi-driver said. "Heard it
> at a meeting on the Parade. Whites act like that because of
> the capitalis' system." "What the hell do you mean—
> capitalis' system?" Michael Adonis asked. "What's this
> capitalis' system you talking about?" (15)

The young man, Michael Adonis, does not understand the property relationship, its origins and development in slavery and colonialism, nor its current relevance to his personal predicament.

    And, in a moment of the most basic human need, he forgot his
status as a man of color and acted just as a man when he talked
back to the white foreman. This Michael understands and concedes, not willingly, but of necessity. How could he not understand? With a permit required to be where you are, and to be doing
what you are doing; a permit required to be in a "white" area, to be
issued a railway ticket, to visit your friends and relatives in a different town or area; a permit which states which particular house
you are visiting, the purpose and length of your visit, et cetera, et
cetera; surely, Michael had had enough—thinking, perhaps, next
he would need a permit to go to the bathroom and not just permis-

sion. What Michael did not understand and would not understand, through the end of this book, is the sadistic, world-wide economic conditions that make his enslavement necessary and perpetual. Again, Professor Kunene:

> ...these are precisely the kinds of conditions that capital, forever seeking areas of investment with the highest returns, will take advantage of, or even create. In order to keep labor cheap, it must be kept under the strictest control, so that it can be sent wherever it is needed. The wishes and desires of the people involved are irrelevant, because they are, first and foremost, labor, not people. (Kunene 1971:70)

For "labor" one should read "property," and, as was the circumstance of the African slave in America, in South Africa too, "The power of the master must be absolute to render the submission of the slave perfect" (Higginbotham 1978:9). The control which the South African courts and police seek is the total submission of Africans and other people of color. It has incorporated into its law-made morality the psychological, social, economic, political and geographical boundaries described by Daniel Kunene, in testimony before the United States Congress (Kunene 1971) and by La Guma in the character of Michael Adonis. Thus the ubiquitous beachcomber, Joe, and Michael can engage in the following dialogue:

> "I hear they're going to make the beaches so only white people can go there," Joe said. "Ja. Read it in the papers. Damn sonsabitches." "It's going to get so's nobody can go nowhere." "I reckon so," Michael Adonis said. (*Walk*, 9)

This, indeed, is another example of the profanity of the white supremacist South African system.

A society that has convinced itself, with the support of its legal, economic and political system, that Africans and other people of color are so inferior that their "subhuman" status deserves no recognition of human value or rights—not even the right to go to the beach. And just as often these white supremacists make no effort at all to find a rationale; they simply terrorize and dehumanize those who are black because of the color of their skin and because they have the military might to do so. In this way, political and social regulations reinforce one another and oppression justifies itself through oppression (Memmi 1967). Africans and other people of color are oppressed because they are considered "subhuman" and they are "subhuman" because they are oppressed. And, since the white South African oppressor denies humanity in others, he regards it everywhere as his enemy (Fanon 1981). The relationship between people of color and white people in South Africa and the world is what it is, we are told, because the people, on both sides, are what (ethnically, racially) they are. Therefore, what is actually a sociological or cultural difference becomes labeled as being biological and genetic. If the police can stop and question and insult Michael ("Where are you walking around...turn out your pockets") without reason, justification, or provocation; if one can't go to the bathroom without permission, then it is as if "you need a permit to prove that your existence is not some terrible mistake" (Walk, 9) and the desecration of the human being and the dehumanizing process is complete, because people of color are legally precluded from responding in a manner thought normal for whites . For example, the white supremacist United States government is the only one in the world, so far, to use atomic bombs. Is this the "normal" behavior the world wants to follow?

Michael Adonis, in answering back to his foreman (his "master"), ceased to be of use and value as an item of labor (property), and was discarded—"endorsed out," as the official terminology has it. In his dual role as person and property, Michael is negated as a human being due to considerations of his value as a piece of property. This, in turn, sets in motion forces that give legal sanction to the African as property (in Africa and America) and ultimately secures him in the position of a perpetual alien in his own land (Patterson-Mudavanha 1978:13). Again, Daniel Kunene gives a cogent explanation for the realistic plight of millions of Africans depicted fictionally by Alex La Guma in the character Michael Adonis:

> ...a tool or vehicle, or any property that you own and over which you have absolute power, is discarded without any qualms once its usefulness to you has ceased." (Kunene 1971:70)

35

Sechaba, a South African journal, reproduced a circular of the Department of "Bantu" Administration of 12 December 1967, in which this "endorsing out," this discarding of human beings, is explained and defended as follows:

> It is accepted Government policy that the Bantu are only temporarily residents in the European areas of the Republic, for as long as they offer their labor there. As soon as they become, for some reason or other, no longer fit for work or superfluous in the labor market, they are to return to their country of origin.... (Kunene 1971:71)

As Ayi Kwe Armah (1973) would say "This is not our way"—this is not the African way; and, as Biko (1978) adds,

> This attitude to see people not as themselves but as agents for some particular function either to one's disadvantage or advantage is foreign to us....We believe in the inherent goodness of man. We enjoy man for himself. We regard our living together not as an unfortunate mishap warranting endless competition among us, but as a deliberate act of God to make us a community of brothers and sisters jointly involved in the quest for a composite answer to the varied problems of life. (45)

It is the idea of the African as property that has gained the full allegiance of white South Africa and white America. This idea becomes for La Guma, in both animate and inanimate imagery, a metaphor for the desecration of human beings, spiritually and physically, in the South African situation. Cheikh Hamidou Kane might conclude this way,"At the same time that work gets along without human life, at that same time it ceases to make human life its final aim; it ceases to value man" (Kane 1972:101). La Guma extends this metaphor of the desecration of human beings to include minor characters, such as Joe—the beachcomber—and the Irishman, Doughty, as well as in the imagery of the physical environment.

James Baldwin once remarked that "dirty socks can make you feel like nothing but a dirty sock." Dirty socks, filthy clothes, cockroach-infested apartments, junk-laden street, can make you feel like and think of yourself as nothing but dirt, filth, junk, or just a loathsome cockroach.

The peripheral character Joe, for instance, is a homeless youth who lives off handouts and by scavenging along the seashore for whatever he can find to sell or eat. The sequence of images creating his portrait is a flashback to the indigenous coast-dwellers of Southern Africa encountered by the Dutch colonists at the Cape, and given the name "strandloper" or beachcomber. He is also a metaphor for the death of the last remnants of independence from the system of international capitalism—one of those who out of stubborn pride refused to become a "civilized" commodity.

Our first impression of Joe reveals him as a dour, abject symbol of a vast ostracized segment of the truculent, inhuman, white supremacist South African system:

> Joe was short and his face had an ageless quality about it under the grime, like something valuable forgotten in a junk shop. He had the soft brown eyes of a dog, and he smelled of a mixture of sweat, slept-in clothes and seaweed. His trousers had gone at the cuffs and knees, the rents held together with pins and pieces of string, and so stained and spotted that the original color could not have been guessed at. Over the trousers he wore an ancient raincoat that reached almost to his ankles, the sleeves torn loose at the shoulders, the body hanging in ribbons, the fron pinned together over his filthy vest. His shoes were worn beyond recognition. Nobody knew where Joe came from, or anything about him. He just seemed to have happened, appearing in the District like a cockroach emerging through a floorboard. Most of the time he wandered around the harbor gathering fish discarded by fishermen and anglers...
> (*Walk*, 8-9)

The theme of this image is organized around one emotion—empathy. The details and force of the image is anything but stolid. Rather, it helps us to see it as a manifestation of social expression, specifically the expression of pity: for the economic, social, human conditions which cause anyone to have to sleep in one's clothes, to have to wear shoes until they are "beyond recognition," or to have to eat fish "discarded by fishermen."

The picture is one that can be objectively seen and subjectively felt; and this "wreck" this "scarecrow" of a man is enlivened, brought into being as a human being deserving of respect, even tenderness: his face having "an ageless quality," and his eyes, "the soft brown eyes of a dog." La Guma presents this image honestly, without any attempt at beautification or glossing over of unpleasant details: and, in so doing, a certain measure of respect is earned by the subject—Joe. He, like any character who exhibits a grossness in his person, retains his human dignity.

At the same time, the principle social and political objective of the image is also achieved. It endows the reader, and other witnesses to this desecration of the masses of starving humanity, with the consciousness of their responsibility to, not just South Africa's but, the world's oppressed and exploited millions; and to arouse the consciousness of exploited people to their belonging to an oppressed class with justifiable antipathy towards their oppressors.

This antipathy, for La Guma, is not a unilateral condemnation of all whites, but as revealed through his careful selection of characters, whites are also desecrated victims of the foul crimes of a white supremacist world order. Doughty, the old alcoholic ex-actor, speaks for numerous members of his society when he recites the words from Shakespeare's Hamlet:

> I am thy father's spirit, doomed for a certain time to walk
> the night...and...and for the day confined to fast in fires, till
> the foul crimes done in my days of natures...nature are burnt
> and purged away.... (*Walk*, 28)

Doughty, by recalling the words of the ghost in Hamlet, is doing so for all the characters in the novella, *A Walk in the Night*, all of whom, in one way or another, experience the terrors of the South African night; where, in a life immersed in violent encounters, imprisonment and murders, the people "fast in fires" of hatred, fear, frustration, poverty and racism. Doughty, too, is one of the pitiful, desecrated millions, and a symbolic metaphor for the condition of many white South Africans:

> In the light of the bulb in the ceiling his face looked yellowish-blue. The purple-veined, greyish skin had loosened

all over it and sagged in blotched, puffy folds. With his
sagging lower eyelids, revealing blood-shot rims, and the
big, bulbous, red-veined nose that had once been aquiline;
his face had the expression of a decrepit bloodhound. His
head was almost bald, as wisps of dirty grey hair clung to
the bony, pinkish skull like scrub clinging to eroded rock.
(24)

This image, and the mood it elicits, might demonstrate to anyone
who has eyes to see, the profound compassion Alex La Guma felt
for his fellow men. Observe how, when La Guma looks at a person, he sees him with the eye of a very sensitive artist and seems to
be using a color-dipped brush rather than a pen to write the words.
Under the light, Doughty's face looks "yellowish-blue"; closer
observation shows his skin to be "greyish," and "purple-veined";
and his eyelids revealed "blood-shot rims," and his nose is "red-
veined," and his head "pinkish" and "almost bald." Using such
words as "sagging," "decrepit," "dirty," and "clinging," La Guma
tries to fashion a picture which would simultaneously express
multiple perceptions of a single calamitous event. Doughty, who
has once been a famous actor, is now a retired, discarded senior
citizen dying of alcoholism, diabetes and old age: suggesting, in a
sense, that Michael's crime of passion   was more an act of eutha-
nasia than some sort of premeditated revolutionary violence.

After exploiting his productive, virile youth, Doughty—a white
man—has now become expendable and is left 'trapped' in a derelict tenement, waiting for death, which comes   even sooner than
expected. And the way La Guma describes Doughty's room inten-
sifies   the effects of the misuse and abuse of the physical environment:

The room was hot and airless as a newly opened tomb, and
there was an iron bed against one wall, covered with unwashed bedding, and next to it a backless chair that served
as a table on which stood a chipped ashtray full of cigarette
butts and burnt matches, and a thick tumbler, sticky with
the dregs of heavy red wine. A battered cupboard stood in
a corner with a cracked, flyspotted mirror over it, and a
small stack of dog-eared books gathering dust. In another

> corner an accumulation of empty wine bottles stood like
> packed skittles. (24)

This image conveys a morbid, deathly quality, the same atmosphere
that elicited the plethora of images of nausea and retching, cited
earlier. The cumulative images of desecration of individuals is
carried over into the description of the physical environment; and
again, "nothing escapes the general foulness" (Aidoo 1968:xii) of
the vulgar white supremacist system; a system that, for young and
old alike, is like an "open tomb"; where people, like Joe the beachcomber, are "unwashed" like the bedding on Doughty's iron bed;
where some people have lost their nerve, their courage to struggle
against this awesome international white supremacist imposition
and have become, at least, metaphorically "backless" as the chair
in Doughty's room that doubled as table; and even the cigarettes
are not whole but rather "butts," and the matches "burnt," the cupboard "battered," the ashtray "chipped," and the mirror "flyspotted."
The complete picture emphasizes the material decadence and harshness of the environment in which most people of color and some
people of non-color have to live.

Portrayals of the physical environment, landscape or cityscape,
also reflect ideology and priorities—especially European-domi-
nated environments, where, for example, once-religious cathedrals
dominated the skyline have been dwarfed by economic "cathedrals";
physical environments have their social connotations, especially
when there are people visible in them.

We see the signs of human use: care or neglect, abandonment
or affection. These images, as well as their related themes and
realistic frame of reference, are a terrifying document of the devastation of human values.

In addition to the psychological and physical environment, a
final aspect of this context, namely, the verbal environment, can
be touched upon. Dialogue, though not the particular focus of this
chapter, deserves at least a comment or two, since it is closely
integrated into the story and plays a dynamic part in its progress.
Also, some images derive much of their expressive force from effects of vocabulary or syntax and renders moods. Lewis Nkosi has
observed that:

> ...what is often overlooked is the masterly and creative way
> in which Alex La Guma handles dialogue, which will yet
> be seen as his major contribution to South African English.
> What he gets into the English dialogue is really the Afri-
> kaans accents and rhythems of the Cape Malay coloureds
> taal and he merges it with English more successfully than
> any South African writer had done, white or black. (Nkosi
> 1968:6)

What La Guma tries to do, and does successfully, is to individual-
ize each character through language, to make speech an expression of personality, ethnicity and class and power. Take for instance the Afrikaans police whom Michael Adonis encounters early
in the book; they say to him, "Waar loop jy rond, jong?" Which La
Guma translates for readers as "Where are you walking around,
man?" Apart from this fragment of dialogue being unrealistic, that
is, it is unlikely that he police would repeat or, more accurately,
translate his question for Michael, still, the use of the Afrikaans
hints at the local situation, an environment that really questions
Michael's humanity to the extent that he understands "Waar loop
jy rond, jong?" As Fanon (1967) puts it, Africans and other people
of color "will come closer to being real human being(s) in direct
ratio to (their) mastery of the (colonizer's) language" (18). On
other occasions, his use of language, in the sense of bringing non-
English words, perhaps, "exotic" words, words that maybe need
not be there, is contexualized in such a way that they need not be
explained, as in this passage of Adonis' interior monologue:

> You ought to get yourself a goose, he thought. You've been
> messing around too long. You ought to get married and
> have a family. Maybe you ought to try that goose you met
> downstairs. Her? Bedonerd. When I take a girl she's got
> to be nice. With soft hair you can run your hands through
> and skin so you can feel how soft her cheeks are and you'd
> come home every night mos and she'd have your diet
> ready.... (*Walk*, 42)

This seems more natural. Here, La Guma is not using the non-
English "exotic" Afrikaans words and then translating them and in
the process destroying the naturalness of the narrative. There is no

need for translation in this passage as it can be understood from the context that, "goose" means woman or girlfriend, that "Bedonerd" means crazy, and that "mos" in this context can mean almost, just about, or sometime. Throughout *A Walk in the Night*, La Guma uses Afrikaans and other non-English words without apology, without explaining or interpreting them for the English reader; a few examples should be illustrative:

> ...I remember the time...I saw Flippy Isaacs get cut up. You remember Flippy? He was in for house-break and theff. ...Well...while Flippy is up at the oubaas he gets word that his goose is jolling with Cully Richards. You remember Cully? He mos used to work down here in Hanover Street.... Flippy gets to hearing about Cully messing around with his goose. Well, ou Flippy didn't like that. Man, that john was a bastard of a hardcase.... Cully was a pretty tough juba himself. Well, when he pulls that knife Cully sees red and he runs back into the butcher-shop and gets a butcher-knife.... Well, ...Cully comes running out of the shop, his face all screwed up with rage, and goes for Flippy. Just one cut with that knife, man. It must have been about a foot long and sharp like a razor.... Just one cut, jong. Across the belly. Right through his shirt. Hell, ou Flippy just sat down on the pavement and held his stomach, with his guts all trying to come out between his fingers, and the blood running down into the gutter. His whole face was blue. He just sat there, trying to keep his guts in. (16-17)

This passage captures the local verbal environment in a way that suggests that La Guma would, perhaps, prefer to write in this language style throughout, but for purposes of audience he must write in, predominantly, standard English. This scene, narrated by the taxi-driver, depicts the climate and reality of internal violence; that violence that is just below the surface of the skin of all the Flippies, Cullies, Williwboys, and Michaels of South Africa who live in a state of permanent tension. La Guma's language, particularly his use of non-standard English, is the thread that connects *A Walk in the Night* to the specific fabric of life that can only be South Africa; the events, the images of characters, environment, of the desecration of human beings could be anywhere, the language could not. La Guma has commented, "our community culturally has been Europeanized. We speak European languages...as a result of the colonialization of the Cape province in particular" (Abrahams 1991:22). In *South African Literature and Culture*, Njabulo Ndebele (1994) remarks "Indeed, the history of the spread of the English language throughout the world is inseparable from the history of the spread of British and American imperialisms" (100). English and Afrikaans were the country's official languages until the first free elections of April 1994 and Nelson Mandela's installation as president on 10 May 1994.

Indeed anything associated with government, like signs or brochures, is still in both languages. Now, there are 11 official languages: English, Afrikaans, Ndebele, Northern and Southern Sotho, Swati, Tsonga, Tswana, Venda, Xhosa, and Zulu. Eight are spoken by more than one million people. There are various Indian languages and plenty of dialects within languages.

Ndebele, "a provocative thinker in the reassessment of values that is important to South Africa in this era of transition" (Gordimer), observes:

> Firstly, South African English must be open to the possibility of its becoming a new language. This may happen not only at the level of vocabulary (notice how the word "necklace" has acquired a new and terrible meaning), but also with regard to grammatical adjustments that may result from the proximity of English to indigenous African languages.
> (Ndebele 1994: 112)

Of relevance here is The Reconstruction and Development Programme's (RDP) aim to "establish and implement a language policy that encourages and supports, financially and otherwise, the utilisation of all the languages of South Africa...particularly the historically neglected indigenous languages" (ANC 1994:70-71); about which Ndebele (1994) warns that "the teaching of English will have to be freed from the functional instruction of corporate English...Where...African languages hold a mainly functional, manipulative interest. They are a means towards a more efficient use of African labour" (112-113). English, on the other hand, is said to belong to all who use it provided that it is used correctly.

"It is assumed, of course, that it is the native speakers who will determine the standards of correctness" (100). As in the case of La Guma and other South African writers, however, "If English belongs to all, then it will naturally assume the cultural colour of its respective users" (113).

A Walk in the Night was a great beginning to Alex La Guma's literary career, one of the most significant contributions to South African literature in recent years. La Guma's struggle to establish a pattern within the images of this novella is very well suited to the themes of social description, concerning the South African white supremacist system, and the place of Africans and other people of color in contemporary South Africa. The universal themes of unemployment, alienation, power relations, racism and colorism reflect today's urban battlegrounds where contending demands for space and the spoils of industrial society are being fought out.

It is very likely that La Guma's technique of realistic imagery, of imitating the appearance of reality, represents an effort to control reality. Perhaps La Guma thinks we are less likely to be victims of the seemingly capricious actions of the world if we can create images which are accurate and faithful enough to take the place of those portions of the world we must deal with.

44

Chapter 2

AND A THREEFOLD CORD:
IMAGE AND IDEA

...like a sick body to be healed
with painful treatments, bitter herbs
and deep-cut vaccinations...

Purification One
In Soweto
Fires lick walls of hate
Burn the encrustation
Imprisoning the very breath of life

Let the conflagration come
the stubborn weeds
that smother the struggling life

Set the life free
With fire

Soweto!

—Daniel Kunene

And a Threefold Cord, La Guma's second novel, was published in Berlin in 1964. He wrote this book while he was in prison on Roeland Street. La Guma says:

> My attorney brought me the contract to sign for *And a Three-fold Cord*. Again it was a matter of recoding history or

recording situation. The book was about the suburban slums which is a character of the South African scene, whether it is Soweto or Alexandra Township, Cooksbush and so on. (Abrahams 1991:24)

In these suburban slums, there are no paved streets, sanitation, indoor plumbing, drainage or electric lights, and water has to be bought by the canful. This story is about one of many areas in South Africa where as Brian Bunting (1964 notes, "life is short and cheap, where violence flares out of hate and frustration, yet where humanity, love and hope sprout even from the dunghill of eveil and decay" (*Threefold Cord* Forward 15). And Alex La Guma, in writing this book too, still entertains the secret hope that those who read it will be moved to do something about those people who have turned South Africa into a material and cultural wasteland for the majority of the inhabitants (La Guma "Literature and Life," 237).

In this novel, as in his others, the physical environment is rigorously selected and meticulously drawn. *And a Threefold Cord*, set in the shanty towns of the Cape, is dominated by the forces of "nature"—by the northwest winter wind and the long rains it brings; and by political forces vaguely comprehended by its denizens. Still, the effective creation of a physical setting—the symbiosis of theme and the images of the environment—is one of La Guma's characteristic technical strengths. In this work, the imagery of the wind and rain is consistent with the distinctive atmosphere of the work and, along with other time-honored ingredients of poetic metaphor, play their familiar part in furnishing equivalents for human processes. Even the most casual reader is bound to be struck by the frequency and the strange, haunting quality of the rain imagery. The full significance of such imagery, however, can be better appreciated if it is set against the background of the imagery as a whole; that is, imagery that develops themes, imagery that composes and distinguishes characters, and that special kind of imagery of La Guma's that portrays the desecration of physical bodies as a metaphor for the South African situation.

And a Threefold Cord has a very explicit moral: collectivism is better than individualism. The title is taken from Ecclesiastes IV: 9-12:

Two are better than one; because they have a good reward
for their labor. For if they fall, the one will lift up his fellow:
but woe to him that is alone when he falleth; for he hath
not another to help him. Again, if two lie together, they
they have heat, how con one be warm alone? And if one
prevail against him, two shall withstand him; *And a Threefold Cord* is not quickly broken.

La Guma's portrait of the agony of the African and Coloured people
of South Africa is well represented in the suggestively dramatic and
symbolic situations in this novel. Here we are given an insight into the
intense human struggle against the oppressive, almost elemental, pri-
mordial force of the myth of white supremacy. The novel, as Brian
Bunting (1964) eloquently observes, is "drenched in the wet and mis-
ery of the Cape winter, whose grey and dreary tones Alex La Guma
has captured in a series of graphic prose-etchings" (15); for example:

In the north-west the rainheads piled up, first in cottony
tuffs, blown by the high wind, then in skeins of dull cloud,
and finally in high, climbing battlements, like a rough wall
of mortar built across the horizon, so that the sun had no
gleam, but a pale phosphorescence behind the veil of grey.
The sea was grey, too, and metallic, moving in sluggish
swells, like a blanket blown in a tired wind...
    The people of the shanties and the pondokkie cabins along
the national road and beside the railway tracks and in the
suburban sand-lots watched the sky and looked towards the
north-west where the clouds, pregnant with moisture, hung
beyond the mountain. When the bursts of rain came, knocking on the roofs, working-men carried home loads of pilfered
corrugated cardboard cartons, salvaged rusted sheets of iron
and tin to reinforce the roofs. Heavy stones were heaved
onto the lean-tos and patched roofs, to keep them down,
when the wind rose. (La Guma *Threefold Cord* 1988:1-2)

Thus, from the outset, we are aware that "nature," the weather,
that hangs "like an omen over the land," is going to be a factor in
the motivation and explanation of characters and events to follow.
From this, the first paragraph of the novel, La Guma leads us, in the
words of Samuel Omo Asein (1974), "into the heart of a black

location where we watch the pathetic struggle of the Pauls family
in a social setting which denies the individual a purposeful existence and a cosmic setting symbolically alienated from its human
inhabitants" (21). At the heart of this book is the collective life of
the shanty dwellers; their struggle to preserve their humanity along
with their makeshift, corrugated tin dwellings is a measure of the
need to protect the solidarity of community. Asein capsulizes the
thematic thrust of the work when he writes:

> The story *And a Threefold Cord* is based on the premise
> that under the prevailing state of constant fear, uncertainty
> and insecurity such as presented in *A Walk in the Night*,
> black South Africans, as well as coloureds, can only sur-
> vive the assault of apartheid by sheer force of will and col-
> laborative efforts. (21)

In this novel, we follow the Pauls family in their struggle to keep
alive; Charlie and his brothers Ronny and Jorny, his sister Caroline,
his mother and moribund father. With them we live the lesson they
learn: that survival lies in unity, of families and, by implication, of
African and so-called colored peoples. As the author admits:

> This was just another scene in the life of the community,
> another facet of the picture, and I decided again that the
> picture of the suburban slums did not appear anywhere in
> South African writing, so I said well why shouldn't I do it,
> because it is part of our life, our scene so it should appear
> in the picture. (Abrahams 1991:25)

La Guma's gift and stylistic propensity for expressing himself in
images, and the pleasure he seems to derive from the process suggest that he was intent on using and developing this style. In *And
a Threefold Cord*, the imagery of rain is very meticulously woven
into the fabric of the work and plays a dynamic and highly visible
role in the progress of the story and in its final design. As noted,
the rain image appears for the first time in the very first paragraph
of the novel, and by intermittent, repetitive use it becomes a symbolic motif. When it makes its first appearance, its source and
power suggest several comparisons: "The rainheads piled up...like

a rough wall of mortar built across the horizon...The sea was grey...metallic, moving...like a blanket blown in a tired wind...grey-uniformed fog...hung like an omen over the land" (*Threefold Cord,* 17). There is, in addition to La Guma's observed preference for the explicit simile, an interesting double image in the above citation; the first two are concrete, tangible; an allusion, perhaps, to the callously rigid and so-called "natural" divisions that make up the walls of myth of white supremacy. The second part of this double image has an awing, abstract twist suggesting certain intangibles: intellect, emotions, spirit, which must be included in the South African equation. The book, therefore, has opened with an image of great precision and sombre pathos, which strikes at once the keynote of the whole book. It should prove useful here to cite William J. Grace's (1965) distinction between pathos and tragedy:

> Pathos might be described as a feeling of sympathetic sadness, but it has special characteristics that distinguishes it from tragic emotion. The essential difference between the pathetic and the tragic lies in the fact that the tragic situation has an end. And up to that very end the hero is an active agent...
>
> In pathos, the hero is more sinned against than sinning; he is caught in the web of circumstances through which he cannot cut his way either triumphantly or unsuccessfully. We cannot really fear (as in tragedy) for what he will do, because basically he cannot do anything. The development of conflict as necessary to the tragic emotion cannot take place. (123)

This is not to be construed as meaning that La Guma intended to write a tragedy, or to speculate on his "intentions" at all; rather, the hope is that by making use of certain definitive and specific "literary" words we might share a perspective on the explication of the work before us.

The imagery of the rain, the wind, the fog, is not just the thing itself, but is also La Guma's and his characters' relationship to these things, and it is the relationship between things and feelings which compels the author to metaphor. And this is not just metaphor for the sake of proving some sort of "literariness" but for the sake of clarity, mood, tone, sensual appeal and thematic emphasis.

Certainly, La Guma must try "to see things as they really are," but nothing really is in isolation, pure and self-sufficient. Reality involves relationship, and as soon as you have relationship you have, for human beings, emotion. So, La Guma cannot just see things as they really are, cannot be absolute about them, unless he is also absolute about the feelings which attach him to the image. Every image recreates not merely an object but an object in the context of an experience, therefore an object as part of a relationship. Thus, the imagery of the rain does not have to engender feelings of pathos or tragedy—the rain itself is neutral—and we find these terms useful only now, in helping us to better understand La Guma's metaphorical choices. For these choices represent La Guma's desperate attempt to expose, elucidate, and extol man's—especially African and so-call Coloured peoples—effort to relate to those forces that govern the universe, both material and non-material, both the natural and the artificial man-made universe. *And a Threefold Cord* is drenched in pathos precisely because the characters that inhabit its pages, and the reality that is its specific point of reference, "cannot do anything" and are clearly "more sinned against than sinning," caught in a web of circumstances from which they cannot be extricated either successfully or unsuccessfully.

The rain imagery, and the enigmatic, elemental strength it portrays is the dominant image of this work:

> When the burst of rain came, knocking on the roofs, workingmen carried home loads of pilfered corrugated cardboard cartons, salvaged rusted sheets of iron and tin to reinforce the roofs. Heavy stones were heaved onto the lean-tos and patched roofs, to keep them down when the wind rose. (*Threefold Cord*, 18)

Rain imagery plays a dynamic part in the development of the implicit moral message and provides the primary symbol for the theme of adversity. This symbol of the rain, and wind, nature's effects on the shanty dwellers, epitomizes the inner meaning of the novel in a terse and apposite image. Portrayals of this kind also have their social connotations: "workingmen carried home loads of pilfered corrugated cardboard cartons...to reinforce the roofs." And in the next paragraph we read: "children played in the puddles and the muddy soil, bare toes squishing into the wetness" (18). Both images describe objective social conditions that imply a subjective relationship. That is, the workingmen did not buy the cardboard cartons, they "pilfered" or plundered, stole them—which immediately raises certain moral and ethical questions of cause and effect, of motive and objective, of behavior and need. And the children, in spite of their innocent gaiety, deserve better, perhaps and cultural or recreational center, even a YMCA. As it is, however, La Guma succeeds in using visual facts to convey meaning beyond the visible. His attention to detail, "bare toes squishing into the wetness," helps to establish the moods of harsh reality and pathos, strongly represented in the image of the workingmen and the children. By the symbiosis of objective and subjective reality, La Guma constantly creates a sense of immediacy, the illusion in the reader's mind that she is in the actual spot described, experiencing the same emotional and conceptual response as the characters. We can see the workingmen carrying the corrugated cardboard cartons; we can hear the rain knocking on the tin roofs of the rickety hovels; we can, vicariously, feel the naked toes of the children squishing in the soft, wet mud. There is an insistence in La Guma's writing that all of the reader's senses should be engaged, not merely that of sight, but those of hearing, touch, and also smell.

Vernon February (1981) says, "La Guma has this naturalistic bent to portray the sound and the taste of objects and landscapes" (155). One of the greatest characteristics of La Guma's treatment of the world of natural phenomena is the implication that the scene is not simply decorative and passive, but is itself an actor in the human drama. It is the sustained image of the rain that provides the background and tempo and that occurs as an effective counterpoint to the intensity or lethargy of human action or inaction. It is, for example, "The sound of water coming through the roof of the Pauls' house," that awakens, and introduces us to the protagonist, Charlie Pauls at the beginning of Chapter Two. And as Charlie and the rest of the Pauls family begin to rise, the rain, in parallel momentum and personified animation, rises with them:

> The rain leaned against the house, under the pressure of the wind, hissing and rattling on the corrugated iron sides, scouring the roof. The wind flung the rain against the house with

> a roar, as if in anger, and then turned away, leaving only a
> steady hissing along the poorly painted, blistered metal.

Charlie turned in the sagging, loose sprung, iron bedstead...He heard
the downpour outside through his sleep, and still sleeping, hauled
the old Army blanket up over his shoulders. (*Threefold Cord*, 20)
The weather and even the time of day add their effects on the mood
of the scene, for both the fictional character and the reader, are
included in this description. The strange, unearthly feeling of early
morning, the tense, boding atmosphere, "the sagging, loose sprung,
iron bedstead...the old Army blanket": are all objective factors
working on the subjective mood of the character(s) and , through
him, on that of the reader. There is, of course, nothing new in the
attempt, thus, to reproduce atmosphere by working in scenic and
atmospheric effects: but, it has seldom been so successfully and
strikingly carried out as by Alex La Guma. February (1981) comments that "La Guma's characters are subordinate to his physical
descriptions. The terror and agony of his characters are rather felt
through his finely drawn settings and minute details" (154). In
other words, the natural features of his images do not appear to be
drawn in simply for effect. The whole is so carefully arranged that
the characters and their setting are absolutely coordinated; so that,
we cannot imagine the one without the other; the result, in the
design of the work and the feeling of the reader, is one of depend-
able continuity, balance and inevitableness.

This technique of La Guma's, of beginning a novel by relating
the state of the environment, materially and humanly, and its
changes due to weather and the time of year, gives a sense of reality and continuity that heightens the sense of being there. His figurations create this wonderful illusion of living in the spot described
and anticipating the changing seasons in their course, changes in
real life that occur gradually and without noticeable gradations;
yet, it must be observed that, in *And a Threefold Cord*, such seasonal changes do not occur at all, and the rain, nay even the season
of rain becomes a sustained, perpetual metaphor—for the sustained,
perpetual storm in the lives of the dispossessed shanty dwellers
clinging to life and hope on the fringes of Cape Town. "Yes," La
Guma seems to be saying, "nature is beautiful, but it is also the
hapless instrument of blind law" and, as such, he is utterly con-

vinced of its amorality (Herbert Grimsditch 1962: 49). By extending the metaphor, La Guma makes an extraordinary comparison
with the "blind law" inherent in a system based on the myth of
white supremacy. That is, if one accepts the tenets of white supremacy one is the luckless instrument (or victim) of an accidental
condition one can neither determine nor control. In a word, people
who come into society by no choice of their own should not be the
instruments nor the victims of "blind law" but of social and moral
laws devised by ordinary, reasonable and prudent human beings.
As Breyten Breytenbach (1971) and so many others have made
perfectly clear, "apartheid"—so-called white supremacy—is the
state and the condition of being "apart". It is the no man's land
between people. It is the blind spot in the white man's being and,
in this condition, what one doesn't see, doesn't exist (138). La
Guma, in metaphorical terms, captures the essence of this voluntary blindness with the following most fitting image, that of a mo-
torist speeding down a highway that borders a shanty town:

> The lights of high-powered headlamps, surging away in the
> darkness, did not touch the lights in the shanties...The rich
> automobile beams swept above the tiny chinks of malnour-
> ished light that tried to escape from the sagging shanties,
> like restless hope scratching at a door. Along the highway
> the night traffic spun past and did not notice the tumbledown
> latrines that circled the listing shacks and shipwrecked
> people like sharks in a muddy sea. (*Threefold Cord*, 87)

As if to leave no doubt, La Guma, in three specific references reveals the "voluntary" blindness of white South Africa: "high-pow-
ered headlamps...did not touch the lights in the shanties"; "rich
automobile beams swept above...the sagging shanties"; and, finally,
"traffic spun past and did not notice." This premeditated, deliberate unwillingness to see is another aspect of the complementary
pattern of theme-images consorting, one with the other, strengthening and holding the work together. The veracity of the metaphorical choice can be easily identified because it has its basis in
the South African social reality. One example of this kind of "voluntary" blindness, structured into the real-life pattern of South
African life, is the Bantustan fraud, of which the ramshackle com-

munity depicted in *And a Threefold Cord* is but a representative fragment. This fraud, the so-called "homelands policy," is an act of denationalization and dispossession in accordance with Pretoria's stated policy that there will one day be no Black people who are South African citizens. According to a November 1981 *Africa* magazine article, in the 1970s 1.6 million Africans were moved by the South African Government form their homes in the rural areas and relocated in inhospitable parts of the country, and their land designated "White." One and one-third million people have been moved from urban areas such as District Six. The explicit message of such a policy is that what one doesn't see does not exist. The majority of white South Africans would rather not see the peoples of color in South Africa, nor the conditions they have forced them to live under, since this very simple act of seeing might torture their consciences and their lives. Whites try to dismiss the Africans and other people of color from their minds and to imagine the country without them. But, the whites also realize that without the cheap, unprotected labor of the Africans (and others), South Africa would no longer have any meaning. Nor do the whites want to change the conditions of the millions of dispossessed people of color because this would destroy the racist myth upon which they base their privileges. This, and much more, is the meaning packed into the image of automobile traffic spinning past and not noticing "the tumbledown latrines that circle the listing shacks and shipwrecked people"—people La Guma stands before us in all their fundamental dignity and oh so unnecessary wretchedness.

La Guma, like every novelist, must grapple with the problems of the human condition, of human character and conduct; and the fact that he approaches these problems as an observer rather than a pedagogic moralist is no reason for the analyst or critic to do the same. The latter, it seems to me, are bound by certain academic methodology that necessitates, or implies, teaching by way of clarifying and interpreting what a more casual reader may have missed, for example, in subtle or esoteric imagery. Therefore, for La Guma, it is inevitable that he should betray a leaning towards certain character types (e.g., the African and so-called Coloured working class), and certain images of the physical environment (e.g., the desecration of physical bodies), and that he should organize these for the reader in such a way as to give an intelligible picture of the mental and physical anguish of the people—thus indirectly championing his own ethical views. It is then not surprising that the darkness and gloom of the socio-political reality of South Africa strongly colors the fabric of La Guma's literary canvases; particularly in *And a Threefold Cord,* but in his short stories and other novels as well.

La Guma's primary purpose, we may safely assume, is the artistic expression of ideas drawn from his experience of life in South Africa, and not the purely didactic inculcation of dogmatic principles. For this latter approach will not bring forth a novel of high artistic value, but leads its practitioner into exaggeration and perversion of fact in the effort to bear out a preconceived theory. La Guma follows the better method of looking at the world first, and then formulating his conclusions form what he finds there. And what he finds in the shanty town depicted in this novel is people, families, individuals engaged in an inevitable battle against indifferent and powerful natural and human forces. In this novel, we find several ways in which the natural environment is closely bound-up with La Guma's stylistic propensity; his sensitivity to minute sense impressions and his meticulous descriptions of these observed phenomena and lived experiences. Natural phenomena, undoubtedly, affect the mind and mood of humanity, usually in an imperceptive way; and it is the mark of artistic achievement that such phenomena open the mind to the significance of such a reciprocal relationship, and gives unity to a series of otherwise incoherent impressions. For instance, La Guma writes:

> The sky was heavy and grey, shutting out the sun, and there was no daylight, but an unnatural, damp twilight. The rain began again with gusty bursts, showering the world, pausing and then pouring down in big heavy drops. Then it settled gradually into a steady fall, an unhesitant tempo of drops, always grey. (*Threefold Cord,* 19)

This image calls up numerous associations and emotions, and gives us the picture of a world completely overwhelmed, deluged by unrelieved calamity. It creates a definite atmosphere, "The sky...heavy and grey, shutting out the sun...no daylight, but an unnatural, damp twilight" and gusty bursts of rain—making the reader particularly conscious of the disturbing, ruthless, capricious nature of a rainstorm: and its sodden, bedraggled after-effects are depressing and disfiguring, "always grey." The "unhesitant tempo" of the rain runs parallel with the tempo of events and the ebb and flow of emotional and psychological moods the author wishes to evoke in a given scene. For example, in the final chapter, the rain, that has been present throughout the novel, "showering the world," "leaning," "lashing in anger," becomes a devastating torrent viciously aroused:

> The rain tore at the roof and the wind lifted it, spinning and gambolling, through mid-air, a monstrous scythe that sheared through tree-tops and scrub and tore away flimsy fences. The rain scrabbled at the side of the house, groping at a weak overlap, a loosened seam, found a hold and clung on tugging and jerking, until rusty nails and bailing-wire surrendered and the rain and the wind ripped away a great flap of tin and wood, and left the interior of the shanty exposed like the side of a shrapnel-sheared face showing all the bloody convolutions of brain, ear and muscle which were drenched furniture, huddled people and slapping pieces of sacks. (166)

La Guma's frequent use of metaphor, especially simile and personification, serves to deepen the sense of the inanimate as a personality as it gropes, tugs, jerks, rips, and tears at the homes and lives of the people in this Cape Town ghetto. Rain, the dominant natural image in *And a Threefold Cord*, is, thus, endowed with human form, character, traits and sensibilities. It thereby establishes a firm metaphorical link with one of the major themes of the novel—the theme of adversity. The storm of social and economic adversity is likened to an indifferent, amoral, literal rainstorm. Therefore, the images which compose and distinguish characters are etched against this awesome, terrifying environment; awesome and terrifying, not in and of itself, but because abject poverty and wretchedness of the people makes them ill-equipped to deal with it. As Vernon February (1981) has observed, the Pauls family and the other residents of the shanty town are only incidental to the setting:

> Alex La Guma's characters are all isolated elements in an atmosphere which will eventually devour them. The author paints a landscape of annihilation without being maudlin...There is no political rhetoric, no trumpeting of slogans with La Guma. The force of his social protest gains momentum from his rather naturalistic depiction of the physical and spiritual landscape in which his characters dwell. (156)

Yet, in spite of the terror of their environment and the agony of their lives, La Guma's characters "cling defiantly to life" (166). He presents man's, particularly the man of color's, predicament in relation to a demonic landscape of barren earth, isolating wind and stormy weather. Man's tragic predicament, this novel suggest, is that of an uncaring, hostile and blind universe; the environment being one in which change and chance, death and decay prevail and is a recognized conclusion to human effort.

Like the image of nausea and vomiting in *A Walk in the Night*, the image of the rain forms a distinct pattern which recurs like leitmotivs, the controlling image and theme in the story. Images of rain are placed at crucial points in the story, and the close similarity in wording, mood and tempo of the scene ensures that they will be noticed. The rain motif begins at the very beginning of the novel and is sustained to the end. The reappearance of the rain image, within this framework, heralds the intervention of fate and the resumption of adversity. It becomes a major factor in the motivation of Ronny Paul's crime, providing a kind of incentive or psychological explanation for his murder of Susie Meyer.

The critical point is reached when Ronny goes "wandering about the dark settlement" alone and sees the girl, Susie Meyer, emerge from George Mostert's garage. One would have to quote in full the three pages of this chapter to show the metaphorical structure of the scene: the crescendo of the rain and action of the characters, culminating in the fortissimo of the short factual sentences about the murder itself. The main strands of the image, however, will reveal something of the mire in which all the characters' lives are stuck: "Ronny was just about to step down the muddy, leaf-strewn embankment," when he sees Susie, he "stopped short under the growth of trees that dripped down on him" (*Threefold Cord*, 143).

And as the pace of the prose and the action quickens, "anger tore at him with sharp claws," and "the rain was beginning to fall faster now, a regular, straight downpour, but Ronald did not feel the soaking chill, for his guts were hot with rage" (143). We are prepared for this. We have been inured by La Guma's consistent use of the parallel movement of natural forces and the events of the narrative, and the convergence of this parallel movement in an appropriate image, like the following:

> The rain beat down on her and she felt the burn of the knifeblade in her breast, through the chill of the rain. The blade slashed and thrust, slicing her face and driving into her chest again. She tried to scream, but it was a retching sound for the knife had already cut into her throat, through flesh and wind-pipe and vocal cords. The force of the stabbing knocked her, floundering, into the mud....Under the savage, enraged, cutting caresses of the blade she could do nothing but surrender as to another lover. (145)

Ronny Pauls, like all the Ronnies of this and all the slums of South Africa, America—indeed, the world—is trapped in a vicious "maelstrom of cause and effect" (February 1981) paralyzed and then animated by forces which he cannot control and which reduce his desires and needs to animal-like proportions. He kills the girl, Susie Meyer, without qualms; and the knifing is depicted in graphic, animal, sexual terms: "...the savage, enraged, cutting caresses of the blade" (emphasis added), to which Susie surrenders "as to another lover." The rain too plays an active part in this murder scene; it too has no qualms as it "beat down on her" at the same time it had begun to "fall faster...a regular, straight downpour" as the scene commenced. Interestingly, given the hostile and destructive reputation of the rain, up to this point, one could easily substitute "rain" wherever "knifeblade," or its correlates appear and not lose anything as far as the meaning of the image is concerned. In fact, in foreshadowing this scene, La Guma writes "The rain...possessed a certain personality, a cutting, muttering, gurgling, sucking, bubbling personality, like a homicidal imbecile with a knife" (126).

Seen from within, through the eyes of Ronny Pauls, and rein-
forced by a powerful battery of images depicting the merciless,
hostile, and destructive force of the rain, the explanation of the rain
as a motivating factor in Ronny's crime acquires some measure of
validity. The rain plays an intensely interactive role in the converg-
ing attack of overpowering sensations: for example, "the soaking
chill" and indifferent violence of the rain, the internal violence of
frustration, jealousy, anger and fear, which seem to throw Ronny
off his balance.

Like the rain, Ronny's temperament has been a steady crescendo
from the very beginning of the novel. In Chapter Two, as intermittent jabs from the rain strike the tin roof of their hovel, "a tiny
rumbling as the drops struck the metal, and then gradually became
a dull tinkling": a parallel movement is taking place inside the
one-room shack, where Charlie Pauls is busy teasing his brother,
Ronny, about his infatuation with Susie Meyer:

> He yawned loudly, and then pretended seriousness" "She
> got a blerry nice pair of poles, though." Ronald...howled
> and reached down for one of his shoes and flung it...He
> shouted, almost in tears, "You better stop it, hey. I'm tell-
> ing you, you better stop it." (24-25)

In other words, the gradual increase in the inner turmoil of Ronny
is parallel with the gradual gathering of rainclouds; while the intermittent showers are counterpoint to Ronny's intermittent emotional outburst, until the parallel image sequence converges in a
final downpour of uncontrolled, thunderous, rage and violence.
Then, La Guma, like a master conductor, orchestrates the final pia-
nissimo, as he gently describes Ronny's "rain-washed face like
lusterless pearls," as he stands, primevally, over Susie, "the huddle
of old clothes at his feet" (145).

La Guma's organization of the events leading up to Susie's
murder is presented by a series of intelligible pictures, footage,
that when seen as completely as possible, makes the reader aware
that it is the conditions, elemental and human, that create the consciousness of the characters. In other words, the idea, whether the
characters in the narrative are conscious of it or not, of the impact

of the environment on psychological and emotional states is inherent and inseparable from the image.

The parallel image sequence of natural environment and character is particularly vivid and intense and is closely integrated into the meaning of the story. The cruelty of the apartheid system, the institutionalize myth of white superiority, is felt as a social catastrophe with tragic consequences, disguised as "the natural order of things."

Along with the rain imagery in *And a Threefold Cord*, La Guma also uses the image of fire. Occasionally, as we have seen in the episode involving Ronny Pauls and Susie Meyer, images are developed into little scenes. Such is the case in the imagery of fire, an apposite image masterfully juxtaposed with the image of rain.

La Guma presents man's painful predicament in relation to a demonic landscape (both topographical and human), of barren earth, apathetic urbanization, isolating wind, stormy weather, and creative-destructive fire. Fire, that is, as an answer to darkness can be creative or destructive: an instrument of mastery or chaos. Readers will see in Charlie Pauls a character who will, to some extent, master his environment through active participation in it. He creates a livable pattern of life in the midst of the chaos that surrounds him. The scenes that carry the underpattern show other characters acting out their ritual roles as bringers of light or darkness to the pattern of human fate prescribed by a system predicated on the notion of white supremacy. In terms of the novel itself, this must be understood on both a literal and metaphorical level. In the former sense, we notice that the book opens (Chapter Two) in the darkness of early morning, where La Guma writes of Charlie, "Darkness enclosed him with the blackness of a sealed cave, and he lay in darkness...." (20) but it is also Charlie who brings the first light into this darkness, strikes a match and "protecting the match flame with his cupped hand while he turned up the chimney of the storm-lantern, and lit the wick...so that the flame swelled and brightened, throwing light around" (21). In the latter, metaphorical sense, Charlie is the bringer of intellectual light to the shanty-town community, as during his conversation with Uncle Ben he reports what he had heard on a job:

> "This burg say, if the poor people all got together and took everything in the whole blerry world, there wouldn't be poor no more...."Further, this rooker say if all the stuff in the world was shared out among everybody, all would have enough to live nice. He reckoned people got to stick together to get this stuff." (83)

To which Uncle Ben, one of the bringers of darkness responds:

> "Sound almost like a sin, that. Bible say you mustn't covet other people's things...I heard people talking like that...That's communis' things. Talking against the govverment." (83)

Even though there is no trumpeting of slogans or political rhetoric here, one is forced to smile at the simplicity and political naivete' of Uncle Ben. All this, however, is merely background to the build up of a major scene where the forces of light (fire) intersect with the forces of darkness, in this case (poverty), where image and idea converge in an explosive scene conveying the full impact of the theme of adversity inherent in this work.

Throughout the early chapters of the novel, the contiguous development of the rain and fire imagery has been suggested and subtlely foreshadowed as decisive in the outcome of the story. From the very beginning, when Ronny flung his shoe at Charlie for teasing him about Susie Meyer and Charlie scowled, "Cut it out, man. You almost set the blerry place alight"; to the anxiety the reader feels at the beginning of Chapter Three when "Charlie opened the door and went out into the dark kitchen. He struck a match and found another storm-lamp. It hung from a beam across the bulging cardboard ceiling"; and in Chapter Four when we notice, "A candle burned, trembling in the draught, on a limp chest of drawers which stood lopsidedly on the uneven floor," we are tense with anticipation of the latent (to the characters) and blatant (to the reader) danger in these conditions (cardboard ceiling, and a lighted candle on a limp chest of drawers standing lopsidedly on an uneven floor).

The fire and rain imagery is so interwoven in the psychological texture of the story that they are symbolic as well. One of La Guma's main concerns in this novel, which he probes deeply, is the relationship between man and "nature"; with "nature" symbolizing the much more blatant, much more willful desecration of human lives by the local and international system of so-called white supremacy. The fire and rain are thus seen as an actual reality and as symbolic. These symbols, as has been stated, are primarily an aesthetic device for carrying a burden of meaning, that is, theme in a compressed package. These symbols offer an analogy for something not directly stated, but yet essential to the meaning of this work. The balance and harmonious development of these forces creates tension, by bringing together, as in simile and metaphor, associations that are remote or opposed to one another; also by reconciling various discordant qualities, of literal meaning and metaphorical meaning, of the abstract and concrete, of tone and rhythm, and so on.

As such, La Guma uses the symbols of fire and rain as structural principles (balancing, organizing the material of the work), and as principles containing meaning holding the work together. In other words, they present a repeated pattern (motif), and a meaningful theme throughout the work. They convey meaning on many levels and frequently on more than one level at one time. A specific and concrete meaning is presented on the literal level, a transcendent and no less important meaning on the metaphorical level. Consequently, any meaning we assign to these symbols is at best partial, and does not presume to exhaust the possible meanings they contain. As a realistic writer, La Guma arouses deep pity and compassion in the reader because of the contrast between the metaphor and the actuality, and these emotions are quite appropriate to the tragic sequence of events in the story. As with the rain imagery, the cumulative imagery of the fire prepare us for, and help us to anticipate, what is to happen. For twenty-five chapters, La Guma has made subtle and repeated references to the latent, duplicitous image of fire; we know it is going to be a factor. He has also taken time to develop the inconsistent, but affectionate affair between Charlie and Freda; an affair based on spontaneity and convenience, where Charlie is unable to get beyond a superficial, external, inebriated appraisal of Freda's "body, breasts, hips, pelvis" (85); and the "something more than desire for her inside him...worried him a little" (61). Still, La Guma establishes the emotional connection between these two characters early in the novel, and keeps it alive just on the periphery of the main lines of the story to create suspense and curiosity. This suspense is the result of the reader's attempt to evaluate and interpret the theme of the story and the kinds of meaning or ideas that are to be derived from the image-symbol of rain and fire.

In preparing the reader for the rising, devastating role of fire, it is helpful to note that at the beginning of Chapter Twenty-Six, "The rain had stopped" (155) Also, La Guma keeps the somewhat deceptive image of fire active and positive, latent and dangerous as in the following image:

> In Freda's shanty it was warm and dry. She kept the primus stove going most of the time, and the cardboard and paper-covered walls kept the hear in. (155)

Fire, as a positive force, can dry and warm the damp, cold shanty, while at the same time it threatens the flimsy cardboard, paper-covered walls. In addition, our anxiety is intensified when we notice that the stove is precariously propped-up with an empty match-box because one of its legs is missing. Just as there are two types of fire, constructive and destructive, La Guma has also defined two types of water:

> There is water in the threatening sky, and water in the healthy earth; water in copper pipes and iron cisterns. Water to boil coffee, or to wash scraps of clothes. Water with which to wash the dead. Water is precious, and in the yards of those whose sand-lots had been laid with plumbing, the queues of scarecrow children form up with buckets and cans and saucepans. Those who owned the plumbing and the taps sold the water to those who lacked such amenities. Because a man's got to live, hasn't he? (113)

So, there is life preserving and life threatening water, and there is life-preserving and life-threatening fire. What gives them their value, positive or negative,(in their metaphorical social equivalent) is people's material, premeditated capacity—within a given socio-political context—to use these forces for good or evil.

La Guma selects concrete, specific detail to build up the poetic mood and sequence of rain and fire imagery. It takes us from the physical effects of the coldness outside, where "The wind swished through the trees, waving their mustard-yellow flowers like fans, and rattled loose the walls and flapping sheets of tin" That is, where the rain lets up the wind takes over in the same magnificently contradictory way, "swish(ing) mustard-yellow flowers like fans" and simultaneously "rattl(ing) loose the walls" of the shanties; and now the rain lay dormant, but "Overhead the sky lurked in ambush, treacherous as a bog"; to inside Freda's shanty where the simple desire of children yearning for human fulfillment is depicted against the background of these capricious forces—as, "Klonky, the little boy, thought they should make a tent of the settee cover and pretend to be camping. But the little girl, Gracie, turns down the suggestion, saying that mother would be cross and wouldn't give them the sugarsticks..." (156). Then, simple childish desire is metamorphosed into ubiquitous (for the African world) human need, as Klonky whines, "I want a piece of bread."

Like a set-designer for theater, La Guma carefully and thoughtfully builds the scene, every object, and every character in just the right place. There is bread in their rude hovel, and it's on the table "by the basin of dishes and the primus stove" (157). This development of the scene is so profoundly appropriate: as it tends to suggest, metaphorically, that what the children need is within their grasp but to get it they must go through fire. The image easily becomes a metaphor for a human condition that is universal and daily. For, as the stove-fire (now a symbol of the flames of oppression and destruction) "roared and growled...

> The little girl picked up a knife and started to saw at the bread. The table shook on the uneven dung floor. The shaking upset the match-box prop, and the stove toppled over with a clang. Then it exploded.
> The old, clogged, faulty stove, dangerous as a mine, went off with a slapping bang, like the bursting of an immense paperbag, exploding like shrapnel and sending pieces of hot brass and iron hurtling in all directions. Burning oil spat into the little girl's face, set alight her clothes and danced up into her hair. Flames ran like water across the table and caught at dry paper and cardboard lining of the wall. The wall crackled into life. The child shrieked in an atrocious agony and rushed blindly into the curtain across the room. The curtain caught alight from the blazing torch of her body, and screaming, the child tore it down, and doing so, dragged it into the oil lamp hanging from a nail in the ceiling. Oil splashed everywhere; it caught the screaming boy who was trying to hobble on one foot to the door, and washed

him in a bath of dancing yellow as he plucked frantically at
the lock. (157)

The two children, Freda's children, Klonky and Gracie, African
children—in Hunters Point, San Francisco, in East Oakland, California; in South Side Chicago; in Brooklyn, New York—are weekly,
it seems, certainly monthly, burned to death, as "fumes and fire
choked them, boiled their skin into blisters, spluttered through layers of fat, roasted flesh, cartilage, membrane" while "Overhead
the sky sneered" (158). Here, the image-symbol of fire which
carries the burden of meaning intersects with a terrifying image of
extreme desecration of human beings. It is a tragic image arousing
both fear and pity; tragic, too, because the suffering is so unnecessary, so undeserved.

The implications of this event transcend the immediate story;
since there is a universality about man's dread of fire, and his suffering from fire: "God gave Noah the rainbow sign, no more water,
fire next time." Even racial injustice, which plays its part in this
event, has its overtones. And the abject poverty which pursues the
people of the shanty town, the "uneven dung floor" the "cardboard
walls" of the peoples' shacks which dominate the story, have their
own kind of universality. Pain and suffering are universal themes
in literature, themes that are not unique to African writers.

This deep and all-too-common and unnecessary tragedy is,
above all things, human. Like the novel itself, this event focuses
on that most familiar and basic of institutions - the family; in this
case, the two children and the mother, Freda: "Her own husband
had died in a lorry smash two years ago, and Charlie had a suspicion that she now expected him to marry her" (56). This is a typical single-parent family portrait. It is representative, the look of
ordinary people (if by "ordinary" we mean what the majority of
humanity is experiencing everyday) including the borrowed, makeshift furniture, the cheap clothes, malnourished children, poorly
constructed hazardous living quarters; and on this level, La Guma's
depiction acquires universality, and for the compassion he hoped
and believed this heart-rending, distressing narrative image would
arouse.

We are made to feel some curious sense of responsibility about
or for this tragedy, a sort of personal involvement, that we owe

something more than just awareness of the victims. La Guma imbues this image, it seems to me, with everything that he had ever known about fire, as he represents it as having life and human qualities: "Burning oil spat into the little girl's face...and danced up into her hair. Flames ran like water...fumes and fire...roared and snapped and snarled" (emphasis added)—and the collapse of the shanty itself is described as if the death of a person, as it "sagged and lurched like a drunkard...and the tin walls flopped and groaned as if in agony" (157). We are made to feel, to hear, to even smell as well as see, vicariously, the red, yellow, blue, white fire and heat snarling at the helpless onlookers, "holding them at bay."

Yet, the image La Guma creates is not so much one of a disaster per se; rather the emotional tone that surrounds disaster; what we might call inner disaster. He sought and created an image in which this inner feeling is embedded, not just an image of fire. In fact, a fire can be a cheerful affair. It is full of bright colors and moving shapes; it can make people warm and happy. But, obviously, it was not La Guma's purpose to tell about fire, not to describe fire. What he did formulate is the terror, the heart-rending fear that fires can and do cause, the agony of a parent, a mother, losing her only children, for:

> ...through the cries and the crackle of embers came another sound. At first it was a wail, and then it became a sort of shrill, horrid gobbling chant, an awful sound-picture which might conjure up the abominable death-rites of some primitive tribe. It rose to a high, nerve-plucking ululation which was something more then a scream or a shriek, the sound of an impossible sadness, a sound beyond agony, an outcry of unendurable woe, forelorn beyond comprehension, a sort of grief beyond grief. It was Freda. (158)

This image evokes the culminating emotional response to this calamitous event. Images and symbols, as has been stated, must not be thought of as restricted merely to the pictorial. They can be auditory as well. In the above citation, the effectiveness is in the precision with which the auditory aspects of the scene are suggested (":shrill, horrid gobbling chant...nerve-plucking ululations...a sound beyond agony, an outcry of unendurable woe"). The anguish of these sounds of grief themselves symbolize the dramatic tension in the novel itself, standing autonomous as a vivid mental event. As such, the effect is not the separation of image and meaning but their fundamental and essential unity.

Although the children killed in this fire hold the sense of all the helpless and innocent children in the world, one sympathizes with them, not because they represent a generality, but because they are so individual and specific. Injustices embitter one, and one sincerely hopes for and works toward mass improvements; but that is only because whatever mass there may be is made up of individuals, and each of them is able to feel and have hopes and dreams. The dilemma of children is summed up by Vernon February (1981) when he writes: "In children then, are found all the horrible and traumatic effects of the system" of so-called white supremacy (71).

La Guma's synthesis of image and idea is concomitantly the synthesis of objectivity and subjectivity. The challenge is not to abolish either or both from the interpretation of an image, but rather to unite them into a single impression: an image of which meaning (theme) is an inalienable part, in which form and content are inseparable. Alex La Guma's descriptions in *And a Threefold Cord*, his recreation of the animate and inanimate, includes both the object and the emotional and psychological sensations connecting him with the object; that is, both the facts and the tone, the author's attitude toward the experience.

The imagery of rain and fire clusters primarily around the themes of adversity and unity while, at the same time, implying metaphorically the effects of apartheid on the material environment, as well as on the physical, mental, and emotional health of the characters portrayed. In this way, the private experience La Guma depicts becomes a universal experience, because his private experience illuminates the private and personal world in which each of us lives the major part of our life.

The principle that organizes the images is a concord between image and theme, the images lighting the way for the theme and helping to reveal, step by step, the theme as it thus evolves controlling more and more the deployment of the images. La Guma's images of nature, of rain, wind and fire, and of an oppressive and depressing physical environment, do not appear for their own sake only, nor to suggest states of mind only, but to illuminate theme and action. His landscapes and cityscapes are usually with figures, people; contemplating the people inhabiting his environment—both real and imagined—we are better able to understand why Ronny or Susie is what he or she is, does what he or she does, or to view the human characters in perspective with the presence of the universe or capricious fate. The main function of the imagery is to elucidate certain political and socio-economic ideas: one of the most important ideas being the effects of the South African myth of white superiority on the people, particularly people of color.

The principal characters of *And a Threefold Cord* are members of one family—the Pauls family: Ma Pauls, Dad Pauls, and their four children: Charlie, the protagonist, through whose eyes most of the story is revealed and understood: Ronny and Jorny, Charlie's younger brothers—respectively: and Caroline, a teenager recently married and expecting a child. Some demographer would be quick to say that the size of the family itself is the cause of their poverty; that without "so-many" children they would not be poor; mistaking effect for cause. Professor February puts the matter this way:

> Procreation is the only form of creativity and creation allowed to the poor, for in this special realm, the white world cannot impinge. The third world child is not enshrined in his childhood from birth, as is his white counterpart. He cannot at all times rely on that special form of protection from his family, his birth is largely an accident. Right from the start, he is surrounded by the socio-economic conditions of poverty, illiteracy and the vain attempts to survive at all. (*Mind Your Color*, 72)

It is the misfortunes of this family, the Pauls family, that are followed throughout the novel: from the death of the head of the household to the birth of a grandchild. It is, among other things, the faithfulness of La Guma's story to this time-honored cycle, these inevitable "rites of passage" that gives *And a Threefold Cord* its tight structural unity and coherence. Other, minor, characters include: Freda, for whom Charlie has had a long unexpressed liking and will marry: Susie Meyer, the "flirtatious coquette," for whom Ronny has a jealous passion and eventually kills: and George Mostert, a white garage owner, and Roman whom Wilfred Cartey

(1969) describes as "living statements of alienation" (131). Cartey's description is certainly consistent with La Guma's portraits of these two latter characters, as the following examples indicate:

> Life was there, no matter how shabby, a few yards from, George Mostert's Service Station and Garage, but he was trapped in his glass office by his own loneliness and a wretched pride in a false racial superiority, the cracked embattlements of his world. (*Threefold Cord*, 67)

And of the callous Roman, La Guma writes how:

> A common labourer, Roman had drifted from one mean job to another, earning a few shillings here, a few shillings there. Finally, despairing, perhaps, about the upkeep of his offspring, he took to petty thieving, robbing the weaker ones around him. Now and then he robbed out of bounds, and found himself in jail. (103)

In their poignant simplicity, these images succinctly sum-up George's and Roman's tragedy: Their alienation and aloneness, their lack of meaningful relationships or rapport with anyone in their respective, white or black, communities. February (1981) says of Mostert, "He is doubly cut off from the main stream of existence. He is white, but lives outside their normative structure; he lives in a 'coloured' area, but through his skin, is largely precluded from the warmth and proletarian exuberance of the shanty towns" (156). Mostert and Roman are "bringers of darkness" to the illuminating message of unity inherent in the central focus on the Pauls family and Charlie Pauls' pronouncement in particular—"Is not natrual for people to be alone" (168).

These characters are all introduced in the early chapters of the novel in a series of scenes. As the wonderful Wilfred Cartey (1969) summarizes: "We are given their family relationships, their idiosyncratic gestures toward members of the community. Then we see them playing out their roles opposite those with whom they have relationships or rapport, after which we are shown the results of these relationships, results brought about partly by society and partly by their own inner qualities" (131). The tone of the images used to describe each character's behavior with other people corresponds to the nature of the relationship. For example, Charlie Pauls, the eldest child, is the most likely successor as head of the household; even his physique—tight, muscular, strong—and his colorful, extraverted personality shines through a number of images:

> Charlie's face, brown-skinned, glowed in the light which picked up the wide curves of his high cheekbones and the thick, solid jaw running into a chin as curved and hard as the toe of an army boot. There was a dark stubble in the hollows of his cheeks, and deep grooves bracketed the wide, heavy, humorous and sensual mouth. He had a wide forehead, and low, with the dark, thick, kinky hair growing forward. There was a mole on his right cheekbone. His eyes were dark-brown, the colour of chestnuts, gleaming in the lamp-light, the eyeballs yellowish. (22)

And a couple of pages later:

> Charlie was tall and had the big shoulders and chest of one who had worked with his muscles. The muscles bunched and knotted under the long-sleeved, soiled flannel vest. (26)

These essentially physical portraits of Charlie can suggest visual elements of his heroic prowess, which he quickly proves in the fight with Roman: a fight that also provides a moral portrait of Charlie, because he did not want to fight Roman, but in defending the threat to his brother, Ronny, he ends up having to defend himself. When Charlie approaches a group of toughs, La Guma describes as "a motley collection of scarecrows, dummies stuffed with the straw of poverty" (46), Roman says to him, "I was just reckoning to these jubas I don't like that Ronny must worry with my goose. See?" The "goose" to whom he is referring is Susie Meyer: to which Charlie replies, "you can mos tell Ronny that yourself. Don't I say?" (47) Charlie had decided to call it off, but Roman pressed him, "Like an aggressive power waiting for an excuse to start a war" (49). And the elements of nature, the sky, the stormy horizon are summoned by La Guma to comment on, to play their familiar part in furnishing metaphorical equivalents for this action as, "The sky had a flat, battle-grey look" (51). In keeping with his heroic stature, Charlie wins the fight and warns Roman "...leave my brother alone" (52). It can be noted that the short and simple image of the "battle-grey" sky adds a fleeting note to the narrative action, provides an effective link with the predominant elemental images of the work, without holding-up the narrative or diverting attention from its subject.

An atmosphere of latent and active violence, in the 'natural' and societal environment, is everywhere present in the imagery of *And a Threefold Cord*. The elements, the people, everything seems to be drawn-up in battle array marshaled for fight; everywhere, the destructive images of war-torn scenes are presented in their stark materiality (Cartey 1969:132). This is precisely the tension I felt while visiting South Africa in December of 1996. From the moment of our arrival at Jan Smuts International airport and the obvious color hierarchy visible even in the airport restaurant, to the restaurant near Cape Town University that carefully refused us service; the only time we, my wife and sons, did not feel this way was when we were visiting her relatives in the various townships. Thus, there is a plethora of such military, battle references, even in the description of characters such as Charlie who has "a chin as curved and hard as the toe of an *army boot*...the round skull, hard as a *bullet*...he peered out sadly past the petrol pumps which gazed like petrified *sentries* across the concrete no-man's land of the road...It was as if all the leaving of a modern *battlefield* had been collected and dumped there..." (22, 50, 67 and 70; emphasis added). These images demonstrate La Guma's vision of South African society, as an embattled, violent, hostile environment, in which the forces of nature and man seem to join hands to defeat the peoples' very will to exist. And, how much of a chance they will have to exist, and reach their highest worth, depends on the relative strength of the forces, both human and elemental, acting on and through them, as well as their collective and individual responses to these forces. In a sense, the Pauls' family troubles, and by metaphorical implication the troubles of African and other peoples of color in South Africa and the world, spring from their unwillingness to accept the capricious laws of "nature". Especially if the definition of "nature" includes the notion that the myth of white supremacy (racism) is the "natural" order of things.

The forces acting on Roman are, in a general sense, the same ones acting on Charlie and the other inhabitants of the shanty-town. Why, therefore, is Roman's response to these forces so much more magnified, more violently aggressive and irrational than, say, Charlie's? The answer seems to be that despite their common poverty there are qualitative differences in the individual circumstances. And it is La Guma's selective delineation of representative characters that provides depth, complexity, and individuation to each character's unique responses to this dehumanizing environment.

Charlie, for instance (as his mother is quick to point out to him on one occasion) has no wife, or children, or job: this latter aspect of his experience, his unemployment, being the point of intersection, of convergence, for him and Roman. Roman, on the other hand, "lived with his family in what looked like an amalgamation of a kennel, a chicken-coup and a lean-to shed...Within it, he, his wife and eleven children crowded like rabbits in a hutch, whenever shelter was necessary" (103). It may be of interest to note that Charlie is poor with "no wife, or children," whereas Roman is also poor with "his wife and eleven children"; La Guma seems fond of this kind of dialectic. Roman's personal condition, however, has a determining effect on his pessimistic and aggressive consciousness. Frustrated, unemployed, his wife giving birth "as regularly as clock-work...as smoothly as a grease-gun gives grease," despairing about his ability to provide for his eleven offspring, he takes his frustrations and anger out on the weaker people around him. This character type is a favorite of La Guma's, appearing both in his short story "Tattoo Marks and Nails," and as Butcherboy in his novel *The Stone Country*. In size, attitude, and behavior, Roman is representative, a metaphor, a certain type of character: a type, however, that is a microcosm epitomizing, not just individual traits, but those of nations. For example:

> When he was home, all who lived near them could hear the sounds of Roman's brutality. He beat his wife's head with faggots, or her face with his fists. He kicked her ribs and broke her arms. When he became tired of beating her, he whipped the children. Most of the time he was in a state of drunken savagery, and when he had wine, or the means of

procuring any, he was dangerous as a starved old wolf, ready
to turn on anybody who got in his way. (104)

Like Willieboy (*A Walk in the Night*), or more precisely like
Willieboy's father, and Constable Raalt, Roman's antisocial (violent) attitude and behavior has something to do with the brutal
society around him, and most probably his own brutal upbringing.
Roman's insouciance, like that of Raalt's and Willieboy's father,
and Willieboy himself, his disregard for social ethics, his quixotic
violence, is a result of his society, and his philosophy of life stems
from this society.   Roman, like Willieboy, for example, lacks affection and companionship, and when he is dying, after having
been shot by Constable Raalt, he can only recall the drunken brutality of his father, and the lack of concern of his mother, both of
whom appear to him in his painful delirium (Cartey 1969:129):

> His father's leather belt crashed against the sides of the van
> and snapped through the air, its sharp edge ripping at his
> legs and buttocks, the pain jumping through him....Once
> his mother woke up and turning her head shouted at him to
> stop complaining. (*Walk*, 86-87)

Such a comparison is useful in again pointing out that La Guma's
characters represent both specific and general human qualities. Put
another way, while the social and environmental factors to which
the characters are exposed may be identical, the responses are
unique to each particular character. This portrait of Willieboy's
father could very easily be that of Roman. For La Guma's study of
character is not just a study of character for its own sake, but is like
a drama, where the two major actors are the characters on one side
and their whole environment on the other. Roman's defeat, therefore, is not just a victory for Charlie, but for the entire community.
Roman, like South Africa, must learn humility, to humble his pride,
to discipline his strength and reckless violence with that of the
community, and thus achieve his freedom. Roman is, in the final
analysis, a simple type. We do not see a complex individual who
changes and matures over a period of time. La Guma does not
employ elaborate analysis to bring out the complexities of his per-

sonality or to explain the motivations for his feelings and behavior. What we know about Roman is from the outside only.

Yet, Roman, as an autonomous portrait, is consistent with the pattern of imagery related to the elements of nature and shares similar characteristics: capricious, whimsical, unpredictable—characteristics which are by definition oddly constituted, fickle, and without reasoned motivation. Roman's relationship to his environment is neatly summed up in his fight with Charlie and in the picture of his violent domestic life. The main function of the image of Roman, it seems to me, being to elucidate the, admittedly, hackneyed theme of brain over brawn; and the inanity of incestuous violence and its logical extreme—fratricide. Whatever its artistic merits, such images—as those depicting or related to Roman—make it abundantly clear that such images are not a passing fancy with La Guma, but symptoms of a deep-rooted and serious interest. One has only to contemplate, momentarily, a La Guma character sketch or portrait, and it will be apparent that he has not only a great interest in human character, in human feeling, but also has a great love for the people he portrays.

It is a tribute to his concern for individualizing each character that we can observe Charlie's and Roman's unique and specific responses to the same physical and socio-political environment. And how their private (family) context, like Willieboy's, inured them to their reality. Of concern, naturally, is the value of these comparisons to the delineation of characters, and to the overall meaning and design of *And a Threefold Cord*. Wilfred Cartey (1969) has said, with regard to the difference in characterization in *And a Threefold Cord* and *A Walk in the Night*:

> ...in *And a Threefold Cord* the family unit is intact at the beginning of the novel. Of course, Dad Pauls is very ill, Caroline is with child, Ronald is petulant and an angry, truculent young man. Yet, Ma Pauls is strong and resistant, and by her hard toil, she manages to keep the family together, above water and relatively happy. Charlie, too, is a good person—sweet-natured, optimistic, kind, and jovial. The characterization in this novel differs from that of *A Walk in the Night* in that the qualities of the protagonist are directly and at times shrewdly delineated for us. The char-

acters' relations to the community sustain them or bring
about their down-fall. (130)

Charlie's relation to his community is a non-antagonistic one;
whereas, Roman's relation, like that of Ronny's, is an antagonistic
one. Charlie, symbolically speaking, is a "bringer of light"—intellectually and in terms of his actions; Roman "brings darkness";
Charlie is "a good person...sweet natured, optimistic, kind, and
jovial"; Roman is a bully with a sour, pessimistic, mean, and humorless outlook. Each of the characters has his or her (e.g., Caroline
and Susie Meyer) peculiar, idiosyncratic responses to their oppressive environment where whites exercise an almost total control.
Charlie, for instance, is a more alert character, more interested in
the people and the ideas around him, more extroverted. This makes
for greater variety in content, in the levels of meaning, as well as
style. He is a logical link between his younger brothers, Ronny
and Jorney, and his parents, Ma and Pa Pauls; he is a transitional
stage in intellectual physiognomy, the dawning of a new consciousness among the so-called Coloured people of South Africa. David
Rabkin punctuates this view when he comments: "Charlie Pauls...is
an occasional worker, in whom the roots of class-consciousness
have taken a precarious hold" (February 1981:159).

Though the subject of a more extensive treatment later in this
chapter, it is, at this time, worthwhile to note some specific characteristics of Charlie that reveal La Guma's conscientious control of
his subject in ways that anticipate the former's heroism, evolving
consciousness and basic sensitivity. It is no accident that early in
the novel, when the Pauls family is just waking to the monotonous
drumming of the rain, it is Charlie who rises first. And when Ma
Pauls shouts,"Get up or go to sleep, but let your pa get his rest,"
the petulant Ronald echos with a small sneer "Your pa got to have
his rest," and adds, mockingly critical "The ou rest all bladdy day."
And Charlie, alert and good-natured, chastens his arrogant brother:
"You leave ou kerel alone. You got no right raising that sort of
voice about the old man" (*Threefold Cord*, 25). Charlie's relation
to his family sustains him, just as it helps sustain the Pauls family.
His words, like his actions, reveal him as a man, his values, are an
index to his personality; and the same can be said of Ronald.

So, from the beginning, Ronny's relation to his environment is diametrically opposite that of Charlie's, even though they confront the same specific environment. The truculent, hostile dimensions of Ronny's personality are strengthened by La Guma's physical portrait of him:

> Ronald crouched *morosely* at the table, gulping down his breakfast. The lamplight glowed on the pomade on his hair. Adolescence lay heavily on him, reflected in his *mean* brown eyes, in the twist of his *bitter* mouth, and the *reck-less* truculence scratched at the *hard enclosure* of his mind, vicious as a *watchdog* at a gate. (32; emphasis added)

This kind of figuration, essential for understanding the imagistic technique of La Guma,s delineates Ronny's physical qualities, at the same time it suggests intellectual physiognomy: moral, attitudinal, and subjective qualities to an otherwise objective portrait. Such imaging also provides an emotional tone appropriate to the action going forward at the moment. For instance, as Ronald "crouched morosely at the table, gulping down his breakfast," the following dialogue ensues:

> ...the mother said...''The whole house look like it's falling in. I don't know what to do with your pa sick." "Sick," Ronald said...."''That ou been sick a helluva time." "You stop talking about your pa like that," the mother said, sharply. Charlie looked at his younger brother. "You go nothing to say, hey. Helluva lot *you* do around this blerry place." (33; emphasis added)

Ronald's attitude is indeed an anomaly, not the ordinary feelings a son should have for his father. But the conditions of life in the shanty-towns of South Africa, the shanty-towns of the African world, are not "ordinary" conditions; if anything, they are extraordinary. Ronny is angry and hurt because of his father's illness, then too, he is the only Pauls working, so he is resentful and indignant; because the family owes the doctor who said he wouldn't come unless they pay cash, "And there's no money till Ronny get pay Friday" (75). Yet, in the face of his father's irreversible, terminal illness and Ronny's bitterness, meanness and reckless speech, Charlie remains an assiduous optimist: "Ach, Ronny's awright....He will still come right, you see, Ma" (34). And Ma Pauls, in a flash of candor, castigates Charlie's gratuitous and perhaps myopic optimism with:

> Goddamit,...Everybody's awright by you. Isn't so bad. Is awright. Everything is going to be okay. You not bringing up no children yet. (35-36)

Charlie, with characteristic equanimity, capitulates, "Awright Ma. Awright, man. don't go on so." To explain Ronny's attitude beyond what has already been suggested, we should recognize that when he was just a "dirty-nosed youngster" hanging onto his mother's skirts, "whining like a hurt pup" (39), Charlie and Dad Pauls had worked desperately to have their house built in time for the birth of Caroline. Consequently, and along with all that it means to be the first male child, Charlie and his Dad are closer, for example:

> Dad and Charlie had scavenged, begged and, on dark nights, stolen the materials for the house. They had dragged for miles sheets of rusty corrugated iron, planks, pieces of cardboard, and all the astonishing miscellany that had gone into building the house. (39)

Charlie and Dad Pauls are like a team from which Ronny is, nonmaliciously, excluded. Thus, when Dad Pauls finally dies, Ronny stands in the yard in front of their shack accepting "the formal commiserations of the arrivals," but "looking more sullen than sad" (116). Even while shoveling dirt into the grave, "Ronald shovelled the earth in sullenly, his mind somewhere else, ignoring the damp thudding as the bright metal engraving of Dad Paul's name and date of birth and death was covered up" (121). Ronald's indifferent attitude is possibly motivated by a sense of personal, psychological, emotional, and financial relief; and also by his obsessive attraction to Susie Meyer, whom he had gone to see the night before; and Susie's mother, with Susie's, it appears, willing approval, shut the door in his face. Apart from his glib remarks, noted earlier, we know nothing about what Ronny Pauls thinks of his father, or any other member of his family, or for that matter what he thinks of himself.

A recognizable picture of Ronny, like that of other characters, emerges after fitting together a multitude of fragments. Indeed, Ronny's self-portrait is vacuous without the inclusion of Susie Meyer. And, though the image of her bears the imprint of the narrator's, La Guma's judgement, one is still left to wonder what attracts Ronny to Susie:

> ...a crudely pretty face, the cheekbones brightened with rouge, and the lashes too heavy with mascara, the heavy mouth smeared with glaring lipstick that didn't match her complexion, and the wiry hair held in a number of plastic curlers gave her a ludicrous golliwog appearance. (100)

La Guma's description gives her the appearance of a grotesque doll, with staring eyes and fuzzy hair, and also of being rude, insensitive and disrespectful. For instance, when her mother complains about the successive late-night visits of Ronny and then Roman:

"Always blerry men. If it not one is the other one. Just staying with men, men, men." (99) Susie angrily responds, "Shut up! Stop your mouth! Is it your blerry business?" (100)

It is also Susie who attempts to seduce George Mostert, the white garage owner, and has an illicit affair with Roman who is married.

Ronny is extremely jealous; both because of what he suspects (the relationship with Mostert) and because of what he knows (the affair with Roman), and his jealousy becomes a motivating factor for murdering Susie. Ronny is very sensitive to all those things that threaten his definition of himself and his manhood, of being capable of fighting his own battles, and of being the principle bread-winner in the Pauls family. For example, he is particularly angry when he learns that Charlie had fought Roman for him, and he says to Charlie, "I'm not asking you to fight my battles, understand? You stay out of my business, hey?" (91) And when his mother doesn't have his breakfast ready as early as he thinks she should, he exclaims, "How, man, must a man always wait for his diet?" Ronny's inability to make a meaningful connection, with individuals, his family or his community, together with Susie's inability to give herself up completely to any impulse or pursuit or to another human being, speaks directly to the thematic center of this work: "Two are better than one...how can one be warm alone?"—and it is from this characteristic of alienation that the book takes its title. For Ronny, the final straw comes when Susie's mother shuts the door in his face, and Ronny ruminates:

> She better not bogger around with other jubas or I'll give her what for. He stumbled away through the oozing muck and strewn bricks, rage and disappointment mingling with the unravelling knots of hatred.
> ...He stood there, watching the house, his mind wriggling with anger, and his damp fingers touched the two-and-sixpenny jack-knife in his pocket. (98-99)

This bit of foreshadowing is of crucial significance to the thematic and structural design of *And a Threefold Cord*; therefore, Ronny's sensations, his rage, anger, and disappointment as a result of Susie's rejection, must be described as accurately as possible; since it is the quality of that reaction alone that provides a clue to his otherwise incomprehensible behavior.

The parallel movement of images involving Ronny and Susie is careful and deliberate; it appears that La Guma intended for this image sequence to comprise an autonomous picture of the measure and substance of character of these two people. Like Ronny, for instance, Susie is also rejected; when she follows the white fellow George back to his garage, "he burst suddenly through the doorway and slammed it in her face, leaving the smile to fade away like a once-gaudy pattern on cheap material" (130). Ronny and Susie stand alone; yet, their meaning would be lost if they were understood as being absolutely exceptional, if La Guma had chosen them because they are exceptional. To make their individual and combined portraits representative, La Guma sacrificed, deliberately, protracted treatment of other potentially worthy relationships; between Ronny and any of the other members of his family, or between Susie and her mother, for example. All that we know about Ronny, from beginning to end, is in relation to Susie—and conversely. What links their scattered scenes into one picture is the theme of alienation, and the sequence of moral portraits that express vividly and intelligibly the power of love, the impetuousness of youth, the fallacy of individualism, and the effects of moral indifference or apathy.

In spite of the anger and violence that ultimately engulfs this failed relationship, it is an image of truth and beauty—beautiful, no doubt, because it is true: perhaps, for all time and all places. However, La Guma does not show them simply as the embodiment of youth; but as youth who are the product of a particular society, a particular generation formed by specific historical conditions. The most important aspect of their individual and combined behavior and completed portrait, is its representative character, its universality; in today's context of universal apartheid, universal white domination, universal white racism; for it cannot be denied, that wherever white people and people of color co-exist in the world today, the white people are on top, socially, politically, economically and militarily. This fact alone will go a long way toward explaining Susie's otherwise irrational, anomalous attempted seduction of George Mostert.

There is no hard line between the life in *And a Threefold Cord* and the life beyond it. And Ronny's spontaneous, apathetic, capricious anger and violence is analogous to these same qualities as they are manifested in the imagery depicting the elemental world, as these metaphorically comment on and define the socio-political world of apartheid. Ronny, therefore, is first an object and then a product—an unwitting agent—of these forces working on and through his consciousness. In understanding the motivation for Ronny's murder of Susie, it is efficacious to bear in mind the symbiosis of the environment and character portraits, a complete realistic interpretation of cause and effect. Wilfred Cartey, our African Demodokos, sees clearly the relationship between Ronny's crime and the South African environment—understood in creative fiction or in reality—when he observes (1969), of South African literature generally, that:

> ...it may be said that criminality and amorality become the ethic of this society....There is no judgement by the authors, no moral condemnation. There seems only to be accep-

tance of a fact of life. In a society where one group is faceless, a criminal action gives corporate stature to anyone who has the courage to perpetrate it. (116)

Alex La Guma, in *And a Threefold Cord*, provides ample evidence of the "corporate stature" given to criminal acts, when in Chapter Twenty-Five Jorney Pauls, playing with his friends on the rubbish dump along the edge of the settlement, boasts excitedly:

> "Hell, man, my other brother, Ronny-boy, killed a goose. He's in jail now, reckon and think. Chopped her dead with a knife." And he stabs himself in the belly with a grubby finger and screams in a mockery of assassination, staggering about the hill of muck. Everybody laughs, and he cries, proudly: "Further, Charlie reckon they might hang Ronny-boy up on a rope." He clasps his hands about his throat, choking and gurgling, while the others shout and chuckle with glee. (*Threefold Cord*, 153)

This, the most developed portrait in the novel of the young boy, Jorny, is pathetic. Even though it is dramatized in an assumed mood of humor and comedy, it is not funny; instead, it excites the reader's sense of pity and sympathy as he contemplates the maturation of Jorny and the other youth in this same environment of violence, fear, and hopelessness. Ronny's identity is recognized and known to Jorny as someone who "Chopped her (Susie) dead with a knife...(and) might hang'...choking and gurgling, while the others shout and chuckle with glee." This is the image of his brother that Jorny, at the most vulnerable and impressionable period of his life, must bear for the rest of his life. "This search for identification through criminality," notes Cartey (1969), "this quest for otherness, is the highest point of alienation experienced by the characters" (116). Ronny's crime is nothing more than a microcosm of South African society. Violence is endemic in the South African social structure and South Africa easily deserves its reputation as one of the most violent countries in the world. While the victims of black violence are mostly other blacks, the white minority and its political leaders have set an example of violence for black youth by its historical acts of aggression against African and colored peoples in South Africa. Nor can we ignore the emphasis upon violence in the mass media, in popular pulp literature and movies, as undoubtedly related to acts of violence among African youth. It was, in fact, violence that enslaved and colonized African people, and it is the same violence that maintains white military and economic dominance in Southern Africa today. It should not, therefore, be surprising that La Guma's characters, particularly Ronny and Susie, should exhibit certain thoughts, and desires and habits of the enslaved and colonized mind "they take their pride in the servile imitation of those who oppress them" (Alexis De Toquville). They are dehumanized. Frankinstein, created, will act like Frankinstein.

One of the more paradoxical effects of the colonizer/colonized relationship is that the Ronnies and Susies of South Africa too often admire their oppressors, rather than despise them. Ronny's jealousy and sexism is analogous to and directly parallel with European jealousy and racism, particularly in the era of colonialism. Ronny, for example, seeks mastery and ownership of Susie; just like Europeans seek mastery and ownership of the world (certainly its minerals), and for similar reasons—their sense of inadequacy and inferiority. Ronny because of his inability to realize his full potential as a human being as a male; and Europeans, perhaps, because of their numerical inferiority in a world dominated (numerically) by people of color. Francis Welsing, M.D. (1991) states: "in the majority of instances any neurotic drive for superiority and supremacy is usually founded upon a deep and pervading sense of inadequacy and inferiority" (4).

If Europeans can be cruel, aggressive, violent, dominant, and suffer from none of these behavioral deficiencies, but are rather admired and gain prestige and privilege precisely because of these dubious attributes, Ronny wants merely to be like this magnificent model of virility and supremacy. Susie, on the other hand, exhibits other dimensions of this obnoxious imitation: taking pride, for example, in her Bing Crosby and Frankie Lane records. And of even greater significance, perhaps, are the names of the characters themselves, which are not just names La Guma gives them, but names the so-called Colored and many in the African population, give themselves: Charlie, Ronald, Jorny, Caroline, Susie—or, lest we forget, Nelson, Daniel, Kenneth, Jerry or Lewis. I am reminded of Kunta Kinte in Alex Haley's (1974) *Roots*, cruelly beaten until he succumbs to be Toby. Names are important: Are these choices an indication of admiration and imitation of European conquerors and ancestors, as opposed to their recognized but too often denied and disowned African ancestors?

An understanding of La Guma's characters, therefore, is greatly enhanced if one's knowledge of them is aided by knowledge of South African history and culture; such knowledge is also helpful in the aesthetic experience, in clarifying certain cultural if not psychological propensities of the characters. Even though such propensities are not intended to be the center of the aesthetic experience, they can enrich the apprehension of La Guma's character portraits.

This quest for otherness, through imitation and admiration of one's oppressors, has as its corollary a sense of "nobodyness," of alienation from the total society, from the immediate community, even from one's family and self. Yet, the single man can be saved from this total alienation. This can be achieved by shared participation in the immediate and larger society, by communal action, and by defining one's self—individually and collectively—and this is the path taken by Charlie Pauls (130). As Wilfred Cartey (1969) observes, "Charlie's optimism is his way of expression an inner strength, of resisting his complete ruin, of suppressing the rage that controls the gestures and thoughts of his younger brother, Ronald" (117).

Charlie, by himself, however, is not the subject of *And a Threefold Cord*. What La Guma proposes to exhibit is representative characters, acting in selected, representative ways in just such a world as they occupy. There just isn't enough complexity or depth in Charlie to make him the sole major character of the drama; he could not sustain an interest that would depend solely on his behavior. He is a type, a representative type; and his life is more a picture than a drama. There is no purposefulness to his actions. The actions he does engage in—struggling against the wind and rain on the roof of their shanty to plug a leak; fighting with Roman to defend his brother and himself; inviting George Mostert to a Saturday night party; comforting Freda after her children are burned to death; explaining to Uncle Ben the necessity of working-class unity; burying his father, Dad Pauls; proposing marriage to Freda— are all elements of the picture creating Charlie. These episodes—

external, isolated—are unconnected to Charlie's inner life; they do not depend on the volition, on the deliberate, premeditated choice of action decided upon by Charlie. They are, indeed, spontaneous in every instance. It is as if the action is chosen for the sake of the pictures they can present: as if the picture is in the foreground and the drama in the background. The result is a character (and a novel) that is more pictorial than dramatic.

What helps to control the story is La Guma's unmistakable consistency in the treatment of his characters. They are always true to themselves wherever we meet them. Charlie thinks, and talks, and acts consistently with his nature, exactly as the story demands that he should. La Guma has a design, a slice of life, a point of view that he wishes Charlie to express and represent, and there is no vacillation in the portrayal. Charlie, as a character, is easily knowable; he stands firm and clear, without the least bit of ambiguity.

This same clarity and orderliness is evident in La Guma's depiction of the other major characters as well: the serene dignity of Papa Pauls, the static repose of Mama Pauls, the virility and youthful arrogance of Ronny, the sensitivity and intellectual maturation of Charlie, suggests various states of life, ways of responding to their common environment, in what might otherwise be considered a rather simple, uncomplicated, and depressing world. But Charlie and Ronny and the others do not inhabit a "world of their own," they inhabit our world, in an unbreakable symbiosis, like anybody else; at the same time we recognize, and accept, that even if he were more complex, Charlie would still be infinitely less complex than the most superficial of "real" human beings. As such, Charlie Pauls must, and does, represent both specific and general human qualities. He provides, both in the work and for the reality beyond it, a lofty but not inaccessible example; he is astonishing but not incredible; and it is this dual quality which makes him convincing and gives validity to his heroism. This is nowhere more obvious than in the scene in which Charlie knocks down the policeman.

This particular incident is very significant to the psychological portrait of Charlie: because the question of propriety, of the "rightness" or "wrongness" of what he does is important to the meaning of Charlie's character and to the meaning of the story. In the following image, La Guma is giving us simply and directly a key to Charlie's character:

> ...the policeman turned his face slightly, to call for assis-
> tance, and Charlie hit him suddenly on the exposed
> jawbone...a hard snapping blow...and the policeman's feet
> left the ground....(*Threefold Cord*, 141)

Charlie's actions are derived from this principle of propriety, of
the "rightness" or "wrongness" of what he does. To get the full
meaning of this episode, however, it is necessary to establish the
context in which it occurred. The occasion is a police raid, one of
the frequent acts of harassment by the South African police—to
check for passes, that contemptible document that purports affir-
mation of one's right to be where one is, to be doing what one is
doing, to exist; also, police raids are simply to humiliate and insult
those militarily weaker. The police find Charlie in the home of his
girlfriend, Freda, whom they accuse of being a "Blerry black
whore." The police, and this is most important, are not just the
whites, there are also three African policemen accompanying the
sergeant who insults Freda; they are, of course, nothing more than
appendages, lackeys, imitators, who "followed without a word"
(136) and, in their silence, consenting. These African policemen,
despised by the whites and hated by the other Africans, are motivated by a deep sense of inferiority to the white world, into excessive brutality against their brothers, who ask, bewildered, "Why
do you do this, brother? Why do you do this to your own people?"
(133) It is left to Charlie, a most worthy hero of the moment, to
show his mettle, to act—not just in defense of Freda's honor, or his
own, but on behalf of the community:

> "Charlie, " Freda cried. "Where you going?"
> "Going to see what goes on."
> "You mustn't. There might be trouble."
> He said, stamping to get the boots on, "Don't go on like
> that. I'm going to see. To see what's happening to our
> people." (138)

His concern goes beyond himself, to a sense of collectivity and
unity or purpose and action. Finally, we return to the scene where
Charlie, in a completely gratuitous and impulsive act of rage, re-
leases his latent anger and knocks down one of the policemen (141).

It is through this kind of action that we know what kind of character Charlie Pauls is. Gerald Moore's perceptive insight in his Twelve African Writers is appropriate here:

Charlie Pauls' simple humanity is the main antidote to events...He does not give up, and as long as he doesn't, the current of life, even the current of hope, seems to flow through these wretched streets. (111) Moore goes on to say that La Guma has shown in Charlie, "the dawnings of an ideological consciousness...the first emergence in La Guma's work of someone who is fumbling his way towards a philosophy of resistance rather than one of endurance" (112).

What a wonderful distinction. So, the powerless are not so powerless after all, and it is this quality of resistance that Charlie is charged to valiantly and nobly represent. Though embryonic, latent, and spontaneous, his actions and ideas are an example for his family and community.

Charlie Pauls is a fighter; one in whom the roots of class-consciousness have seemingly taken hold. He dissociates himself from his mother's naive reliance on religion and capricious fate, saying to his Uncle Ben on one occasion, "Ma read the Bible every night. It don't make the poor old toppy any better" (82) and identifies instead with the class-conscious views of a "slim rooker" with whom he once worked:

> This burg say, if the poor people all got together and took everything in the whole blerry world, there wouldn't be poor no more...if all the stuff in the world was shared out among everybody, all would have enough to live nice. He reckoned people got to stick together to get this stuff. (83)

Charlie reenforces the concept of community, togetherness, unity-especially class unity—in his own mind, while at the same time politicizing his community, in this particular instance Uncle Ben, his mother's brother. Though we hear "Workers of the world unite" echoing in the background, Charlie's dialogue with Uncle Ben is a much more mundane, pragmatic application of the African proverb "Gather sand where you are." Charlie's political sophistication is, therefore, consistent with his character, his intellectual physiognomy, and not that of the author's.

It would have been obviously improper for Charlie to launch into a diatribe using esoteric and sophisticated Marxist terminology,

given La Guma's intellectual portrait of him in this story. Therefore, Charlie starts at home, with Uncle Ben and Ma Pauls, exposing and explaining to them the contradictions he has witnessed—
for example, people with houses "mos, big as the effing city hall...And
a juba like me can't even touch the handle of the front door" (83)—
and the solutions he believes will resolve specific contradictions;
solutions like, unity, compassion, courage, and resistance, that could
help to explain the apparent impotence and malaise of the community, generally, and Ronny's tragic isolation in particular; solutions
that would facilitate the evolving ethos of the group and the stabili-
zation of individual personalities.

For it is the formidable power of unity, a mere fragment of revolutionary insight, that Charlie snatches from an anonymous colleague and fashions into a comprehensible and functional explanation that could help create a higher level of consciousness, identity, and solidarity. Because there has been such profound dis-
agreement on what fundamental definitions of the South African
situation should be inculcated in the masses at large, as an ideologically biased, but no less committed, writer, La Guma offers his
perspective regarding what self-images or definitions of identity
so-called Coloreds and other South Africans should be encouraged to adopt. A measure of the importance of class consciousness (versus racial consciousness) to La Guma's character and
thematic formulations in *And a Threefold Cord*, is the monotonous, repetitive use of this theme. La Guma's final portrait of
Charlie, on the last two pages of the novel, has him again recalling
the poignant comments of his anonymous colleague, and he does
so in much the same language as before:

> There was this rooker I worked with when we was laying
> pipe up country. A slim burg, I reckon. A clever fellow.
> always was saying funny things. He said something one
> time, about people most of the time takes trouble hardest
> when they alone. I don't know how it fit in here, hey. I
> don't understand it real right, you see. But this burg had a
> lot of good things in his head, I reckon...Like he say, people
> can't stand up to the world alone, they got to be together. I
> reckon maybe he was right. A slim juba. Maybe it was like
> that with Ronny-boy. Ronald didn't ever want nobody to

> he'p him. Wanted to do things alone. Never was part of us.
> I don't know. Maybe, like Uncle Ben, too. Is not natural for
> people to be alone. Hell, I reckon people was just made to
> be together. I—" Words failed him again, and he shook his
> head, frowning. (168)

This "fellow worker" or "rooker I worked with," then becomes one of the central themes of *And a Threefold Cord*, and Charlie is an appropriately chosen vessel to convey this simple, yet profound truth to the characters in the work and to the reading audience. In fact, the intensity of the message is so concentrated, so narrowly focused on the Marxian concepts of class consciousness and class unity that it threatens, perhaps by design, to obfuscate entirely the racial and color dimensions of oppression in South Africa and the world. Given the thoroughness with which La Guma promulgates his ideological bias, albeit through the medium of creative fiction, predisposes the literary critic and analyst to be equally as thorough in explicating and analyzing the meaning of his perspective to the work as a whole and to the delineation of African and so-called Colored ideological and ethical perspectives in the South African and international context.

It is this writer's view, for example, that the African struggle for economic and political power and dignity in South Africa and the world has both a race (color) and class character. Africans, everywhere, are not only at the bottom of the economy, they are kept there on a race (color) basis. Standing Fanon's "You're rich because you're white and white because you're rich" on its head, we might say, "You're poor because you're black and black because you're poor." It is not just an economic system (capitalism) against which African people struggle, as many Marxists (including La Guma) would like to have it; rather, in South Africa, color and race—and not class—is the real determinant of status. A purely class-based interpretation of South African society does not square with an African's most infantile political awareness of reality. Africans in South Africa and the United States are kept at the bottom of the economic ladder by another race which keeps them there because of color and race, and which benefits—economically, socially and even psychologically—from keeping them there. As such, all those people above the Africans (i.e., all the whites, including working-class whites like George Mostert) become responsible for the Africans' position, either actively or passively, directly or indirectly. It is not just the multinational corporations, management, or the controllers of the economic system who are allied against African people. It is the white world—kith and kin. And this alliance is not just economic, but political and social and psychological and theological and, indeed, iconographic. Psychologically, to take just one example, George Mostert affirms this alliance to the insult of African women and men. La Guma describes George as a man whose "solitude clung in the half moons of black grease under his uncut fingernails, and in the wrinkles of his rugose neck, in the dirty overalls and the lank, uncombed, brittle, greying hair the colour of dusty floor polish" (66). Yet, with the false pride of racial superiority, George has the temerity to violently refuse companionship with a young, seductive, Colored woman, Susie, who literally throws herself on him. And it is not the apartheid law, which comes as an afterthought, but the mere "association" that bridles his sexual need and his simple need for companionship; needs we have come to recognize as the fulcrum of human interaction are submerged, sacrificed to the "glory" of the myth of white supremacy (racism). It is quite possible that Susie was only teasing and flirting with George, making fun of him; but what is at issue here is what is going on in George's mind, or at least what La Guma is suggesting is the mentality of the white working class through George. As Susie makes her obnoxious advances to him, George thinks, "She was a woman, probably easy to get with a drink and a few shillings, but he ewas afraid of the association. One didn't go with coloured girls; it was against the law, anyway" (128).

"Easy to get with a drink and a few shillings" and this, mind you, from a derelict white man who "drank without pleasure, as if he needed the alcohol only to anesthetize the bitterness and solitude that gnawed at him, persistent as a toothache" (164). When these psychological and physical portraits of George and Susie are combined with those of George and Charlie—specifically, on the occasion of the latter's visit to the former's Gas Station, junk yard, to get a piece of metal to patch the roof of the Pauls' shanty—we are forced to question the desperateness of La Guma's quest for class unity, on both the personal and universal (Marxian) levels. The fact that George later decides to honor Charlie's invitation and attend the party in the shanty-town, only to be thwarted by the police raid, indicates that La Guma believes such an alliance is possible: not because George initiates it or wants it, but because Charlie makes him such an attractive offer: "You haven't got a wife, hey, Mister George?...People got a right to have some pleasure, don't I say?" This is not an invitation to attend a political caucus, or even for a friendly social visit, but to satisfy George's need "to have some pleasure." This, it must be admitted, is too often the tactic, the purpose, and the sine qua non of most appeals for class unity, i.e., to satisfy the respective groups' pathological craving for the "forbidden fruit." Charlie, it seems, is blind to all considerations except those of class in extending an invitation to George, or at least it appears this way on the surface. What about those deeper motivating complexes of dependency and inferiority? Why doesn't Charlie think that the unity and solidarity of his own group, the so-called Coloreds, is enough challenge for him, or certainly a priority? Could it be that the so-called Coloreds, viewing themselves as a separate people, must likewise view themselves as a minority, and thereby feel more inclined to make appeals to multiracial unity? There is a very similar tendency among Mulattos and Negroes in the United States: as if Socialist white supremacy is somehow superior to Capitalist white supremacy.

These are some of the political questions raised by the two scenes involving Charlie, Susie, and George, and there are others; because, *And a Threefold Cord*, like La Guma's other novels and short-stories, is regarded as political—not after being extracted from a matrix of allegory and symbol, a subjective process, but on the basis of overt, objective imagistic and thematic evidence: e.g., "...if the poor people all got together and took everything...there wouldn't be poor no more." It is difficult to be more politically explicit than that. Charlie, the protagonist who speaks these words, and La Guma himself, is not about to become cynical about politics and just decide to look out for himself. Nonetheless, mouthing these pseudo-intellectual phrases and half-understood ideas, Charlie appears too eager to ally himself with "the poor people" making poverty or class the pre-eminent criterion for unity.

It is clear from the "Colored" girl, Susie Meyer's attempted seduction of the white derelict, George Mostert, that poverty—of the most abject, severe, economic, psychological, emotional, and spiritual nature—as a basis for unity among individuals and "national" groups, of African and European descent, is an idealistic Marxian hoax. Poverty is an even more unlikely basis for unity among competing groups, especially when there is no clear conception of "one's group." This is a particular problem of the "Colored" or Mulatto, in Africa and the diaspora. And no one has more clearly discerned the wrenching nature of this (essentially) identity problem than Dr. W. E. B. DuBois, who, though writing about the consciousness of Africans in America, described in eloquent prose the essence of this dilemma:

> One ever feels his twoness, an American, a Negro; two thoughts, two unreconciled strivings; two warring ideals in one dark body, whose dogged strength alone keeps it from being torn asunder.
> The history of the American Negro is the history of this strife, this longing to attain self-conscious manhood, to merge his double self into a better and truer self. (1903:3-4)

The history of the South African Colored is also the history of this strife, to merge his African self with his European self. This dichotomy encourages the amorphous Marxist ideology that informs La Guma's works and particularizes his characters' intellectual physiognomy, despite the lack of references to their specific ethnicity. The South African so-called Colored becomes a communist or Colored nationalist because it seems for reasons of an identity imposed on him and which he has subsequently assumed, refuses to become a Pan-Africanist or African nationalist. When Charlie says to George, "People got a right to have some pleasure...we mos men of the world," (69) he is, in a sense, offering his women to George as a sort of token of his sincere camaraderie. Nothing about this appeal, nor Susie's attempted seduction, makes sense unless we keep in the forefront of our minds that George is white; and it is his whiteness, and all it supposedly represents, that makes the seduction and Charlie's ingratiating invitation intelligible. For, in truth, Susie's failed seduction and Charlie's invitation are metaphors for the same behavior of Mulattos in

America and so-called Coloreds in South Africa; they are representative.

La Guma goes to great lengths to make it plain to the reader
that Charlie's invitation is on the fundamental premise that George
is poor and alone, that George's color, or lack thereof, makes no
difference. George, on the other hand, is looking so hard at Susie's
and Charlie's color that there is no way for him to see the Coloreds'
social, economic, and world role in relation to the accumulation of
capital, to the development of automation, and to the world revolution of the "have nots." In other words, it is their color that
matters to George and not their class. And to pursue this tautology, what Charlie fails to see, and what La Guma seems intent on
diminishing in importance, is the decisive nature of color in con-
stituting the world order that we now live in. Note well, that I said
color and not race.

The distinction is crucial, for it recognizes the pervasive nature
of color in determining political and social and economic status.
South Africa, like America, like Brazil (see Twine 1998), is a country where even shades of color count—the degree of Africanness,
or blackness, being a yardstick by which one's human worth is
measured (Nkrumah 1970). As a consequence, it is not at all un-
thinkable that Susie Meyer would have welcomed becoming pregnant by the white George Mostert. Frantz Fanon (1967) gives cogent support to this possibility when he observes, during clinical
investigations, that the colored woman "wants not only to turn white
but also to avoid slipping back" (54). And Charlie, if he had been
successful in befriending George, would have been raised high in
the esteem of the shanty-town community, certainly higher than if
George had been African. What else did George have to offer
except his whiteness?

Now one may or may not subscribe to the view that the consciousness of color was among the earliest sensibilities of man, yet
the persistence of this quality over most of known human history
is, however, an inescapable fact. The history of human relations
has involved, all too frequently, the confrontation and consequently
the conflict of people of different colors. The result has invariably
been the humiliation, insult, and injury of one by the other. As we,
human beings, took our first tentative and bold steps into the twen-

tieth century, Dr. DuBois (1903) declared, eloquently and propheti-
cally:

> I have seen a land right merry with the sun, where children
> sing, and rolling hills lie like passioned women wanton with
> harvest. And there in the King's Highway sat and sits a
> figure veiled and bowed, by which the traveler's footsteps
> hasten as they go. On the tainted air broods fear. Three
> centuries' thought has been the raising and unveiling of
> that bowed human heart, and now behold a century new for
> the duty and the deed. *The problem of the Twentieth Cen-
> tury is the problem of the color-line* . (40 emphasis added)

La Guma's necessary, but excessive, concern with class unity, with
poor people anywhere and everywhere getting together and taking
everything in the world, obscures this fundamental problem of the
color-line. Why, we have to ask, would La Guma do this? And the
answer is not far to find, but first we must resharpen our focus.

There are two social realities: La Guma is a Colored and he is a
communist. As a so-called Colored, in DuBoisian terms, his consciousness is divided; thus, restricting and limiting his potential
commitment to African nationalism and Pan-Africanism. This is,
indeed, a complex and difficult analysis. Walter Rodney (1996) in
a 1974 Dar es Salaam, Tanzania address, "Towards the Sixth Pan
African Congress: Aspects of the International Class Struggle in
Africa, the Caribbean, and America" offers the following:

> Pan Africanism in the post-independence era is internation-
> alist in so far as it seeks the unity of peoples living in a
> large number of juridically independent states. But it is si-
> multaneously a brand of nationalism, and one must there-
> fore penetrate its nationalist form to appreciate its class
> content. (730)

Secondly, as a communist, La Guma's assertive preoccupation with
class unity—particularly in *And a Threefold Cord*—belies the fundamental Marxist perspective: that a racial twist has been given to
what is basically an economic phenomenon; that slavery and colonialism were not born of racism, rather racism was the consequence
of slavery and colonialism. In his recent *The Making of a Racist*

State: British Imperialism and the Union of South Africa, 1875-1910, Dr. Bernard M. Magubane (1996) concludes: "It is difficult to accept the class analysis per se in South Africa. An abstract class analysis not only liquidates the national question, but it ignores critical differences in the exploitation of black and of white workers which are due specifically to racism" (4). Like everything in life, all phenomena, all rational ideas are worthy of investigation, are worthy of our understanding.

There is no chicken-and-egg paradox being suggested here. Research into the history of this problem of the color-line reveals, unequivocally, that the belief in white supremacy (racism) is both the cause and the consequence of the enslavement and subsequent colonization of African people. Before the sixteenth century, Englishmen, in particular found in the very idea of blackness a way of expressing some of their most ingrained values. And the meaning of black, before the rise of modern capitalism, as described by the *Oxford English Dictionary* included, "Deeply stained with dirt; soiled, dirty, foul....Having dark or deadly purposes, malignant; pertaining to or involving death, deadly; baneful, disastrous, sinister....Foul, iniquitous, atrocious, horrible, wicked....Indicating disgrace, censure, liability to punishment, etc." Before the rise of capitalism, University of California at Berkeley Professor Winthrop Jordan (1974) states, "The complexion of Africans posed problems about its nature, especially its permanence and utility, its cause and origin, and its significance" (7). The Africans' color, therefore, even at this early fourteenth century date, had acquired connotations in the European mind relating to differences in mental and biological worth, relating to "inferiority" and "superiority," and not just to superficial physical differences in appearance. With the roots and fruits of so-called white supremacy (racism) buried and bearing fruit in the pre-capitalist soil of the European tradition, it should come as no surprise that a racist social structure is inherent in the colonial situation, inseparable from European capitalist development. Class exploitation and the oppression of peoples of darker complexion are mutually inclusive; to remove one is to remove the other. In the modern world, the struggle against the mythological color hierarchy is the struggle against the class hierarchy. In his 1964 speech "Message to the Grassroots" the insightful and eloquent Malcolm X (1996) noted:

> The same man that was colonizing our people in Kenya
> was colonizing our people in the Congo. The same one in
> the Congo was colonizing our people in South Africa, and
> in Southern Rhodesia, and in Burma, and in India, and in
> Afghanistan, and in Pakistan. They realized all over the
> world where the dark man was being oppressed, he was
> being oppressed by the white man; where the dark man was
> being exploited, he was being exploited by the white man.
> So they (at the Bandung Conference- my note) got together
> on this basis—that they have a common enemy. (722)

This truth gives rise to the basic question, that acknowledges this
hiatus between people of color and the other world: Why is this?
Why is this reality real? Why are the people of non-hue, of non-
color everywhere, at this very minute, on top by most objective
standards of quality of life (excluding moral and ethical concerns,
of course)? Then is heard the unspeakable, the great omission that
confirms the suspicion. The thing that is in everyone's head but is
on no one's lips: Does it have to do with color? The answer we
give to this question is essential to illuminating our understanding
of Charlie Pauls, Susie Meyer, George Mostert, and all the other
characters in *And a Threefold Cord* as well as La Guma's other
works and, perhaps, the author himself.

Charlie, Susie, and George, for instance, know intuitively, if
not consciously, the effects on their own psyches of the tyranny,
the severity, and cruelty of color consciousness on their lives, and
as a motivating factor for many of their actions and thoughts.
George Mostert gives compelling proof of the perspective employed
here, a man whose basic human need for companionship and bond-
ing with other human beings has been repetitively emphasized, but
who refuses to initiate contact, "trapped in his office by his own
loneliness and a wretched pride in a false racial superiority" (67)
and who, in contemplating Charlie's appeal, "felt like a man who
had decided to undertake some desperate adventure: an explorer
who had summoned up courage to enter a territory never yet trod-
den by man" (*Threefold Cord*, 71-72). What induces George to sit
alone "trapped in his office" is his concept of his whiteness: he is,
in other words, a prisoner of his skin; he knows this, accepts this,
and his actions stem from this awareness. What causes Susie and

Charlie to seduce and woo him into their lives is, we are led to believe, their lack of color consciousness, but assumed, somehow intuitive, class-consciousness and affinity. Yet, even in "mutual" poverty, the white man, George is on top; for Charlie and the other inhabitants of the shanty-town must go to him for the scraps of junk metal and cardboard to build and repair their shacks, their homes; and Susie accosts him to get a drink and maybe a few shillings and her idea of a good time. So, even at this level, the white man, the poor white, the white working class enjoys possessions and prestige desired by the colonized man of color. Albert Memmi, in *The Colonizer and the Colonized* (1967), offers cogent insight into the perspective under consideration here:

> The first attempt of the colonized is to change his condition by changing his skin. There is a tempting model very close at hand—the colonizer. The latter suffers from none of his deficiencies, has all rights, enjoys every possession and benefits from every prestige...The first ambition of the colonized is to become equal to that splendid model and to resemble him to the point of disappearing in him. (120)

Even as a potential class ally, George's deficiencies pale beside those of the not only economically colonized man of color, but psychologically colonized as well. If George is "trapped by a feeling of magnanimity"—a euphemism for what is actually a feeling of superiority—then Charlie is trapped by his feeling of inferiority. Why else would he need to humor and ingratiate himself to this class ally with "Hell....They [speaking of the shanty-town dwellers] ought to make you the may-or, Mister George" (68). What La Guma, at this point, is not ready to admit is that white Marxists—which George admittedly, is not—have regarded as axiomatic their own involvement and even leadership in the fight for African liberation.

Due, perhaps, to his emphasis on the pictorial, on the external portraiture and physical appearance of his characters; also, because of his essentially materialist perspective, La Guma fails to probe the serious implications of color consciousness on his Colored characters, which are, assuredly, deeper levels of character motivation and internal turmoil. What ought to have served La Guma has ended up dominating him. Lewis Nkosi (1968) lends credence to this point of view:

> When everything is said and done, Alex La Guma is a man fiercely and humourlessly committed to his ideology—communism. I was surprised to discover how conservative and uncritical he was in this commitment. Indeed, there are many independent Marxist thinkers who would be irritated by his brand of pious regard for everything Soviet policy-makers are doing as almost beyond any questioning. (3-4)

La Guma's fierce and uncritical commitment to communism blinds him to the fact that communism is simply another brand of white nationalism, if not, the Kremlin and Peking would certainly be closer together. Neither capitalism nor communism is designed for African people; both have ruling classes that oppress and exploit the masses of their people. And intellectuals and writers are fed and filled with the ideals and principles of both systems. For these they fight and die, screaming and regurgitating these ideals as if they were intoxicated: "if the poor people all got together and took everything...there wouldn't be poor no more."

Such a division of wealth is not going to affect the thinking of Europeans about the humanity of African people; it is not going to change the thinking of the mixed African, Coloreds, who often think they are superior to the unmixed African, since the status of both is a result of genetic factors (the complexion of one's skin) and not economic factors; nor will it affect the thinking of Africans who, unfortunately, have internalized the idea of their color as ugly, their culture as primitive, their ability to organize, govern and control their own nation as idealistic, that there is nothing or no one in their past that needs celebration or holidays, that their languages and traditional names have no value, that their noses are too wide, lips too thick, hair too kinky, buttocks too big, and legs too skinny. How does Karl Marx deal with these deep scars on the self-concept of African people? Marx may have discovered the importance of the economy in socio-political relationships, but this relationship has other characteristics which cannot be summarily pre-empted by Marxism—or, for that matter, Freudian psychoanalysis. How else can we explain the fact that even the poorest white, using George Mostert as an example, thinks himself to be—and actually is—superior (socially, economically) to the colonized African and other people of color in South Africa?

There is one important difference between capitalistic and communist countries, and that is: the people in the latter countries know they are powerless. Between these two giants of white nationalism, the choice for African people can only be a choice between two groups of white masters. Chancellor Williams, in *The Destruction of Black Civilization* (1976) sums up this argument succinctly when he states:

> ...When the African people achieve enough unity to develop the ideological guidelines for their own advancement, they will draw what is best for them from any or all existing systems as a simple matter of course. (336)

Elementary common sense dictates no less. African people can extract what they need from capitalism or communism without apology and without becoming capitalist or communist. La Guma, we can now say, by making Charlie Pauls the repository and the parrot of communist ideology, make him one-dimensional, largely predictable, and a substanceless subject as a Colored victim of apartheid. Charlie is a victim of race (color) and class oppression; yet, there is no indication from La Guma that he suffers at all from the fact of color and color consciousness; there is no interior monologue, no omniscient narrative insight that indicates that either the Colored characters or the author is grappling with the vital color dimensions of Charlie's experience; a characterization through thought and authorial insight is just as important as characterization through action and dialogue. Charlie lacks an inner life.

The dual consciousness, the divided psyche of Colored people in South Africa is a primary ingredient in the emotional and psychological experience of Colored South Africans, and by skillful application of interior monologue, La Guma could have explored and exhumed these deeper and valuable aspects of Charlie's (and other characters') personality. But he fails to make use of it by putting his priority on the class aspect of his characters' existence. And all this is because Marx once wrote or is reported to have written or implied that racism is a consequence and not the cause of capitalism and imperialism. In his article "Culture and Liberation" La Guma

(1976) echoes this notion with "...contrary to the belief that racial preju-
dicial ways existed, racism is a phenomenon of capitalism and did not
exist as a social phenomenon before the advent of the system" (33).

Let us, once and for all, extricate ourselves from this circular
tautology, and to do this, it is necessary for the past, as a whole, to
be recognized and admitted, Racism (white supremacy) predated
capitalism by at least five hundred years. In a monumental study,
The Image of the Black in Western Art, (1979) Jean Devisse
offers the following conclusions with regard to the iconography of
African people from the early Christian era to the "Age of Discovery": all that was known about African people, he writes,

> ...was an abstraction—blackness itself. As human beings,
> the Black and African in general presented no direct prob-
> lem, physical or metaphysical, to the Western European.
> Hence a total hostility to blackness could take root, appar-
> ently, without jeopardizing the fundamental idea of the vo-
> cation of all men to salvation. The fears and terrors of the
> Occidental were centered on blackness itself. (57)

If La Guma had firmly grasped this understanding, that it is "blackness itself" that is the basis of the fears and terrors of white people,
along with his Marxism, then his characters and thematic thrust
might have been more rounded and objective. For Devisse, in a
lengthy explication of ancient sources, involving ideological, intellectual, folkloristic, biblical, and inconographic dimensions, refutes
the optimistic view of the African American historian Frank M.
Snowden, Jr. (1979), that "among the men of antiquity there existed not a trace of antiblack racism, nor was there even a consciousness of racial differences" (50). Rather, Devisse (1979) found
"the linking together of the four ideas—black, other, sinner, dangerous—runs throughout all the manifestations of Medieval Western
Christian thought" (61). Even more interesting, Devisse found that
in many thirteenth-century representations, in stone and paintings,
depicting scenes of martyrdom, the executioner of John the Bap-
tist, the Stoning of St. Stephen, even the executioners of Jesus, as
well as representations of Judas are all depicted as African or
"Negroid," contrary to all reliable historical evidence ancient and
modern. This iconography of Africans by Western Europeans of
the ancient world and Middle Ages compels Devisse to ask a fun-

damental question concerning Europeans' intellectual and imagistic inheritance: "How many generations of Christians have been conditioned by looking at a grimacing black man torturing Christ or his saints?" (80). By virtue of our knowledge of the state of white supremacy (racism) in the world today, we would have to conclude that all subsequent generations of Western Europeans from (at least) the thirteenth-century onward were so conditioned. In fact, the 1960s musical play "Jesus Christ Super Star," quite consistent with the aforementioned precedent, portrayed Judas as an African. The past is not dead; it's not even past.

From all of this it emerges clearly that Alex La Guma, in *And a Threefold Cord*, stresses class consciousness and class unity at the expense of—or in deliberate preference to—color consciousness, African unity, and Pan-Africanism, and that he does this for reasons peculiar and unique to the ethos of South African Coloreds; an ethos and history "of miscegenation over a period of three hundred years (i.e., from the time of the arrival of the Dutch in 1652 until today)" (February 1981:12). Unmixed Africans are not immune to this dilemma, for they too exhibit characteristics of a dual consciousness; having assumed a European language, they have also taken on European culture, including religion, dress, names, music, jurisprudence, cuisine , and etiquette. The problem of the Coloreds deserves special attention, not just because La Guma is a Colored, but because of the invidious and sinister way the white power structure is able to use them, and the way they too often perceive themselves, as a socio-genetic link between Africans and Europeans, deigning even to be considered African or "Black" tentatively for strategic leadership reasons. Concern, therefore, is not just with Charlie's economic and material well being, but also with his emotional, mental, and spiritual health, and with what these latter aspects have to do with the condition of being Colored in South Africa. How, for instance, does the European side of his nature appear in his social affectation and preferences? How does the Coloreds' confused race instinct manifest itself in their understanding of group loyalty and choices of political allies? How do shades of color and texture of hair, to be quite banal, affect social status and self-concept within the Colored community? And, alas, how does the Coloreds' perception of themselves affect their perception of Africans, particularly as revealed through literary images?

As stated earlier, Charlie, the main vehicle for theme in *And a Threefold Cord,* acts out of a sense of class consciousness; while George, the only significant white character in the novel, acts exclusively out of his sense of race (color) consciousness and loyalty. For George, a representative white working-class mind, civilization, culture, and genius is carried in the genes, in the blood, in pigment, in whiteness: if you change the economic class of all African people, that will not change the meaning of blackness and all that the very idea and reality of blackness itself denotes and connotes.

It is quite possible that La Guma could have achieved a greater depth in character portrayal if his characters were also motivated by even a cursory awareness of the tyranny of color consciousness on their thoughts and feelings and actions. If, for instance, Charlie were lighter in complexion than Ronny: or if Ronny's hair were straighter and his nose more aquiline than Charlie's (which could account for the fact that he's working and Charlie is not—tacit recognition of the fact that whites attribute preeminence of one man over another on the basis of the degree of "white blood"), we could, perhaps, know the characters better if there were some indication of how they, individually, thought about their ethnic uniqueness, and some of the consequences of this thought in terms of internal and external conflicts. For the other, and even more devastating aspect of the tyranny of color on the consciousness of people of color (particularly concerning the African and so-called Colored people of South Africa) is that, just as color constitutes the basis of justification for conflict between people of different races and cultures, color also constitutes the basis for differentiation and preference within a given society or even within a racial or cultural group.

The viciousness and pervasiveness of South Africa's apartheid system, its Bantustans and color classifications, its balkanization and retribalization of African people under the insidious misnomer "separate development," infects the victims to such an extent that they too unwittingly—and sometimes consciously—inculcate within themselves a belief in a color hierarchy: "If you're white, you're all right, if you're brown, stick around, if you're black, get back" is an African American folk-axiom that nauseatingly expresses this differentiation and preference within the African experience. Nor is Alex La Guma immune; his political and social commitment have not been enough to exorcise the demon of race (color) preference and demeaning portraiture of African people, particularly African women. This is a most revealing and disheartening insight, one that critics of La Guma's writings have overlooked or deliberately avoided, yet one that must be dealt with: for it is like an open wound, a deep scar on La Guma's character portraits. Whether unconsciously, in the heat of creation, he snatched at these stereotypical, caricatured, derogatory images of African women; or if he consciously and premeditatedly intended to create such insulting portraits, in either case, it demonstrates the inveterate and pernicious nature of the laughable and lamentable doctrine of white supremacy (racism) and the system of apartheid. It is clear from careful and comprehensive reading of La Guma's texts that he is unable to depict an image of an African woman whose sensual beauty compels one to admiration and respect: not on the basis of what they do or say—for they act in very human, compassionate, and even revolutionary ways—but on the fundamental basis of how they look, that is, on La Guma's idea of the African woman.

A few examples from his four novels, at this time, will serve to illustrate this assertion. First, from *And a Threefold Cord*, there is Missus Nzuba:

> The whole house creaked and sagged as this woman entered.... Given a huge black currant jelly that had been moulded into a series of connected ovals, spheres, elipses and sundry bulges representing head, torso, arms and legs. Attire this jelly in a vast dress, washed out and then once more soiled with grease and spilled food; pull over the dress a man's coat, old and bursting at the seams, and refusing to button in front; a man's stretched, darned and holed socks over the elaphantine calves, and a man's cracked and shapeless, cast-off shoes on the great feet. Result: Missus Nzuba. (110)

And, as if this were not enough, La Guma goes on, poetically, as if inspired by this repulsive image of African womanhood:

> Her mouth, when she spoke or smiled, became a swelling
> and contracting bubble on a boiling sphere of chocolate
> blancmange. Whenever she moved, even if only a little
> finger, the whole vast mound of her body shook and bounced
> and quivered as if a million slack little springs had been set
> into action beneath the undulating expanse of her skin. (110)

To add insult to injury, La Guma says later on that when Missus
Nzuba talked "she clucked with a sound that seemed to come from
some gigantic bird" (110). Here, then, is a picture—supposedly
representative of the African woman—whose features are distorted
and exaggerated to produce an absurd effect; it is the description
of the only African woman in the novel, recognized as such: first
by her name, Nzuba (she is not a Susie, or Caroline, or Freda) and,
secondly, by La Guma's word-color choices, "black currant
jelly...boiling sphere of chocolate blancmange." The human body
should be, in itself, an object upon which one's eyes can dwell
with pleasure and which we are glad to see depicted. And although
the human body, and its desecration in the South African context,
is no more than a point of departure for La Guma's imagery, it is a
pretext of great importance. Such images are an index to La
Guma's—and, by extension, Coloreds'—perception of African
women. Missus Nzuba is—if not in fact, at least in fiction—a
pathetic mass of jelly, totally unattractive and undesirable, in spite
of the fact that she does very human things, such as comforting Ma
Pauls when Dad Pauls died, and helping Caroline give birth. The
compassionate or revolutionary African woman does not have to
be a "boiling sphere of chocolate blancmange."

In *The Stone Country*, La Guma again rolls out the "Aunt
Jemima" stereotype. The African woman visiting Solly, in prison,
is described as a ...jiggling woman in a gaudy dress as big as a
beach tent, and fat hands like blown-up rubber gloves, decorated
with cheap Woolworth jewellery...She was prespiring and the powder on her face was turning to paste and starting to run. (*Stone
Country*, 116-117)

Upon leaving from her visit with the inmate Solly, "The fat
woman winked again at Solly and said good-bye, and went out of
the cage, swaying like an elephant" (118). This woman, too, performed a very courageous act: she smuggled the hacksaw blades to

Solly that Gus, Morgan, and Kope later use in their attempted escape. But is it necessary that she be portrayed in such an inept, ridiculous, elephantine way in order to perform this task? It is certainly a noticeable proclivity in La Guma's writings. Then, in the novel *In the Fog of the Seasons' End*, there is the following portrait of Henny April's wife, Maria:

> From the kitchen came a big African woman. She was made even bigger by advanced pregnancy which she carried under a stained apron. She wore an old beret and held a long spoon like a spear at the trail... She laughed boomingly, and gestured with the spoon at the swollen belly. (*Fog*, 167)

La Guma appears determined to make a decisive and meticulous distinction in his concept of an African woman; for here she is not only fat and pregnant, but "held a long spoon like a spear at the trail." This too is a demeaning stereotype of African women; and by stereotype is meant not just the exaggerated image, but also the function of a stereotype, which is to justify or rationalize our conduct in relation to the image, in this case the African woman. No self-respecting African man or woman can accept images that denigrate African women, and it is of crucial importance that we try to understand and appreciate the consciousness of (in this instance, Colored) writers who support such images. Stereotypes of African women and their concomitant myths are indispensable to the maintenance of the South African and worldwide color-caste system. They suggest values that are inconsistent with La Guma's clarion calls for unity and togetherness of all poor people.

By freezing African women with these essentially negative physical and verbal characteristics, he simultaneously ascribes to them the sensuous portrayal of untouchables. It should be understood that a positive, attractive image of the African woman would threaten and shake the very foundations of so-called white supremacy. On the other hand, negative, stereotypic images of African women are indispensable to maintaining color-caste restrictions especially those against intermarriage between Africans and non-Africans, and between members of the upper and lower classes.

Negative images of African women deprive them of their womanhood, self-respect and social status, and thereby help to dissuade members of either the Colored or the White group from any contemplation of marriage with African women. La Guma, by "defeminizing" the African woman, putting her in "a man's coat...a man's stretched, darned and holed socks...and a man's...cast-off shoes on the great feet," opens the door for the most outrageous exploitation of African females by African and non-African men and by the harsh and indifferent South African labor system. "Defeminizing" the African woman has the added "advantage" of providing psychological succor, security, and stability to Colored and White women. I have actually seen very fat Colored women and very fat White women; yet, such depictions are seldom used as representative of these women. Perhaps we're back to Dr. Welsing's (1991) formulation that "Any neurotic drive for superiority and supremacy is usually founded upon a deep and pervading sense of inadequacy and inferiority" (5). That is, one of the primary reasons white people hate black people is because white people are not black people. Is it not also possible that, like White people, Colored people in South Africa have a profound sense of numerical inadequacy and color inferiority when they consider the massive majority of South African black people? It is, therefore, not just the images that we are explicating, but the consciousness behind them, creating and directing their deployment and significance.

La Guma's stereotypic, caricatured images of African women, as huge, as massive black currant jelly, as vast mounds, and all other metaphors, images and myths, he uses to satirize, nay desecrate the physical appeal and beauty of African women, false though they may be, become central in determining political and cultural values, criteria and standards of beauty, and general attitudes toward African women. To be a comforting mother and sensitive wife, there is no genetic or cultural proclivity that precludes the African woman from being shapely, slim, and sensuously arousing. Ma Pauls is the mother of four Colored children would it be fair, (that is, politically and aesthetically correct) for an African writer (as consciously distinct from a Colored or Mulatto writer) to depict her as, say, "a big yellow woman, holding a belt like the reigns of a mule," or some such metaphor. By having Henny April's wife, Maria, hold "a long spoon like a spear at the trail," La Guma petrifies a hackneyed symbol of Africaness in a way that precludes her entrance and relevance to the twentieth century. It is in this stereotypic sense that the image is appropriate: it leaves no provision for mistaking the "Africaness" of the woman, from La Guma's perspective: she's fat, pregnant, coming from the kitchen, holding a long spoon like a spear; and, to complete the stereotype, like all fat people happy and laughing. While Beukes, the Colored protagonist in *In the Fog of the Seasons' End*, is busily creating clandestine drawings of modern handguns and rifles, the African woman, Maria, stands at the trail with a spear.

Petrifying African women as obese and in atavistic poses represents not just La Guma's vision of African femininity, but also his willingness to project this image to all throughout the world who read his works. For the masses of Coloreds, Whites, and Africans, through his vision, will acquire, share, support and believe in his vision. For example, the reference linking the Colored, or Mulatto, to the mule is by no means fortuitous; the mule is a hybrid, ordinarily a cross between a mare and a jackass. That mules have no ancestors that are mules and no descendants at all is common knowledge, and many references and jokes about Coloreds or Mulattos have been built upon this theme. Ultimately, the idea was that as the mule dies, so too dies the Mulatto. The cruelty of such metaphorical references is obvious. No less cruel are La Guma's derogatory images of the African woman.

Finally, from *Time of the Butcherbird*, the first African woman depicted by La Guma is "A fat black woman (who) came once a week to dust and polish and take away bundles of washing" (31). Are we to believe that in South Africa it is only fat, black women who perform these tasks? Aren't there some fat, yellow women who are midwives, domestics, nannies, de-feminized, tough, and manly? Aren't there some very attractive, beautiful and shapely African women who perform these tasks—which, no doubt, partly accounts for the Colored population anyway? Does La Guma consider the Colored woman too feminine, too fragile, to be revolutionary? If the imagery in his novels is any indication, one would have to answer this latter question in the affirmative. La Guma, just as any white writer would do, has turned the African woman into a strong, self-reliant Amazon and deposits her in the kitchen or as a matriarch, manly and de-feminized, at the front lines of the

liberation movement where no man, African or otherwise, would
have the slightest romantic inclinations toward her. Mma Tau, the
African woman heroine of *Time of the Butcherbird*, exemplifies
this kind of masculine portrait:

> A heavy square woman, she looked as if she had been con-
> structed out of blocks of dark wood of various sizes, the
> uppermost of which had been roughly carved with eye-sock-
> ets, nose, nostrils, cheekbones, a great gash of a mouth,
> and then sanded and polished to a shiny smoothness. She
> wore a dusty headcloth, a vast dress like a tent strapped
> around the middle with an old leather belt, and on her feet
> a man's boots, cracked and down-at-heel. (45-46)

It's as if La Guma no longer cares to delineate his African women
characters, as if they are spontaneous, stock characters fixed in his
imagistic repertoire that he rolls out as the occasion requires: Missus
Nzuba in *And a Threefold Cord* wore a "vast dress" and a man's
shoes; the African woman who visits Solly in *The Stone Country*
wore "a gaudy dress as big as a beach tent"; and Maria in *In the
Fog of the Seasons' End* was "even bigger by advanced pregnancy"; and now, Mma Tau in *Time of the Butcherbird* wore, "a
vast dress like a tent...and...a man's boots." La Guma hardly even
bothers to change the language from novel to novel.

These few examples (and there are others) are illustrative of
what can only be referred to as racism, Colored racism. There is
no justification or need—save for the feeling of inferiority and
inadequacy, and a kind of variation on the Oedipus complex, that
finds Coloreds often hating their African matrilineal heritage and
clinging to their preference for their European paternal line—for
an African woman, a Missus Nzuba or Mma Tau, to be stereotyped
in this way in order to be "heroic." And when La Guma's images
of African women are compared with his descriptions of Colored
women, we know that there is no genetic, or cultural propensity in
African men that compels them to prefer obese, fat, vast, bubbly,
huge, elephant-like, jiggling, big, swollen, heavy-and-square, pon-
derous-as-a-hippopotamus, great, massive, bulging, shapeless, expansive African women; who, presumably out of shame and the
internalization of the notion of even their hair as inferior or bad,

having no concept of hair grooming or styling, must always be quickly wrapped in a bandana or headcloth or even a beret to conceal their "curse," their "shame."

With Colored women it is a different matter. For instance, in *And a Threefold Cord*, Freda (Charlie's significant other, who loses her two children to fire) is describe by La Guma as:

> ...a good looking woman, thickly built, but soft and big-breasted and big-hipped under the soiled and faded overall she wore....She had thick eye-brows and a broad, kindly, heavy face, the full lips soft, and her coarse black hair was tied back with a scrap of cloth. (1988:30)

No, a woman does not have to be thin to be "good looking"; also, in an ideal world a Missus Nzuba, Mma Tau, or Maria does not have to be massive, bulging, and shapeless.

Admittedly pedantic, however, such matters are of moment in a South Africa trying to create a multiracial democracy. Naomi Wolf, in *The Beauty Myth* (1991), says that one of the vital lies in the "ideology of 'beauty'" allowing for the discrimination and sub-jugation of women is that "'Beauty' had to be defined as a legitimate and necessary qualificaiton for a woman's rise in power" (28). Wolf also says, "An economy that depends on slavery needs to promote images of slaves that 'justify' the institution of slavery" (18). South African Whites, Coloreds, and even some Africans today (1999) depend on the domestic servitude (slavery) of African women (see Sindiwe Magona's *Living, Loving and Lying Awake at Night*). Tracing it a step further, in *In the Fog of the Seasons' End*, when Beukes meets the Colored girl Frances at the fun-fair, La Guma writes:

> Beukes...saw the smooth texture of her skin and the wide, slightly slanted eyes that were a strange color in the glare of the fun-fair; he noticed the full, drawn bow of her mouth as she smiled and he thought, coffee and cream, she's all coffee and cream. (37)

The idea promoted in this image inclines one to view "coffee and cream," the near-white woman, as more aesthetically beautiful and desirable than just "coffee" and certainly more attractive than "a boiling sphere of chocolate blancmange." La Guma, whether unintentionally or not, is playing right into the racists' hands, since "fairness" or "whiteness" was and is the standard of European femininity; yet, for millions of quite contented African women, black skin is the most natural and beautiful thing in the world. Obviously, La Guma intended for Coloreds, if not Africans, to feel proud of this "coffee and cream" mixture. Such images are, therefore, important in assessing La Guma's attitude to not just African women but to African people. The perceptive and insightful feminist writer bell hooks (1997) has commented:

> This need to look as much like white people as possible...is related to a desire to succeed in the white world....In a culture of domination, one that is essentially anti-intimacy, we must struggle daily to remain in touch with ourselves and our bodies....Especially black women and men, as it is our bodies that have been so often devalued, burdened, wounded in alienated labor. Celebrating our bodies, we participate in a liberatory struggle that frees mind and heart. (247, 251)

It seems as though La Guma is portraying the African woman as big and fat and tough, or stuck in the kitchen, but never desired romantically, as a sort of amusement; certainly not a "celebration", and probably not out of any sense of malice—that is, if one thinks that an African woman, "ponderous as a hippopotamus...swaying like and elephant...thick and dark as an oak," who "possessed the ferocity of an old African buffalo" and "clucks" when she speaks, is amusing. On the other hand, one can say that La Guma is a man who is committed, but in whom the cancerous poison of the white supremacist monster comes out, as if in an act of creative exorcism. We can continue to respect and love Alex La Guma and treasure what he has written because we understand some of the consequences of the myth of white superiority and the insidiousness of color-consciousness and racism; but we must, at the same time, be wary of depictions of African women because of the way these depictions affect African and Colored people and perceptions of them.

Therefore, in his portraits of African women, La Guma denies African people a full measure of pride and dignity with themselves, as well as the legitimacy of an aesthetically attractive and sensuously appealing African identity as a distinctly artistic, social, and psychological force in the struggle for African liberation. The problem of the twentieth century is still the problem of the color-line, but not just in the international arena; it is also a problem of differentiation and preference among darker and lighter people of the same races, and of the African and Colored women who are selected and depicted as representative of each group. For it is the whole family, rather than the light or the dark, that must be affirmed.

La Guma may not even be aware of the extent to which color-consciousness has influenced him, but, as the foregoing examples indicate, in crucial situations and important portrayals, this influence will inevitably surface. Vernon February, himself a so-called Colored South African states that, "The 'Cape coloured' has been the greatest dupe of white stereotyped portrayals than any other group in South Africa" (1981:164). An important issue, therefore, is the author's own definition of himself and his work. La Guma is doing no more nor less than any other artist in bringing the influences of his life, background, and culture, to his canvas. I have been using the term "so-called Coloured(s)" intermittently to stress the view posited by February when he observes that:

It is not the shame of identification with being 'coloured', which prompts the 'coloured' to refer to himself as a 'so-called coloured'... It is rather the connotations attached to the word 'coloured', as found in the white political ethos, which cause the violent rejection. ...A comparative analysis will bear out that the facts of negritude, Pan-Africanism and soul-brotherism are increasingly being reflected in 'coloured' thinking and writing. There are similar indications that the 'no past, no myth through taught belief' image, as imposed on 'coloureds' by white South Africans, is also being expunged through a greater political awareness. (165)

It is no mystery that 'coloreds' owing their origin to various groups at the Cape: African, European, and Asian, making them the most heterogeneous of groups in South Africa, South Africans would have imposed upon them the image of "no past, no myth through taught belief," nor that many "coloreds" would not take pride in being classified, or referred to as "coloreds". This is quite understandable, given the eternal drive to glorify "white blood"; and most certainly there has been "colored" or "mulatto" achievement; and I really don't know if Alex La Guma was raised in a family like that of "Soaphead" in Toni Morrison's (1994) *The Bluest Eye*, who "had been reared in a family proud of its academic accomplishments and its mixed blood—in fact, they believed the former was based on the latter....With the confidence born of a conviction of superiority, they performed well at schools" (167-168). What is mysterious and surprising is La Guma's cognizance of this "colored" classification, his political awareness, yet his persistent use of desecrating images of African women. It may also be important to understand that the classification "Coloured" is a result of South African racial legislation. The classification itself suggests that the persons responsible for it are most uncomfortable with color distinctions and consciousness of color that it implies. "Coloured," even once used by Africans in America, is a term that vaporizes; it is about as close to nothingness and invisibility that you can come. It is a vacuous, meaningless word used in a pre-eminently color conscious society, where color means everything, which is a contradiction. In addition, the term "Coloured" like the terms Negro, Black, Afro or African, all of these words exemplify and are an index to one's perspective on the meaning of struggle, change, and even history for African people. The meaning, goals and objectives of struggle for Coloreds, Negroes or Mulattos is not always the same as those of Africans, especially at the personal, individual level.

As the African revolution matures, writers like La Guma must put away those terms and identities which belittle this struggle and are suggestive of an identity crisis, and ideological infantilism. They must substitute those figurations and images which elevate the African people to the height of universalism and dignity they justly deserve. "African" is the only identity, it seems to me, that brings dignity, that speaks of a history, a land, a people, a culture. The term "Coloured" makes impossible a vision of nationhood, it gives no direction, no focus; it is the reason why Charlie Pauls reaches for the universal before he has grasped the immediate and local; it is the reason La Guma can mock and amuse himself with sardonic images of African women. One can easily understand, though not accept, why La Guma—like too many so-called Coloureds—want to escape their African identity and are pushing for an identity of color with "their kind" in a country like South Africa where they can sometimes "play white" and are in a class distinctly superior to the subordinated Africans. "Indeed," states Chancellor Williams (1976), "the race would experience the joyful relief that comes with a new birth of freedom if this particular group would stop trying to operate in both the white and Black worlds, stop straddling the fence and get down decisively on the side of its choice" (357).

Williams, however, despairs of their ever doing this because of the double advantage the so-called coloreds have of shifting to whatever side it is expedient to be on from time to time. The Afrikaners know this, February notes, "and are still trying, to forge a 'colored' myth. Sadly, however, what has emerged (if anything at all) can only be classified as folklore" (1981:167). And in the conclusion to his very timely book, *Mind Your Colour*, February states, emphatically that "Nothing, however, has been solved and nothing will be solved, as long as the 'colored' is seen as a separate problem, which must be solved separately" (178). La Guma and other so-called Coloured writers, in fact all the people of South Africa laboring under the misnomer "colored" should embrace unequivocally, in spirit and in pride, an African identity.

Precision of language and naming is an essential component of the African survival kit. Faulty language soon deteriorates into faulty reasoning and subsequently faulty behavior. It is this ambiguous dimension of *And a Threefold Cord*—La Guma's misguided clarion call for class collaboration with poor whites, and his insulting portraits of African women—that necessitates the foregoing and following discussion.

The second dimension of La Guma's self-definition is: South African. February considers this to be a "blessing in disguise. The African and the white man can, after all, both fall back on a tribal myth, the 'coloreds' are asked to forge one which is all South African" (1981:165). To the contrary, the notion of the "Coloured South African" is a logical absurdity. Neither the Africans nor the so-called Coloreds are legally South Africans; only the Whites are South Africans. If by "Coloured South African" is meant a Colored citizen of South Africa, and if a citizen is one who, by birth or by naturalization under the laws of a given nation, enjoys and exercises all the rights, privileges, and obligations conferred and imposed upon him by the laws of that nation, then it is clear that no Colored or African, either born or naturalized in South Africa, has yet achieved the status of citizenship. Like pregnancy, one is either a citizen or one is not.

Still, with regard to La Guma's characterization, none of his characters in *And a Threefold Cord* is troubled with these questions of color, race, nationality or citizenship; but rather, they attempt, by all indications, to transcend these essential identities in pursuit of the "universal." The occasional glimpse into a character's inner life, as when Charlie tries to console Freda after the fire death of her children, echoes the same central message of solidarity promulgated all the way from the biblical epigraph, to the Marxist - communists' dictum of "workers of the world unite"; as he says to her, "people can't stand up to the world alone, they got to be together" (168).

What does La Guma really mean? What people can't stand up to the world alone? What "world" is he talking about? If he is talking about the so-called Coloured "people" standing up to the "white" world—well, that's yet the nature of the equation, here in the twentieth century. Even in a seemingly trite reference, "people can't stand up to the world alone," La Guma has carelessly lumped together, metaphorically, the so-called "Coloured", White, and Black people in South Africa with exploited people the world over; including the white working class of America, England, France, Russia, as victims in common, rather than as the victims of a distinctly racist society in which their theoretical allies, the white working class, the George Mosterts of South Africa and the world, became and continue to be staunch, de facto, enemies of African liberation.

To take their rightful place among the nations and peoples of this world, Africa and African people must "stand alone" on their own feet. They cannot look to their oppressors (ideologically, economically, or militarily) to liberate them or even to help in their liberation. White people, universally, will and must serve their own interests, which always involves the amazing oxymoronic desire to be "first among equals." White people, universally, have never changed their real attitude toward African people during all the passing centuries and there is absolutely no evidence upon which to base the belief that they (as a people, rich and poor) will change in the centuries to come. There is, on the other hand, compelling and overwhelming evidence that African people must first stand-alone. And when they have achieved enough strength and unity of purpose and direction, as one African people, to develop the ideological guidelines for their own advancement, they will draw what is best for them from any or all existing systems, of necessity and as a simple matter of course. African people, throughout the world, must make these fundamental decisions as a single people.

Even though La Guma recognizes and has stated that "The main concept of the struggle in South Africa today is the liberation of the African majority," (Abrahams 61) rather than be a part of that majority, mind, body and soul, his Colored-communist identity predisposes him to compromise, to equivocate. So he adds "At the same time, the programme of the liberation struggle states that South Africa belongs to all who live in it, black and white" ("Culture and Liberation," 35). It is precisely this kind of thinking that encourages Charlie, via La Guma, to invite George Mostert to a party in the shanty-town and suggest that he can have one of the Coloured women there as a sort of token of their class affinity. South Africa does not belong to "all who live in it" it, presently, belongs to white people who live in it; and if the African people who live in it want it, they will have to take it by revolutionary struggle from these white people. White people in South Africa do not—nor will they ever—share power with African people.

La Guma—and other Marxists—recognize that a revolution is involved in the African struggle, but still they want Africans to depend upon the white worker being with them. The average white worker in South Africa today isn't joining any liberal or revolutionary organizations—in mass. La Guma certainly has some understanding of this because he shows how difficult it is for George to even accept the invitation to the party—with his potential class allies—in spite of his own abject poverty and loneliness. In this episode, La Guma strongly suggests the stranglehold of color-consciousness on the white character; but, in classic liberal Marxist terms, he is careful to deny Charlie a similar consciousness. Charlie, therefore, conveys the grateful, dependency complex of the colonized by initiating this attempted class unity.

La Guma, like his antiquated European Marxist mentors, is still using the slogan "workers of the world, unite" and evading the scientific question of which workers he is calling on. Who is to unite? And with whom? The underclass of Africa, Asia, and Latin America? Or, the workers of highly developed America and Europe and European—controlled South Africa (whose improved conditions and higher standard of living have been made possible by exploitation of the world underclass of African and other people of color)? The white working class of South Africa, America, and Western Europe collaborate with the white power structure and support the system because their high standard of living depends upon the continuation of this power structure and system (Boggs 1970:53-54).

Still, La Guma, in this one scene involving Charlie Pauls and George Mostert, propagates the concept of "black and white, unite and fight," as if African people and white people have common issues and grievances, systematically evading the fact that every white immigrant who walked into South Africa did so on the backs of the indigenous South Africans and had the opportunity to advance precisely because the indigenous South Africans were and are being systematically deprived of the opportunity to advance by both white capitalists and white workers. La Guma finds it perfectly natural to exhort Africans and so-called Coloreds to invite the enemy into their fold. Under the guise of combating the racism of whites, La Guma is actually trying to bring about collaboration between the oppressed race (Africans) and the oppressing race (Europeans); thus, undermining the revolutionary struggle against oppression, which, by virtue of the historical development of South Africa, requires a mobilization of the oppressed Africans for struggle against the oppressing Europeans. Again, there is no historical basis for the promise constantly made to Africans—by Coloured, Mulatto and European Marxists—that the white workers, the Mosterts, will join with them against the European capitalist enemy. To expect the African liberation movement to embrace the Mosterts inside the African struggle is, in fact, as Boggs warns, to expect the revolution to welcome the enemy into its camp (1970:53-54). Charlie's invitation and George's refusal is a metaphor for Coloreds' (as distinct from Africans') invitation to the white working class of South Africa; just as the image of Missus Nzuba is a metaphor for African women. Here too, he reaches for the "universal" unable to portray African women in an attractive, appealing way because "the world" has a different standard of beauty. In this view, Marilyn Monroe, Sophia Loren, etc. are "universal" and the beauty of an African woman is measured by her proximity to that standard.

Fully cognizant that these are decadent standards that focus on the exterior person, these are also La Guma's standards; his characters are known from the outside rather than from the inside. We come to know a character from external appearance not from internal knowledge, which is the only validity in this line of discussion. La Guma does not give any indication of the factors of color-consciousness or national consciousness that move and animate his characters—and no doubt, to the white liberal and Marxist's mind this is the "universal" quality in La Guma's writing—so that what he does portray, repetitively and monotonously, are the factors of class that motivate his characters. What motivates Charlie, therefore, is not the same consciousness that motivates a Steve Biko or Barney Pityana. Pityana, Biko's chief lieutenant in the SASO movement, in an admirable exposition of Black Consciousness, *inter alia*, makes the following prognosis:

> Many would prefer to be color-blind; to them skin pigmentation is merely an accident of creation. To us it is something much more fundamental. It is a synonym for subjection, an identification for the disinherited....
>
> South Africa uniquely demonstrates that a powerful minority will perpetuate social indignities even on the labor force of a vigorously expanding economy. Civil status is determined at birth and for life by color. Whether he is a wage earner, a businessman, an intellectual or a chief, no black can be admitted to the national Parliament....
>
> ...We shall never find our goals and aspirations as a people centered anywhere else but in US. This, therefore, necessitates self-examination and a rediscovery of ourselves.

Blacks can no longer afford to be led and dominated by
nonblacks.... This means that black people must build themselves into a position of nondependence upon whites. They
must work towards a self-sufficient political, social and
economic unit. In this manner they will help themselves
towards a deeper realization of their potential and worth as
self-respecting people...The way to the future is not through
a directionless multiracialism but through a positive unilateral approach. Black man, you are on your own. (Woods
1978:33-35)

Now we can come back to Charlie's (which one can also read as
La Guma's) position that "People cannot stand alone..." and see
that it stands in diametrical opposition to the tenets of the Black
Consciousness movement that "Black man, you are on your own."
And it can be conjectured, if not accepted, that the underlying reason for this dichotomy is the understanding of identity, the degree
of Africaness or blackness, of the respective spokesmen.

The millions of Africans of mixed blood, so-called Coloreds
and Mulattos, in South Africa and in Diaspora, must become steadfast and devoted to an African identity; knowing that when the
whites give them a preferential status above the "unmixed," but
always below themselves, they do so to maintain the myth of superior "white blood." They must bind themselves to African people,
and must be embraced by African people with unbreakable bonds
of love, and fight to the death any attempt to legally or otherwise
classify and establish them as a separate ethnic group with the vacuous misnomer "Coloured."

When this is done, and we note La Guma's imagery of the desecration of the human body, and human beings, as a metaphor for
the South African situation, readers can be sure, without the slightest
dubiety, that the comparison he makes is "universal" precisely
within the context of the African experience, and not a "directionless
multiracialism" with no concrete point of reference to a definable
people. In today's world, Europeans, of all classes, are not the
immediate descendants of slaves or colonized people; they have
not suffered the humiliation of conquest as an entire people; they
have not had their very humanity called into question; they have
not internalized their color (or lack of color) and physical features

as ugly and despicable; they have not been imbued with an inferiority complex, a dependency complex, and a proclivity for imitation. African people, mixed and unmixed, must first heal themselves before they can be effective in healing others. Therefore, African people should be clear, even if La Guma is not, that the desecration of lives, as depicted in the following examples, mirrors the conditions of the African world: Cape Town, Nairobi, Addis Ababa, Cairo, Tunis, Tripoli, Lagos, Accra, Monrovia, Haiti, Jamaica, Miami, Newark, New York, Detroit, Chicago, St. Louis, Atlanta, Los Angeles, San Francisco, Oakland—all the places African people live and often call home—where:

> The rubbish dump along the edge of the settlement is a favorite playground of the children. They can climb dunes of soggy paper and rags, and clamber over the jungle-gyms of rusting iron, see-saw on lengths of decaying and slippery flotsam, breathing the air of disease dotted with flies like currents in pudding. (*Threefold Cord*, 152)

This image is a precise metaphor for the African world, in Africa, in South Africa, and in Diaspora, where the no-longer-useful, the expendable African man and woman is discarded like the "piled and scattered metal debris" in George's junkyard, where:

> ...all the leaving of a modern battlefield had been collected and dumped there: heaped and entangled rusty and broken automobile engines, chasis, fenders, struts, mudguards, radiators, spring-leaves, axles, wheels, coach-work, detached doors, bolts and seat-springs, all the abandoned offal from butchered traffic lay in the yard, flaking with brown rust, clogged with a paste of sand and oil and grease. (70)

It takes no great powers of discernment to interpret this image as a metaphor for the millions of African people, everywhere, who have ceased to be of use and value as "items" of labor or property, and are discarded. The "battlefield" is the military-industrial complex of the white Western world and their South African "kith and kin"; while "collected and dumped...heaped and entangled" there are the broken lives of Pa and Ma Pauls, Charlie, Ronny, Jorny, Caroline, Roman,

Susie, Uncle Ben, Missus Nzuba, Aunty Mina, Freda (and of course
her children), Klonky, Gracie, and the millions of Africans who
have—because expendable due to age, mechanization, or even attitude (let's not forget Michael Adonis)—found themselves "endorsed out" of the labor force; collected and dumped in "homelands," segregated ghettos or "heaped and entangled" in cheaply
constructed high-rise apartments and projects. These people, all
African, (with an occasional George Mostert who can't make it
even in a system designed for his advancement) are the "abandoned offal" tossed on the rubish-heap of history by the inhuman
international capitalist, so-called white-supremacist system.

There is no need for La Guma to attempt any racial rapproche-
ment in this ubiquitous African experience. It is overwhelmingly
evident that it is African people, mixed and unmixed, who, over the
centuries, have been systematically deprived of the opportunity to
become skilled workers, in societies where industry itself has become automated and highly technical, and who therefore have become socially and economically unnecessary. The Mosterts of South
Africa, at least, have the opportunity to become skilled. The systematic underdevelopment of African labor potential, the Charlies
and Ronnies, is the very foundation for the systematic development
of the European community. Surplus from the exploitation of African labor, by unemployment or underemployment, is partly used to
offer a few more benefits to white workers and serves as a bribe to
make the latter less revolutionary. Like their white brothers and
sisters in the United States, bribes come in the form of increased
wages, better working conditions, expanded social service (e.g.,
the hiring of more police and their lackeys, various welfare-type
initiatives staffed at the most critical levels by white liberals and
black Uncle Toms) and, of course, the bribe carries with it the
delightful psychological gratification of being slightly better-off than
the super-exploited Africans. Like George, the white worker of
highly industrialized countries—of which South Africa is one—sur-
vives, but he or she no longer seeks political power, no longer fights
to better his position, is no longer creative nor exercises any independent judgement on the great issues of war and peace, control of
industries, or color (racial) conflict, but rather,

> ...peered out towards the world like an entombed miner
> through a gap in a rockfall, surrounded by the dusty piles

> of advertising literature, the spike of dog-eared accounts,
> and the smudged calendar covered with long-forgotten
> phone numbers.(164)

This simile is an appropriate comparison with the superficially contained and fortified barriers of ignorance and racism erected around
all Southern Africa. There is a decisive contrast between George's
attitude and that of Charlie and Ma Pauls. Ma Pauls, for instance,
is the essence of humanity: fighting for her rights even in the midst
of squalor and little hope, we see her asserting her dignity and humanity, singing to herself, thinking not of her own plight but of that
of her children, relatives, and friends:

> Ma Pauls sat in her chair in the bedroom and rocked slowly
> backwards and forward, her body hunched and her face
> withered with sadness. She sang in her old mind, and
> thought back on Dad Pauls, on young Ronald, on Freda's
> children. Her hands, corded and dry, like skeins of brown
> wool, were clasped in her lap, as she rocked. (166-167)

We pity but admire Ma Pauls and the other inhabitants of the shanty-
town; whereas, with George, we pity him but find him pathetic and
insufferable.

This should come as no surprise. Poor whites in South Africa,
Western Europe, and the United States are allies in the exploitation
and oppression of Africans. What will be borne out in analysis of
La Guma's later novels, particularly in *In the Fog of the Seasons'
End*, and what is evident in the muliracial make-up of the Treason
Trials, is that the only whites (and Coloreds) who join the anti-
apartheid struggle (which must be kept clearly distinct from the
African revolution and African nationalism in South Africa; as distinct as integration is from African nationalism in the U.S.) are
those who are financially most secure: professionals, intellectuals,
and maybe a few college students—individuals who represent no
significant social force.

Since unity, solidarity, togetherness, and like synonyms represent the thematic center, the sine qua non for appreciating *And a
Threefold Cord*, let this be crystal clear: the oppressed Africans
(mixed and unmixed) must deliver themselves from the yoke of
oppression, must take upon themselves—singly, alone, and un-

aided—the responsibility for acquiring the necessary power, genius, and expertise to liberate themselves. The white people, the capitalist system, that enslaved and colonized African people cannot be asked or counted on to free them. It is like asking a chicken to produce a duck-egg: it simply isn't in its nature, its system, to do so (Malcolm X 1996: "Message to the Grassroots").

Further analysis will reveal that in *The Stone Country* and in *In the Fog of the Seasons' End*, La Guma's ideas and images are inclined towards—though not entirely towards—a recognition that there is no instinctive, spontaneous solution; that there is a need for premeditated and protracted organization and struggle. There is also in these two works implicit recognition of the specific need for unity between so-called Coloreds and Africans; though, as noted earlier, this is contradicted imagistically by La Guma's portraits of African women. And for reasons one must try to understand, in *Time of the Butcherbird* he returns to the acts of spontaneous and impulsive violence. Unlike Charlie, in the leading character in each of the novels *The Stone Country* (George Adams) and in *In the Fog of the Seasons' End* (Beukes), George Adams and Beukes, there is development towards an overt political posture: both are fully-fledged political agitators and communists, underground workers imbued with Marxian egalitarian principles.

In *The Stone Country*, a metaphor for South Africa, the barriers separating the prisoners according to color are, literally, erected in stone. And though the imagery may suggest vertical barriers, metaphorically and otherwise, it must be understood from the outset that these barriers are horizontal as well: like a platform resting on the backs of African people and holding them down, while above them Colored and white prisoners enjoy infinitesimal yet noticeable psychological and "material" benefits.

Colored, South African, and Communist explains much, perhaps too much, about the kinds of characters, images and ideas one finds in Alex La Guma's novels: still, they are an index to the meaning of *And a Threefold Cord*, and to the meaning of struggle, change and revolution for Alex La Guma.

Chapter 3

THE STONE COUNTRY:
IMAGE AND IDEA

White people...bless their generous little hearts, are quite
unable to imagine that there can be anyone, anywhere, who
does not wish to be White, and are probably the most abject victims of history the world has ever seen, or will ever
know.

—James Baldwin, *Evidence of Things Not Seen*

Stephen Biko, in *I Write What I Like*, quoting Aime Ceasire's 1956
letter of resignation from the French Communist Party, provides
an appropriate segue to the images and ideas in *The Stone Country:*

We Coloured men, in this specific moment of historical
evolution, have consciously grasped in its full breath, the
notion of our peculiar uniqueness, the notion of just who
we are and what, and that we are ready, on every plane and
in every department, to assume the responsibilities which
proceed from this coming of consciousness. The peculiarity of our place in the world is not to be confused with
anyone else's. The peculiarity of our problems which aren't
to be reduced to subordinate forms of any other problem.
The peculiarity of our history, laced with terrible mis-for-
tunes which belong to no other history. The peculiarity of

our culture, which we intend to live and make live in an
ever realer manner. (1978:66-67)

The Stone Country, La Guma's third novel, in its graphic pictures
of prison life in South Africa, is a metaphor, a deliberate microcosmic comparison, for life in the broader South African society as
lived by Africans and so-called Coloreds. In the rigid internal struc-
turing of the prison, along the same segregated, apartheid lines as
the "outer" South African reality, the "peculiar uniqueness" of the
African and so-called Coloreds' place in the world is concretized
in stone walls and iron bars. Jefferson Mpolo, the African who
was arrested with George Adams, a Colored (and as much as it
may be detested, it must be said this way if the peculiarity of the
African's perspective and "place in the world is not to be confused
with anyone else's), for distributing anti-government leaflets, says
to the protagonist, George Adams:

> "This jail is a small something of what they want to make
> the country. Everybody separate, boy. White, African,
> Coloured. Regulations for everybody, and a white boss
> with a gun and a stick." (20)

Here, again, for reasons undoubtedly related to his Mulatto-Col-
ored-Communist consciousness, La Guma can have a character,
Jefferson Mpolo, talking about apartheid as a possibility, a desire
("what they want to make the country") and not as a reality; (what
they, white people, have made the country). The distinction may
be important. George Adams' response to Mpolo's equivocating,
ambiguous comment is only, "Ja, the hell with them." As one
steeped in Marxian principles and, thereby, intellectually superior
(at least in the context of the story), with a grasp of precise and
correct language and analysis, it is Grorge Adams' (or La Guma's)
responsibility to address and clarify Mpolo's ambiguous perception, to put other words into the mouth of this African, words and
perceptions that would, perhaps, echo Bantu Stephen Biko. For, if
South Africa is, in the words of Mpolo, still wanting to create a
separate society (Black, White, Brown, and Yellow) and has not
in fact already done so, a major task of intellectuals, both revolutionary and liberal, is to work desperately to prevent the separation

from becoming real. In other words, revolutionary intellectuals and soldiers must intensify their efforts for color and race integration before apartheid is really solidified, before "separate development," homelands, shanty-towns, urban ghettos, are really real. On the other hand, if everyone in South Africa is already separated (African, European, Coloured, and Asian) then a task of intellectuals, among others, is to first of all accept this reality as real and then to suggest and implement strategies and tactics for each man and woman in each group "to rise and attain the envisioned self."

For example, if the verbal, intellectual image of Mpolo were the words of Stephen Biko, he might say to George Adams: Each group working autonomously, then concertedly as issues and circumstances permit, "to attain its style of existence without encroaching on or being thwarted by another." In *I Write What I Like*, Biko continues: "Out of this mutual respect for each other and complete freedom of self-determination there will obviously arise a genuine fusion of the life-styles of the various groups" (1978:21). This is how the founder of the Black Consciousness Movement defines "true integration."

As such, this somewhat trite and inadvertent quip by Jefferson Mpolo ("This jail is a small something of what they want to make the country. Everybody separate, boy: White, African, Coloured. Regulations for everybody, and a white boss with a gun and a stick") becomes a gateway for probing some rather significant themes and ideological and moral messages inherent in *The Stone Country*; ideological and moral messages embedded in La Guma's imagery. Images of character (physical and intellectual, including dialogue and interior monologue) , setting or the physical environment, and images of the desecration of physical bodies as a metaphor for the South African situation.

Thematic imagery is not simply rooted in the pages of the book alone, but is part of the intellectual environment, the intellectual context of South Africa at a definable and given historical period (1950s-60s); more precisely, the period when the author is creating his work. Concern, therefore, is with the ideological, political, even ethical accuracy or efficacy of Jefferson Mpolo's comment and its link to a discernable thematic thread in *The Stone Country*.

The image of the prison, the setting for this work, is a precise metaphor for South African society right now (1997) and not what it one day might become. This is more than mere intellectual "hair-splitting," but a concerned and purposeful explication and analysis of sensitive, subtle, and vital ideological perspectives on the meaning, direction, and objectives of struggle, attired in aesthetic language and promulgated through art. One of the ideological perspectives suggested by La Guma in *The Stone Country* is a more concentrated variation of the theme in *And a Threefold Cord*, namely, unity; or, as George Adams tells Yusef the Turk, "We all in this together" (39). As a result, a dominating idea of *The Stone Country* is that life in a South African prison is a mirror image, a lucid reflection, of life in the larger social-political reality of South Africa.

The Marxian-laden theme "we're in this together" reverberates throughout this novel. When the prison guards, coloured and white, like the white-supremacist socio-economic system in South Africa, have completed "separating Coloured from Africans" (26), what "we" is La Guma appealing to? When all the warders and guards are white and colored and none black, what "we" is he referring to? When there is no significant or memorable mention of a white prisoner as a character worthy of a reader's attention in the entire novel, what "we" is La Guma trying to guide our sympathies toward? George Adams is a so-called Coloured; and a lot of the meaning and significance of this novel, and La Guma's perspective as it works its way through and on the novel, will be lost if this fact of the peculiarity and particularity of "colored" identity is not recognized and admitted.

La Guma's perspective, rooted in Marxian dialectics, makes no provision for political sovereignty that is joined to a national or racial community in the figurations inhabiting *The Stone Country*. He seems too quick and eager to transcend the insidious and inveterate effects of the myth of white supremacy on the Coloured psyche and behavior; which makes difficult, if not superfluous, rhetorical appeals to class unity. Coloreds, for example, even under apartheid, could vote, and did not have to carry passes, which means, among other things, that they will have fewer encounters with the South African Police; thus, fewer random jail sentences that make incarceration a way of life for African people in and around urban areas throughout the world.

When George Adams is arrested and cast into a South African prison community where he has little experience with the pattern of life, he feels "like an immigrant in a strange country, ignorant of the habits and customs of its violent people" (92). In an interview with Cecil Abrahams (1991) La Guma confesses:

> *The Stone Country* was based upon my own experiences and the experiences of other prisoners. Most of it is completely authentic, from my point of view. I even personally shared the cell with a young man. I wouldn't say that he is me subjectively, but let's say that the character George Adams seemed to hold together all the other scenes. (23)

On another occasion George Adams ruminates, "Guards and prisoners, everybody, were the enforced inhabitants of another country, another world" (*Stone Country*, 18). George Adams' bewilderment and awe of life in a South African jail is one more small but significant indication that the so-called Coloreds, in South Africa, like Mulattos in America—north and south—and the West Indies, occupy a different place in the social and economic color-hierarchy and consequently have developed their own unique ethos, their own peculiar and distinct problems, attitudes, and responses to those problems.

The position of Coloreds is further distinguished by the vicious and divisive South African practice, like that in America and Brazil, of paying light-skinned South Africans better than dark-skinned in the same jobs; by providing better equipment for light-skinned (Coloured) children than for dark-skinned (African) children. Thus, when we come to La Guma's images of prison personnel, we are not surprised to find that watching the African prisoners "was a young Coloured guard in a washed-out uniform and a big topi that looked ridiculous above his small face...(and) naked convicts were being herded away by the Coloured warder" (22-23). It is wonderful, here, that La Guma engages in a kind of self-criticism; aware of the too often debasing mimicry of his own "colored" people, taking pride in the servile imitation of those who oppress them (DeToquville).

Life in a South African jail, for the daily average of 70,351 prisoners to whom La Guma dedicates his novel—stultified, crippled, rendered useless and made to appear stupid and ridiculous by an exaggerated three-tiered system of black, brown-yellow, white stratification—is a direct and accurate reflection of the same system of color stratification in the larger society. It matters not a lot that there is race-mixing and integration at the surface when there is separation at the very foundation—economic, political, social—of the system. La Guma knows this, yet attempts to transcend it, by manipulating the reader's sympathies and intellectual loyalties to an identification with this surface reality. And it is not that he is unaware of the socio-economic hiatus between so-called Coloureds and Africans, it is rather that he distorts and does violence to this reality to further advance his Marxist idealism.

For example, when George Adams and Jefferson Mpolo are driving slowly through a middle-class Colored community, en route to distribute their anti-government leaflets, George observes:

> ...here were the well-to-do of his community: the professionals, the clerks, the artisans, small-time businessmen and some of the border-liners who went through life sorry they had not been born a shade lighter so they could slip across and be white. (42)

How sad. That mere shades of skin-color have such meaning in today's world. How sad. That one today believes that a change in condition—objective, material—requires a change in skin color. It is interesting that George Adams contemplates here "the well-to-do of his community," that is, the so-called "Coloured" community; as opposed to Jefferson Mpolo's African community; here, the "elite" are those with less color. This middle-class "colored" community quickly reminds one of the Walmer Estate of Richard Rive's novel, *Emergency* (1970): a community that is part of the calculated, structural foundation of the myth of white supremacy, just as much as the "colored" ghetto—District Six—the African ghetto Soweto, and the so-called homelands. The middle-class communities referred to by La Guma and Rive are examples of class and color stratification within the Coloured community. Rive—incidentally, a shade darker than La Guma—seems more deeply troubled by the subtle dimensions of this internal color hierarchy. Andrew Dreyer, Rive's protagonist, while thinking about the relationship between himself and his brothers James and Daniel, observes:

> James was very fair like his mother, went to white cinemas
> and bars, had been a gunner in an artillery regiment during
> the war, and only his responsibility towards the family still
> kept him in District Six. He in turn despised Andrew, whose
> dark skin he found an embarrassment. (*Emergency*, 37)

Similar thoughts trouble him in his relationship with his mother, and:

> He wondered whether it had anything to do with colour.
> She was fair, like James and Annette, whereas he was dark,
> the darkest in the family. Sometimes when they walked
> together in the street, he had a feeling that she was ashamed
> of him, even in District Six. (45)

These citations reveal some rather interesting attitudes of "colored" characters toward color: guilt, embarrassment, shame. Clearly, these Colored attitudes are important to consider when one is advocating "unity" and suggesting that "we're in this together" as a class-conscious Marxian principle; while taking lightly or altogether ignoring such serious and obvious internal contradictions; or considering such contradictions secondary to the idealistic appeal for inter-racial working-class unity. February (1981) says that Rive's "hero... comes across as a confused, wooly-headed liberal and romantic" (162). And one is left to ponder what "wooly-headed" adds to February's criticism.

Within the fictional world of *The Stone Country*, there exists a plethora of imagistic and thematic appeals to unity. Since we know that the prisoners are separated black, brown-yellow, and white, it follows that George, a Coloured, who closely resembles La Guma in attitude, experience, and physiognomy, is segregated along with the other Coloured prisoners. As such, there is the possible interpretation that La Guma is making a direct appeal for unity within the Coloured community, both inside and outside of the prison. After the prison guard had separated the African and Coloured prisoners, George reflects:

"In this half-world, hemmed in by stone and iron, there was an atmosphere of every-man-for-himself which George Adams did not like" (37). George fights aggressively against the anarchistic individualism fostered by the prison system and the criminal underworld, and some of the prisoners begin to appreciate and respect him for this. For example, after Yusef the Turk intervenes and supports George in his confrontation with the prison bully, Butcherboy, George asks:

> "Well, what for did you interfere? You said mos everyman for himself in this place." To which Yusef the Turk answers: "Ja. Maybe is for jubas like me and Butcherboy and the res' of these skolly-boy hoodlums....People like you, we got to look after, mos." (70)

Just as a little aside: the name "Yusef the Turk" suggests that Asians or Indians are categorized with Coloreds on the white supremacists' socio-genetic scale and often show common cause, as in the scene above.

George, a resolute political agitator, demonstrates courage and common cause with the other prisoners and becomes, by example, the standard against which the other characters are measured, by standing up to the prison guards, actually talking back to them, like the time he approached one of the nameless white gendarmes because he hadn't received a drinking mug, like the other prisoners, upon entering the jail:

> "What is your trouble now?" asked the frozen voice.
> "I didn't get a mug when I came in."
> "So it's you again, hey?" The blond moustache twitched slightly.
> "That's just too bad, jong. No mug, no coffee."
> "I'm entitled to a mug, isn't it?" George Adams asked...
> "I can't help it if the man on duty didn't hand out the stuff."
> ..."You donder, " the guard shouted. "Who the hell you talking to? You think I let any skolly talk to me like he was a white man?—off, out of my sight." (75)

130

The prisoners are expected to crawl and beg for everything they get, but George Adams breaks the mold, gives the prisoners a more manly, a more courageous image to emulate. Also, by sharing his food (69) and cigarettes (39), he wins the admiration of other inmates, particularly Yusef Ebrahim, or "the Turk," as he is called, and the Casbah Kid, Albert March. When George offers a cigarette to an anonymous character in a group of card-players, Yusef exclaims:

> "Hell, what for you giving tobacco away? These baskets
> can find their own, mos, don't I say?"
> "Hell," George Adams told him, "We all in this - - - -
> together." (39)

Where La Guma's earlier protagonists, Michael Adonis, Charlie Pauls, are still groping their way towards some definable political posture, George Adams stands bold and courageous, teaching through example. Portraits of his bravery, his unselfish giving, his words of unity and inspiration, the repetitive "we're in this together," must be seen in their wider metaphorical connotations and ideological implications. In order to achieve this, George Adams' appeal can be understood as La Guma's appeal: and that means freeing the images, both verbal and pictorial, from the contained parameters of the fictionally created world of *The Stone Country* and placing them in the broader context of ideological struggles in South African society and the world. There is no question that courage, sharing, and unity are admirable qualities for any person or nation. One relevant question, however, might be: How do these qualities reflect La Guma's perspective on struggle and change in South African society? Is his concern the developing Colored consciousness? Marxist consciousness? Nationalist consciousness? Pan-African consciousness? Is his concern the unity and achievement of a particular people, a peculiar people—African people? Is La Guma, at this stage in his writing and intellectual development, in the words of Lewis Nkosi trapped in the "exigencies of Cape Malay homecooking" (1968:8)?

Some of the answers to these questions are provided in the novel itself, and revolve around the circumstances of George Adams' arrest in the first place. George Adams is a member of an underground, communist network. And La Guma, sensitive to the sharp cleavages in South Africa's racially stratified society, is careful to indicate, even in the naming of his characters, their racial identity. Thus, in a well-placed and informative flashbck, comprising the whole of Chapter 6, we discover the integrated, interracial underground network George is working with. There is Jefferson Mpolo, an African, who gets arrested with George; a "sympathizer" Casim, obviously an Asian; and the unnamed white girl with the "reddish hair" and "a smudge of ink on her chin" (a subtle image that accentuates her whiteness) who runs the copying machine; and, of course, George, a Coloured (41-49).

Here we have it, then—very cleverly and surreptitiously woven into the thematic fabric of the novel—the four basic racial groups in South Africa (ironically, the major racial groups in the world): African, Asian, European, and so-called Coloured or black, yellow, white, and brown, respectively. The iconographic significance of interracial harmony among the supposed intellectual elite, those "we got to look after, mos" (70) precludes any discussion of African nationalism or Pan-Africanism. Africans in South Africa, like African people throughout the world, have not been allowed to give to the world and to civilization the full spiritual and cultural message which they are capable of giving, and surely their destiny should not be a servile imitation of European culture (DuBois 1903: 232-233). Irving Howe (1957), states quite candidly and poignantly this writer's perception of the ideological and thematic thrust apparent in this insidiously ideological image of the four conspirators:

> For both the writer and the reader, the political novel provides a particularly severe test: politics rakes our passions as nothing else, and whatever we may consent to overlook in reading a novel, we react with an almost demonic rapidity to a detested political opinion. (24).

The multiracial communism fostered by La Guma's theme-images is untenable, if not, at times, detestable. And it is not that African intellectuals, writers, and political leaders fear the red bogey: for even Pan-Africanists like Dr. Kwame Nkrumah, Dr. W.E. B. DuBois, Patrice Lumumba, Julius Nyerere, Sekou Toure, George

Padmore, Dr. Walter Rodney, and others, recognize much that is true in the Marxist's interpretation of history—"since" as Padmore (1971) notes, "it provides a rational explanation for a good deal that would otherwise be unintelligible" (xvi). Rather, Pan-Africanism and Pan-Africanists refuse to accept "the pretentious claims of doctrinaire Communism, that it alone has the solutions to all the complex racial, tribal, and socio-economic problems facing Africa" (Padmore 1971: xvi). It is clear from these few examples that imagery is an important vehicle for La Guma in conveying the themes and meaning of his novels, as well as deeping their artistic effect.

George Adams rests comfortably in La Guma's oeuvre as a logical link between Charlie Pauls and Beukes, a transitional stage in intellectual physiognomy of characters. Again, the principle that organizes the images is a concord between character portraits (what they say, think, and do) and theme, the images lighting the way for theme and helping to reveal it.

A new man of action emerges in George Adams. There is neither the apolitical, evasive introvert, Michael Adonis, of *A Walk in the Night*, nor the meditative and ideologically immature Charlie Pauls of *And a Threefold Cord*. When George is thrown into the barren landscape of a South African prison, he meets other victims of the myth of white superiority. They include the jocular minstrel, Solly; the smooth and violent Yusef Ebrahim "the Turk"; the cell-boss, brute, and bully Butcherboy Williams; the fatalistic, enigmatic and youthful murderer, Casbah Kid, "wrapped up in his own personal armor of silence, hiding his secret thoughts under invisible layers of dispassionate blankness" but with whom George's empathy and compassion are ultimately reconciled; nor can we overlook Gus, Morgan, and Koppe, the three inmates busily plotting their escape against the awesome, capricious forces of man and nature.

Then there are the ubiquitous prison guards, sadistic by temperament, who seem to be one single figure. The unnatural and dehumanizing relationship between the prisoners and the prison guards reduces the respective groups to animal level; and this debasement, as we shall see, is expressed in simple but powerful and thoroughly unpleasant images.

George Adams' role in the novel is primarily that of an on-
looker, linking the various parts of the story together. From his
observer position, George, as representative of La Guma's point of
view, does not come between the main substance of the novel and
the reader's perception of it. He sees and hears and smells and
senses and knows intellectually what's going on in the prison, but
remains advantageously detached, strategically estranged from total immersion in the prison life. On several occasions, with slight
variation, he states that he feels "like an immigrant entering a new
and strange country..." (18, 20, and 92). In a moment of intense
reflection, George rediscovers the law of the jungle (or cave), which
he detests because it reminds him of his childhood; a law he is
bound to fight because of the individualism and fratricide it encourages:

> In this half-world, hemmed in by stone and iron, there was
> an atmosphere of every-man-for-himself which George
> Adams did not like. He had grown up in the slums and he
> knew that here were the treacherous and the wily, the cring-
> ers and the boot-lickers, the violent and the domineering,
> the smooth-talkers and the savage, the bewildered and the
> helpless; the strong preyed on the weak, and the strong and
> brutal acknowledged a sort of nebulous alliance among
> themselves for the terrorisation of the underlings. (37)

George had been "locked up in police-stations" before, but this is
his first time in the upper echelons of crime; and when the prisoners, most of whom are "street-corner hoodlums...drunks,
thugs...murderers, robbers, housebreakers, petty criminals, rapists,
loiterers and simple permit offenders..." (19), when these
incorrigibles, otherwise victims of the myth of white supremacy,
discover that George Adams is in for "Political" working against
the government, they quickly promote him to the prison aristoc-
racy as "an equal, an expert from the upper echelons of crime"
(39).
    Indeed, George is involved in "the upper echelons of crime":
he is a political agitator and organizer, dedicated to a revolutionary
ideology, with a clear understanding and acceptance of the consequences of his actions, thinking with conviction that he "did not

have any regrets about his arrest. You did what you decided was the right thing, and then accepted the consequences" (74). He is grateful to Yusef the Turk for fighting on his behalf, but also saddened, as he thinks: "What a waste; here they got us fighting each other like dogs" (74). George's thought, the interior monologue here, though in the form of intellectual imagery, speaks the language of sight. This kind of intellectual image is intended to influence thought and social behavior; to make readers consider certain kinds of socio-political thought and action, or to see clearly the isolating and ostracizing effects of individualism and the idea of "every man for himself" in the microcosmic, concrete situation of prison life; a major obstacle to unity among the inmates and a compelling metaphor for the broader South African reality. Even though George Adams is remanded for only one month, among prisoners some of whom have been in for years, others who will be in for years to come, and still others who, like the Casbah Kid, are awaiting execution: George feels and accepts his responsibility as a teacher ("Professor" as Yusef the Turk calls him), in word and deed, to raise the level of consciousness of each and every prisoner he comes in contact with; knowing every step of the way that he is in

> ...a jungle of stone and iron, inhabited by jackals and hyenas, snarling wolves and trembling sheep, entrapped lions fighting off shambling monsters with stunted brains and bodies amoured with the hide of ignorance and brutality, trampling underfoot those who tried to claw their way from the clutch of the swamp. (81)

George makes the effort, even if he must conclude, as he does, as he sits watching and thinking about the fate awaiting Albert March, the Casbah Kid:

> You poor sod, you poor, poor sod, you going to die and you don't give a damn about yourself and about anybody else; except maybe if you had been shown the way, and right now you're learning, even if it is too bloody late. (92)

The unnatural and dehumanizing relationship between the prisoners and the prison guards, a reflection of the relationship between people of color and the white power structure of South Africa, reduces the respective groups to animal level, and this debasement is expressed in simple but powerful and thoroughly unpleasant imagery: "jackals and hyenas, snarling wolves and trembling sheep" (60) and the lips of one of the guards, "writhed like squirming caterpillars...(and) Something like an impaled worm writhed under the pudgy skin in the guard's throat"(61). Such images are a fitting comment on the prison experience and a natural expression of the narrator's emotional reaction to it and its impact on his mind, vividly imprinted also on the reader's memory, by the repulsive and almost hysterical images.

George Adams realizes that as long as "they got us fighting each other like dogs," this introverted violence will do the guards' work for them. He therefore tries to channel the prisoners' anger and emotions outward. When Yusef complains about the prison food, George says to him, "Prisoners ought to objeck...Strike for a better diet, mos" (74). And when George is bold enough to confront one of the guards because he didn't receive a drinking mug,

> He was thinking. Be damned if I'm going to let him get away with it. They expect you to crawl for everything: Please, boss, can I have this? Please, boss, can I have that? (75)

George's self-concept, his personal dignity, simply will not allow him to crawl and stoop; and, willing to accept the consequences, he says to one guard, directly, "Well, why don't they run this jail proper?" To which the guard could only reply weakly, "So you one of those slim men, hey? A clever darky" (76). The guard realizes he has been defeated, and this disturbs him. What emerges from this small incident is a powerful image of George Adams' courage, which is a major theme of *The Stone Country*.

The theme of courage is central to our understanding of Yusef as well, especially when he stands up to the much bigger and stronger Butcherboy Williams, defending his behavior to George with the simple cliche, "The bigger they come, the harder they fall" (74). Courage is also the quality that embellishes the character of the otherwise pathetic Casbah Kid, who, though obviously nervous— chewing at the cuticle of a thumb, biting his nails, "gnawing at a blunt fingernail," his "fingers with bitten nails..." (14, 141,143, 145 155 and 168)—has, nevertheless, audaciously resigned himself to the imminent inevitability of his execution by hanging. "You's clever."

He tells George. "You got things to talk about, and brains. Okay.
But leave it, hey. Me, I'm going to swing. Who cares? My old
man was hanged, so what about it?" (15) Even the prison minstrel,
Solly, acted bravely, proving his minstrelsy to be an act of convenience, "he had assumed the position of court jester" (122). He
and his woman are also successful in smuggling into the prison, in a
loaf of bread, two hacksaw blades for Gus, Morgan, and Koppe,
which they use in their escape attempt. The escape attempt itself
is a bold and defiant act. When Gus is spotted before he can go
over the wall, he curses the guards all the way down: "Awright, I'm
coming down, you baskets... Your mothers, you pigs of sons of
bitches and baskets...." (159) Predictably, when he comes to within
their reach, the guards club him with gun-butts and truncheons. It
becomes apparent that on the moral plane (of courage, of will, of
boldness, of fortitude) as well as on the physical plane (of abuse, of
hunger, of hygiene), the narrator is haunted by the feeling and fact
of being imprisoned, of being dehumanized: that it is not just the
physical bodies of the prisoners that demand freedom, but their
very spirit, their nerve, their manhood—in a word, their humanity.

From the very beginning of the novel, La Guma paints an image
of the physical surroundings, limiting the prisoners, as cruel and
inhuman, as this image of the prisoners in the prison van en route to
the prison graphically reveals:

> They were jammed tight into the back of the big steel ve-
> hicle, crowded onto the metal benches along side, packed
> in on the floor, and still more stood awkwardly among those
> squatting, clinging to the iron ribs of the canopy. It was hot
> in the truck too, and the air was heavy with the smell of
> cramped bodies and sour breath and unwashed clothes. (15-
> 16)

Sensed through the consciousness of George Adams, there is a
relentless emphasis on the "jammed...crowded...packed...cramped"
environment and the oppressive heat the prisoners must endure.
Typical of the images of setting evoking this oppressive environment is La Guma's description of Adams' cell:

> With over forty prisoners locked up in the middle of sum-
> mer, the smell of sweat was heavy and cloying as the smell
> of death. The heat seemed packed in between the bodies of
> the men, like layers of cotton wool; like a thick sauce which
> moistened a human salad of accused petty thieves, gang-
> sters, rapists, burglars, thugs, brawlers, dope peddlars, few
> of them strangers to the cells, many already depraved, and
> several old and abandoned, sucking hopelessly at the bit-
> ter disintegrating butt-end of life. (80-81)

Figurations of the environment, the setting, with tactile and olfactory images of "heat" and "the smell of sweat" and packed and
crowded bodies, are certainly among the most interesting in this
work and form several distinct metaphorical patterns, leitmotivs in
the story; even the same material reference, "heat packed like cot-
ton wool," is repeated, creating an effective unifying link:

> It seems as if the heat of the day had been trapped in the
> cell with the prisoners, and it was packed in with them like
> a sort of invisible cotton wool, damp and sticky, aggravat-
> ing the smell of breath and bodies...Smells and heat were
> solid, enveloping, engulfing, as was the babble of sound
> in the caserne. (29)

Here, the word sand tone of the image,
"trapped....packed...enveloping...engulfing," establish a firm metaphorical link with the objective conditions of Africans and other
people of color in South Africa, in countless numbers of embarrassing, insulting, crowded shanty-towns, urban ghettos, and so-
called "homelands." The aggravating heat and cramped conditions are a vehicle for George Adams to externalize his inner, spiritual
pain. Imagery of stale air "heavy with the smell of perspiration and
musty blankets," disturbs any comfortable notions we may have about
human dignity, the beauty and value of every human being. This requires a bigger vision, one beyond the military figuration.

Part II of the novel abruptly, but unobtrusively shifts the focus
outside from the prison courtyard to a larger vision and brilliant,
seemingly organic, orchestration and substitution of sensuous imagery, from the fetid environment inside particular prison cells to
the symbolic therapeutic image pattern of the wind. In contrast to
the first part, Part II of *The Stone Country* opens with the following image:

The early evening lay purple in the square outside the Isolation Block, and a wind, little more than a breeze, had sprung up, making small blowing noises through the sprawl of buildings inside the walls of the prison. (89)

And, oh, how refreshing is this breeze..."winds of change." Just as the novel begins and ends in the company of George Adams and the Casbah Kid, the second half of the novel also begins and ends in their company. The novel, therefore, is in the form of a poetic chiasmus whereby the ending appears at the beginning; and the story moves in a circular or elliptical, yet chronological and linear progression, back to the ending. It is the narrative line of George Adams and the Casbah Kid, the central and dominant image and relationship around which the most important ideas of the novel revolve. Gerald Moore, for example, has observed that "the triumph of the novel is in the depiction of the Casbah Kid" (1980:114). Thematic and structural unity are preserved to the end.

In Part I the imagistic pattern establishes a firm metaphorical connection between the stone walls of the prison and one of the dominant themes of the novel, namely, "the whole country that was like a big stone prison, anyway" (58). The irascible, violent behavior of the prisoners is a product of this environment. Part II is, in a seemingly deliberate sense, a comment on and response to the conditions depicted in Part I. So, from prisoners stuffed in the "thick heat" of their cells, we encounter the cooling and strengthening ocean breeze. The image pattern of the wind begins imperceptibly and builds in intensity, in parallel movement with the plot, particularly the planned escape by Gus, Morgan, and Koppe. In the opening pages of Part II, the presence of the wind is only a faint suggestion, a mere hint of the force it will become:

The *wind* had died away, and the early summer sun, splashing through the back window, made a strippled pattern of meshwork on the floor. (113; emphasis added)

And moments later, when

George, Gus, Morgan and Koppe are jogging in the courtyard, Obliquely above them the sun hung like a red-hot coin in the sky. Although a canopy of *wind cloud* lay motionless along the top of the mountain, there was not a *breeze* moving in the late-morning *air*. (113; emphasis added)

So, from inconspicuous, unpretentious beginnings, the wind imagery develops side by side with the plot, the escapees, motionless, whispering, hissing, until they intersect on the roof of the prison—prisoners and wind—and the wind unleashes its powerful fury, tearing and lashing at them like an evil spirit intent upon their downfall, and Gus, who teeters on the wall, is swept back into the prison by the wind "as easily as it would a leaf." The wind—fate, inevitability, nature?

The wind, a breeze, capricious though it be, is the natural, organic antidote to the heat of the summer sun and the stultifying atmosphere of the prison cells; and as La Guma is wont to suggest, the wind and heat stand in the same dialectical relationship as spontaneity and premeditation, as colonized and colonizer. The impulsive reactions of the prisoners to each other and the prison system in Part I gives way to calculation and premeditation in Part II as the three inmates plot and attempt their escape. It is outside, in the courtyard of the prison, that the prisoners witness the confrontation between the prison cat and the mouse; a brilliantly constructed metaphorical segue that is a deliberate and direct response to the repulsive conditions depicted in Part I.

The parallel between the physical environment and the human condition is effectively connected in the image sequence involving the wind and the escapees.

La Guma develops the figurations of the wind and those of characters concurrently, compelling the reader to watch their parallel progress while relating them all the time to their common theme. La Guma's predilection for this technique of parallel image sequence and the well-timed convergence of this movement is the result of an emphatic and intense harmony of image and idea.

Early in *The Stone Country*, there is a reference to the "Wind coming up" (46) with only vague hints about "the three men in the cell...a nondescript trio" (36). Then, as the references to the wind increase, "stiff in the open country, moving the tops of trees so that they swayed like a choir," (50) its dynamic role is more tellingly, more strikingly personified; as in "The breeze which had sprung up during the night died away like a ghost returning to the grave at dawn" (89). This methodical, building imagery of the wind is never obtrusive, but just at the elbow of the reader, nudging, whispering, "making small blowing noises through the sprawl of the building inside the walls of the prison...blowing all night, and now was dropping with gasping sighs, like an old woman on her death-bed" (101).

Parallel with the developing portrayal of the wind is the surreptitious planning of Gus and his unwitting companions, Morgan and Koppe:

> Gus...had not told the other two anything about his scheme. He would have to let them know at the last minute. They would be compelled to go with him...through the window onto the roof, anyway. After that, they would have to take their chances on their own. (99)

The stealthy actions being planned, the whispering tone of the prisoner, Gus, is similar in action and tone to the wind, "like a ghost...making small blowing noises." Like the developing imagery of the rain in *And a Threefold Cord*, La Guma skillfully prepares the reader for a denouement; for nature, that capricious mistress, has designs of her own, and compels our inarticulate, dumbfounded respect, if not surrender. Thus, as we move closer to the attempted escape,

> The wind made whistling sounds through the prison, soaring down passages and through the deserted yards, leaning against the stone walls and turning away in frustration, cooing plaintively, plucking irritably at eaves and doorways. During the night it would grow stronger and howl in rage at the immovable obstruction of the stone, tear at the gates and bars, pound the concrete and brownstone, thrust futilely at the walls and then growl on its way over the city. (112)

The wind, therefore, is a fitting image exhibiting human characteristics comparable to those of the inmates: "cooing plaintively," or sometimes, as the pressure and frustration of their incarceration grows, we can well-imagine that they would "howl in rage at the immovable obstruction of the stone" or "tear at the gates and bars" in gestures of futility and impotence. This particular image of the wind has similar characteristics as the rain imagery in *And a Threefold Cord*; only here it is the wind that leans, coos, howls, tears, pounds, and thrusts. Also, in like manner, as the plot progresses, it is as if the volume of stereophonic music is being turned up, slowly and deliberately, until the two—wind and dramatis personae—come violently together. As the three would-be escapees made it to the roof of the prison, the wind caught and tugged at their clothes, "howled and roared across the roof, slapping...stinging" their eyes; and as Koppe "shivered with fright...The wind wrestled with him, trying to pluck him from the wall and blow him like a scrap of paper into the dark yard below" (152). And Gus too wrestled with the same fateful adversary as "The wind grabbed...held, pushed and pulled, and for one awful moment he thought he was about to be blown into space"(153). Morgan and Gus are finally overpowered, and not just by the prison guards, but by the wind, nature, inevitable fate clawing at them "like a frenzied woman," ripping, clutching, screeching "like an evil spirit" intent on their demise.

Through the recurrent use of the image of the wind, together with the step-by-step development of the attempted escape, La Guma provides a sense of continuity and gives the imagery of wind and character structural and thematic consistency and depth. The audience is thereby inured to the final convergence of this parallel movement when,

> Gus drew himself up, poised on aching feet in the dark-
> ness, for the leap downwards into the street. For a second
> he teetered on the wall, and then a great gust of wind
> shrieked at him, swept him as easily as it would a leaf, back
> into the prison. (160)

Just as the motif of rain reaches the maximum of its expressive force in the scene where Ronny Pauls murders Susie Meyer, the motif of the wind does likewise in this secondary plot of the escape attempt of Gus, Morgan, and Koppe. This tends to indicate that once a striking and expressive image, or image pattern, has been formed, it is likely to suggest itself again to a writer, with appropriate variation and specificity, and may even develop into an habitual mode of expression. This is where the early texts of La Guma's apprentice years are of particular importance. For example, in an earlier short-story, "The Lemon Orchard," La Guma's unnamed protagonist and nature follow a similar parallel movement. The protagonist, a man of color, is led away into a dark corner of the orchard by two anonymous white men to, (we assume at the begin-ning of the story) be "executed" for having "taken the principal, and the meester of the church before the magistrate and demand payment for the hiding they gave him for being cheeky to them" (*A*

Walk in the Night And Other Stories, 128). In the final scene, La Guma does not describe the actual act, the murder of the colored man, but rather allows the image of nature, which has been a developing force ("a chill in the air; and the moon...hidden behind long, high parallels of clouds which hung like suspended streamers of dirty cotton-wool in the sky"), to convey an emotional atmosphere and to give a metaphorical explanation of what is taking place. The man, we know, is terrified, "clenching his teeth to prevent them from chattering" (*Walk,* 126), and there's logic in the ending, as man and nature meet:

> The blackness of the night crouched over the orchard and the leaves rustled with a harsh whispering that was inconsistent with the pleasant scent of lemons. The chill in the air increased...Then the moon came from behind the banks of cloud and its white light touched the leaves with wet silver, and the perfume of lemons seemed to grow stronger, as if the juice was being crushed from them. (129)

Here, nature, the "harsh whispering of leaves...The chill in the air...The blackness of the night" portray the inevitable answer, the ultimate witness to secrets and lies. Nature, in other words, has final proof of what took place this night in the lemon orchard and, as if to say, "what is done in the dark will come to the light," "the moon came from behind the banks of cloud" as if final witness to this crime. It is the disharmony and inconsistency in the sensual, objective environment that leads to the inevitable conclusion that the colored man is murdered; his death likened to "the perfume of lemons...as if the juice was being crushed from them."

In this short-story, as in *The Stone Country,* Alex La Guma's imagery is strikingly appropriate and perfectly adapted to the distinctive atmosphere he wishes to convey. Each image and image pattern helps to underline the themes of adversity and the desecration of humanity in South African society. In addition, the tone of a particular image is well-adapted to the context in which it occurs. Each carries conviction because it is rooted in the author's personal experience. The desecration of human beings due to the psychological effects of prison life is described in a series of vivid images for which the natural and physical environment runs parallel in dramatic and effective counterpoint. Although there is, in this imagery of prison life, an element of pathos which is motivated by the context, its prime purpose is to give some accurate accounting of the prisoners' state of mind or evolving consciousness. Part I begins with George Adams and the Casbah Kid in the Isolation Block; however, in the linear narrative development of the story, George and the Kid are not confined to the Isolation Block until Part II. The intervening chapters account for the growth and development of their relationship with each other and the other inmates. In this regard, George proves to be not only courageous but also giving and compassionate. His impact on the consciousness of The Kid and other inmates is depicted in a number of poignant images. A particular incident that reveals the impact of George's compassion occurs after the death of the despised bully, Butcherboy Williams, when George remarks "Well, I'm kind of sorry for that poor basket, Butcherboy." To which The Kid exclaims with a sneer, "Sorry?...You? You're a funny ou, mister" (90). George boosts The Kid's ego by complimenting him on his ingenuity in getting tobacco to a neighboring cell: "That was a helluva trick," he tells The Kid, "I would never have thought of it, pal. A helluva trick, that" (94). In fact, it is his somewhat instinctive compassion that finally gets George Adams confined to the Isolation Block with this young man. The guard, Fatty, becomes irate when George picks up the prison cat and pets it, and shouts at him, "You think you here to play?...Now put that cat down and come with me" (110-111). Still, The Casbah Kid, Albert March, has to think long and hard before he opens up, even a little, to Adams:

> The Casbah Kid was thinking reluctantly that perhaps he could tell this man here in the cell with him about it... This john was okay, he admitted grudgingly. He had shared his food and had not grumbled when he parted with a cigarette. That made him strange, but at the same time, an all right bloke. (129)

This image of The Kid reveals him as a reflective, thoughtful, and sensitive man of nineteen years. He is making serious choices about what to say and to whom. He is evaluating not just words but deeds, specific acts that confirm for him that this is "an all right bloke." And George is conscientious enough to know not to pry, not to push; instead, he ponders:

> When a dam bursts, a mighty flood is released. If a man is
> habitually abstemious, liquor will loosen his tongue; when
> a persistently taciturn man decides to talk, he can be ex-
> pected to say a great deal. Some men talk under torture;
> others when they are delirious; still others when they are
> positive that they are soon to die. (139)

It is this sort of understanding and mutual respect of the two characters that makes their intimacy the more touching. The challenge
George has accepted is to give hope to a man sentenced to die in a
matter of days. The implications of such a challenge are profound.
Surely, if a condemned man can hope for a better life there is no
cause for despair and political negativism for those who are not so
immediately and prematurely condemned. The pervasive ideas in
their relationship are those of courage and hope for change. There
is a qualitative difference in the fatalistic and deterministic outlook of The Casbah Kid in the opening chapter of the novel, when
in reply to George Adams' reluctant querry about the possibility of
a death sentence, The Kid answers:

> "Crack. Look, mister, you going to die someday, don't I
> say? We all got to die...Is put out, like. Everybody got his
> life and death put out, reckon and think."
> "Put out?" George Adams asked. "You reckon so? Man,
> if our life was laid out for us beforehand, what use would it
> be for us to work to change things, hey?" (14) Compare
> the attitude The Kid assumes in Part II of the novel, after
> his association with Adams:
> ...Appreciation was strange in the boy's mouth, like the taste
> of medicine.
> "Here, have a cigarette, mate. Help yourself, chommy."
> "You's funny people, mister." The child-face with the
> ancient bitter eyes, frowned. "Here me, mister...All this
> stuff about our people getting into the government, too.
> You reckon it will help people like us? People in prison,
> like?"

George Adams said to this strange boy who was also a murderer:

"There will certainly be more sympathy, I reckon."
"You reckon that time will come?"
George Adams said, feeling sad: "You'll see." (118-119)

Here we notice a shift in the position taken by The Kid as his responses become increasingly more sensitive, positive, and optimistic. In fact, the class and ideological barriers which have separated the two begin to crumble, barriers that struggle to reassemble themselves in the interior monologue of Mrs. Isaacs, George Adams' landlady, who thinks naively: "One left the authorities alone and let them do what they pleased; God would see to everything in the end" (116); who thinks George is too good, socially, morally, to be with the other inmates and should be kept "in some special place, instead of among all these thieves, hooligans and good-for-nothings" (116). Still, George Adams' every effort is to direct the introverted rage and anger of the Coloured inmates, like those of the African revolution, toward the social structures and those who control them: "Strike for a better diet," he admonishes The Turk when he complains to him about the prison food. And this is a lesson he wants desperately to impress on The Casbah Kid. For it is, indeed, The Kid, as Gerald Moore has observed, who "provides a measure for the fate of the other inmates, who are at least not destined to hang; who may hope for a term they can see the end of; who do not have as their earliest memory the horror and complicity this boy has never been able to bury" (1980:114).

The "horror and complicity" Moore is referring to here is The Kid's memory of having seen his mother kill herself, and his father convicted and subsequently hanged for the crime, and the memory that he could have saved his father, but during the trial refused to say what he knew, what he had actually seen. Positive, now, that he is going to die for a murder he had not intended—like Michael Adonis and Ronny Pauls—but had just somehow let happen, in this case because The Kid's victim would not "give up straight. He want to struggle..." (14). The Kid, now, pours out his soul, in confidence, to George:

"Listen," said The Casbah Kid, raising himself up onto an elbow. "They hanged my father for the murder of my mother."

...."Your pa murdered your mother? And was hanged?"...
"He was hanged for it, mister," replied the boy, and the
bruised mouth twisted into the parody of a smile. He added,
"And I could have saved him, hey." (140)

This dialogue between George Adams and The Casbah Kid takes
place in Part II, Chapter 14, and it is a continuation of the dialogue
that opens the novel in Part I, Chapter 1. In Part II, however, we
are given the particulars of the environment surrounding and causing The Kid's predicament. The subtle but harsh dynamics which
led him into crime and that shaped and proscribed his domestic
environment are encompassed within a larger social dynamic—
the myth of white supremacy—which was in motion long before
his birth.

The relationship between intrapsychic functioning and the larger
social environment is exceedingly complex. The psychic violence
of white supremacist (apartheid) laws, the physical violence of
malnutrition and police brutality, the intellectual or mental violence of substandard education, and the economic violence of unemployment and underemployment—these multiple levels of violence together form the environment in which all "The Casbah
Kids" of South Africa are entrapped. Bloke Modisane (1963) puts
the matter this way: "Violence exists in our day-to-day relationships, the expression of the public conscience; it is contained in
the law, the instrument of maintaining law and order" (59). No
doubt these "Kids" want to change inside, but find it difficult to do
unless things outside are changed as well. The ultimate power is
the freedom to understand and alter one's life. It is this power,
both individually and collectively, which has been and is denied
the African man and woman in South Africa and throughout the
world. The Kid's father can do nothing about his unemployment
or occasional underemployment; he is not responsible for the
mechanization, the automation, or the racism that daily throws
African people out of work; and this causes deep psychological
and emotional scars. As a consequence, he takes out his anger and
frustration with his environment on those closest to him—his wife
and children. As The Kid confides to George:

"For so long as I can remember, my old man, he was a drunky
and a bully. So many times I have seen him beat my ma
without mercy, with a buckle belt or his fists.
    Sometimes he hit her with a chair. He would knock her
senseless with one blow and then kick her while she lay
there. So many times, also, he whipped me. Most of the
time for nothing, for no reason. I don't know where he got
money, but he spent it on wine. Most of the time we had no
food to eat. My ma sent me out to beg at people's doors."
(142)

This image reveals The Casbah Kid's perception and understanding of the South African environment and his place in it. It is a
pathetic, heartrending portrait of a man, a woman, and a child—a
family. All day long, the South African police have the right to
strike African men, women, and children, to insult them, to deny
them work or work them like pack-animals, to make them crawl or
beg; and, until there is full support for resistance, intellectual and
military, to the notion of white supremacy and its behavioral manifestations, the last resort of the dehumanized, like The Kid's father, is to defend his personality vis-à-vis his family and neigh-
bors.

Mr. March's behavior, his mental pathology, is a direct product
of oppression: this does not excuse his behavior, but it does help to
explain it. His brutality against his wife and child is his way of
trying to regain his importance as a man. Such incestuous violence is not the result of the hereditary character of a person of
color, nor of the organization of his nervous system, and it is only
in the war of liberation that the true criminal, the real villain, comes
to the fore. It is likewise true that The Kid's father, and The Kid
himself, as representative characters, can never regain their dignity except through real freedom and independence. Their violence against each other must be seized and rechanneled, redirected
against the European-controlled apartheid system.

On the specific question of violence, therefore, in *The Stone
Country*, La Guma is ambiguous. He is violent in his words and
reformist in his attitude. His indirect and unqualified Marxist slogan "We're in this together" leads him—by a curious twist of logic

profoundly misleading—to embrace within his "together" even the prison guards, as his character George Adams thinks at one point:

> ...all the guards in a prison were practically prisoners them-
> selves, that they lived most of their working life behind
> stone walls and bars; they were manacled to the other end
> of the chain. (106)

One idea inherent in this image is to bring about an attitude of class identification or even sympathy with the prison guards. The image may be very clever and literary, but it is objectively false. Prisoners who are not simply "visiting" for one month, like George Adams, must see the guards as their mortal enemy, an enemy with the power of life or death over them; with whom, if anything, they would like to exchange places; which involves a great deal more than simply changing ends of the manacle, with persons, ostensibly, bound equally. This is the kind of troubling imagery one creates with slogans directed at universal workers' unity, forgetting that, in South Africa and throughout the African Diaspora, it should be nationalist slogans that are first in the field. The absence of a nationalist perspective in La Guma's writing is further complicated by the problem of self-definition, as Gail M. Gerhart (1978) states:

> The lack of consensus about whether or not to identify
> themselves as "black" was symptomatic of deeper uncer-
> tainties among Indians and Coloureds about whether their
> best political interests lay in supporting Africans or in main-
> taining their separate identities as intermediate groups en-
> joying relatively greater incomes and legal rights. (279)

This "relative" difference in economic and social status manifests itself in the "relative" but significant ideological difference that African people must be perceptive and analytical enough to recognize and critique. There is similar ambiguity in the intellectual position of United States Marxists, like Angela Davis, who insist that the issue is not "race" but "class"—meaning, as James Baldwin says, "those who find themselves on the bottom belong there" (1985:38). For too long, the Colored or Mulatto has been the white world's secret weapon against Africans, confusing and baffling the

African masses (and leadership) by their chameleon politics and abstract humanitarianism. For example, La Guma has stated that:

> ...whether we are European writers or African writers or
> American writers, all human activity which does not serve
> humanity must be a waste of time and effort. (Wastberg
> 1969:24)

"Gather sand where you are," I once heard Dr. Maulana Karenga quip. Doing something for African people, who are at the bottom of society everywhere in the world today, is doing something for humanity. The question is one of priority and focus. Coloreds and Mulattos must, or should, come down on one side of the fence or the other. Thus, in his conversation with The Casbah Kid, George Adams represents ordinary, innocent, reflective humanity; he is different from his fellow prisoners, separate in kind, a slave who in individually free. He is , ideologically speaking, demanding the right to multiply the emancipated and the opportunity to organize a genuine class of emancipated citizens, "Government by the workers." In this, there is the clear desire to assimilate himself and his multi-racial class allies into the government structure as a cadre of enlightened Marxists; as opposed to overthrowing and replacing completely the existing structure. The Casbah Kid naively glimpses this reformist tendency, even though he doesn't understand it, when he asks George:

> ..."Her me, mister. All this stuff about our people getting
> into government, too. You reckon it will help people like
> us? People in prison, like?" (118)

And because George Adams' position is essentially a reformist one and not a revolutionary one, he can only answer The Kid weakly, "There will certainly be more sympathy, I reckon." If George were a revolutionary, in the truest sense of the word, and not just imbued with Marxian egalitarian principles, he would have informed The Kid right away that "our people getting into the government" is not the objective of the movement of which he is a part; rather, seizing power, taking over the government by any means necessary is one of their objectives. Dr. Frantz Fanon (1981) illuminates this matter:

> ...the mass of the people have no intention of standing by and watching individuals increase their chances of success. What they demand is not the settler's position of status, but the settler's place...For them, there is no question of entering into competition with the settler. They want to take his place. (60-61)

The repeated theme-image in La Guma's writings, is the mythology of multiracial working-class unity: Mr. Doughty, George Mostert, the red-haired copy-machine operator, are now, fantastically, linked, "manacled" to the prison guards. This persistently recurring image of multiracial working-class unity, no matter how shrewdly or subtly structured into the intellectual imagery of La Guma's novels, is inextricably bound up with the basic texture and meaning of his creative fiction. The genesis of the image is La Guma's historically determined Coloured consciousness and his fanatical Marxism, which is a by-product of that consciousness—"by-product" because the peculiar position of Coloreds in South Africa, like Mulattos in America, inclines them towards a radical, transcendent, and all-embracing humanitarianism. There is no question that Communism in South Africa is a multiracial movement. There is likewise no question that these so-called allies of African people often seek to impose upon Africans an ideology and strategy of "revolutionary" struggle that is alien to the nationalistic requirements of African life in South Africa. To get the full impact of this perspective, there is no choice but to quote in full the following lengthy citation form Richard Gibson (1972), who speaks to the very heart of the matter under consideration here; that is, La Guma's images of multiracialism in the intellectual or ideological environment of South Africa:

> Multiracialism as a concept, offering guaranties to the minority against arbitrary and discriminatory rule by an African majority, could only have been justified if there had been—as there was not—a substantial number of Europe-

ans and Indians who were prepared to close ranks with the oppressed majority. As it was, the paltry numbers of European, Coloured, and Indian allies that came forward under the Congress Alliance blunted the driving force of African Nationalism, the only ideology likely—as the subsequent history of PAC demonstrates—to appeal to the broad masses of the black proletariat. In addition, while non-violence might have been acceptable in the short term as a tactic, nothing in the record of African struggle against European encroachment indicated that it could have any deep, long-term appeal to the African people, who passed their daily lives in conditions of often extreme social violence and brutality, harassed by white bosses and anti-social black thugs, as well as the ever-vigilant and violent South African police. Only a political programme of counter violence on massive scale, decided upon years earlier by an African organization, might have mobilized the masses and permitted them to force an early clash with the regime before its repressive apparatus had been installed. The want of such action should not be blamed only on the Christian pacifists of South Africa and the white liberals with their illusions of justice and democracy, but principally on the leaders of SACP (South African Communist Party-my note) whose reformist, revisionist views and naive faith in their ability to provoke a crisis of conscience among the white minority, bringing about the restoration of some form of democracy, preventing them from ever taking a revolutionary road inside South Africa.(64)

Alex La Guma, like his protagonist, George Adams, is one of the small number of Coloreds who comes forward under the South African Communist Party, and whose reformist, revisionist views is blunting the powerful force of African Nationalism, whose "naive faith in their ability to provoke a crisis of conscience among the white minority" help to divert, if not prevent, the struggle of the African majority from taking a revolutionary path inside South Africa. It is the subtle, albeit skillful, imagery La Guma invokes of Jefferson Mpolo (the African), Casim (the Asian-Indian), the "red haired" white woman, and George Adams (the Coloured) that makes his position that much more pernicious and ideologically dangerous.

For no greater reason than this, it should be remembered that
The Stone Country takes place in a predominantly Colored milieu.
Throughout the book the images of environment and character are
related. And in well-composed images, as in well-composed music, motive has some relevance. So much depends on the attitude
of the artist toward the subject. It is because of La Guma's attitude, his avid Marxism, that his images assume the meaning and
impact that they do. Every touch of La Guma's pen on paper is
laden with his interpretation of life. His images, both physical and
intellectual, convey the essence of his characters and themes. Again,
La Guma's early texts are illuminating. For example, the motif of
introverted, incestuous violence began to crystallize quite early in
the short stories "Tattoo Marks and Nails" and "The Gladiators."
"Tattoo Marks and Nails" had already introduced less developed
versions of some of the characters in *The Stone Country*. It provides us with prototypes of Butcherboy and Yusef the Turk in the
two characters named The Creature and Ahmed the Turk, respectively. In *The Stone Country* there is the following description of
Butcherboy:

> Gang leader, and incidentally cell boss by virtue of his bru-
> tality and the backing of bullied and equally vicious toad-
> ies, he was mean as a jackal, blood-thirsty as a wolf, foul as
> a hyena, and the group whom he trapped in the corner
> shuffled nervously on their feet, and avoided the
> palaeoanthropic glare. (*Stone Country*, 30)

And in "Tattoo Marks and Nails," The Creature is described as:

> The gang-leader, and incidentally cell-head by virtue of his
> brutality and the backing of equally vicious hangers-on, was
> pointing at the poor joker's bare chest on which something
> colorfully gaudy had been tattooed....(Walk & Other, 93)

The recurrence of an image is not necessarily a symptom of deep-
seated emotional involvement with the image: it may simply be due
to the appropriateness and expressive force of the image itself.
Many of La Guma's characters are portrayed or ridiculed through
the idiosyncrasies of their faces and bodies. The image of

Butcherboy, though only a faint echo of the original "Creature," is probably called up by the experience and same setting with which it was originally associated; it may also been seen as an amplification or even consummation of the original image. The analogies which La Guma takes from the animal world—a jackal, a wolf, a hyena—are not unique to him in any way, but La Guma has fully exploited the emotive potentialities of animal metaphors to convey nuances of Butcherboy's portrait which would otherwise have remained unformulated. The image is, therefore, a fitting comment on a representative character type, and in this way the images of Butcherboy and The Creature assume a certain social significance. The perception of them in both the real and fictional world is not just how they look but also how they act:

> Butcherboy...turned his back, broad as a door, on the little man and looked around the cell. He started to kick his way through the tangle of bodies on the floor....(*Stone Country*, 33)

From "Tattoo Marks and Nails," there is the same unity of appearance and behavior:

> The Creature made his way across, kicking bodies and legs out of his path, swearing at the impeding jumble of humanity. (*Walk & Other*, 100)

There is a unity of image and idea that illuminates theme and action. These, like all images, must be perceived with feeling. A particular image or portrait must be understood as possessing vivid qualities: happy, sad, brutal, kind, et cetera. We should, in order to grasp the idea in the image, let all that is present in the image appeal to us in the fullest and most vivid way possible. We should get inside the image, submit to its lead, become a part of the prison community: the tangle of bodies, the jumble of humanity, the brutal Creatures, the violent and self-hating Butcherboys, the sneering and insensitive guards, as another element of the aesthetic experience, as another method of clarifying the content of the image for a fuller perception of it. A part of this aesthetic enjoyment is the accompanying awareness of analogies and equivalencies that are knowable, relevant, and definitive.

Because of the analogies and metaphors describing Butcherboy, we know him and his "type" that much better. The embellished description of him is itself a kind of commentary, one that, to La Guma, obviously deserves repeating. Yet even in this repetition, the original image has been reworked—a word or phrase is added or deleted, more descriptive detail is added—thus he preserves his initial vision of the character with all of his pleasure and displeasure manifested in the portrayal. For the first condition of any image, or portrait, is interest in the subject; something the author, La Guma, wants to say definitely about this subject, this type of character and behavior. It is also possible that La Guma's refinement of this image is because, for him, nothing will do but the most precise iconography. He wants, it seems, everything in the picture of Butcherboy, The Creature, and their like, to be constructive—embroidering theme and expressing an emotion. He wants the reader to vicariously experience kicking and being kicked, bullying and being bullied, as well as just being a fighter.

Yusef the Turk is a fighter. He is also a bully. He is the balancing element in the cell, between George Adams and Butcherboy Williams. La Guma describes him as being

> ...thin and lean...he had a lean, smooth, handsome face tan-coloured, with dentures flashing in it when he smiled...his shirt was a flamboyant green, his pegged trousers neat and clean...he took pains to maintain his flashiness...the gentleman gangster, a member of the underworld aristocracy. (*Stone Country*, 38)

Elsewhere La Guma describes him as "sharp and tough and dangerous as a polished spear" and that "under the smooth, tan skin muscles rippled like lizards and the long body was really as tough and as flexible as a sjambok" (81 & 83).

Yusef's personal history, like that of George Adams and The Casbah Kid, is illuminated just enough to reveal the immediate cause of his imprisonment—a robbery. And like the other prisoners, except George, Yusef lacks completely any concept of a future. The Casbah Kid's future is sealed, and can even be measured in hours and minutes; whereas Yusef and the other prisoners, though one day they will be released, still do not express any hope or plans at all for that eventuality. It is as if not only their bodies, but their

minds, their spirits, and their dreams of tomorrow are also imprisoned in stone. It cannot be said with certainty, but it appears that
La Guma's intent is to record the experience of one sector of humanity in a specific time and place, trusting his audience to understand the genesis and broader social reality responsible for the
condition of each of his characters. Poverty, as we know, is the
parent of crime and, for that matter, revolution. There is no need
to give an extensive personal history of each and every character:
the pervasive oppression of African people and other people of
color in South Africa is well known; what is needed and what is
given is the depth of personality and guiding consciousness of the
protagonist, George Adams. It is the illuminating, optimistic consciousness of Adams that distinguishes him from the other prisoners. Yusef the Turk is, basically, a fighter and survivor. His principles are plain and simple: do what is necessary to survive; in-
timidate when you have to without being intimidated. For example,
when George helps a couple of other inmates fold their blankets,
Yusef says to him, "How, let these jubas do it. These small fry do
all the things. They get a little something for it," he is trying to
educate George about prison values that are also, ironically, the
values of the larger "outside" society. And when George responds
with his proverbial "Well, we're all in here together," the Turk
retorts:

> "By Allah, you will learn, mate. You will learn. Hear me,
> the only johns who get by in this place is them what know
> how to get things done for them, them what is hard case
> enough to make others listen, and may be them that licks
> the guards' jack. Most of the time the lickers don't last
> long, anyway." (51)

Is this not the method of unrestrained, unprincipled capitalism, slavery, colonialism? Those who "know how to get things done for
them...hard case enough to make others listen"? Those who claim
the workers, the peasants, the unemployed are lazy, while they su-
pervise, manipulate, and manage their labor or lack thereof? Those
who are the superior "real" men, the inferior half men or less; the
"inferior," of course, work for the superior. Yusef the Turk learned
his values from a society where the most virulent forms of capital-

ist values are manifest: the right to live on the labor and property of others, to prey on weaknesses and use them for one's own benefit or profit. For Yusef the Turk, there are only two kinds of people— those who take and those who are taken, criminals and victims— and he has decided to be a taker, a criminal.

There is no room in The Turk's scheme of thinking for the complexity of human beings, the confusion and contradictions that permeate all human nature. La Guma creates a sort of "pecking order" in the prison that mirrors that of the larger society. An "order" observed by veterinary doctors in farmyards, where the corn that is thrown to the chickens is the object of fierce competition. The strongest birds gobble up all the grains while those who are less aggressive grow visibly thinner. Every capitalist society, and the institutions within them, tends to turn into a huge farmyard, where the only law is the gun or the knife. Butcherboy is at the top of this "pecking order," a vicious and dangerous bully and Uncle Tom, an Uncle Tom because he is "pecked" by the guards, who can "peck" even harder. When, for example, George speaks back to one of the guards, "Butcherboy who stood lounging in a cell door, waiting for his supper to be brought to him...wondered whether he could do the baas a favour by dealing with this clever" (76). The weaker prisoners work for him, and he works for the guards (which, by the way, is a compelling metaphor for neo-colonialism).Yusef the Turk, as La Guma develops him, understands this hierarchy, this "pecking order" and senses in George Adams, though intellectually superior, an ally. It is this possible and eventual alliance that begins to shift the balance of power in the cell from Butcherboy to George and Yusef; a shift that brings about the memorable fight between Buthcerboy and Yusef, with its marvelous quality of freshness and direct observation: "Butcherboy...sensed a threatened shift of allegiance, and he told himself that matters would have to be handled quickly" (77).

To make sure that there is no false sympathy for the physically smaller Yusef in his violent clash with Butcherboy, La Guma provides other useful insights into his character. Of particular value is Yusef's attitude towards women, especially "his" woman, his "goose." At one point, after George had lighted his last cigarette, The Turk declares:

> I hope my goose send me some stuff today. That goose
> missed yesterday, she better watch out for herself. (77)

And a bit later, when the prisoners are all eating the nasty prison
food:

> I wonder why my goose didn't bring me no stuff today. Eat-
> ing this crack. She know she got to bring me a diet every day.
> I'll kick her blerry backside, I get out of here. (71)

Yusef the Turk's predatory strategy for survival includes intimidating and brutalizing "his" woman. He has accepted the "pecking order" and like The Casbah Kid's father, finds no one left for
him to "peck" but the women and children of the society. La Guma
provides this knowledge about The Turk before the fight, so that
this central experience can have its full sway on the consciousness
of the reader; so that the reader's sympathies are even-handed and
balanced; and so that the vicariously real and aesthetic experience
of the fight will force us to favor a moral and ethical choice based
upon justice, and not our subjective judgements as to which character
is "better" than the other. Because of La Guma's skillful and controlled treatment of Butcherboy and Yusef the Turk up to the actual
fight, the reader's emotions and sympathies are neutralized for one or
the other character. Instead, as the fight builds in viciousness and
intensity, one finds one's emotions quite evenly divided; until it is real-
ized that it doesn't really matter who wins the fight, since they are in
the same situation, both men are already "losers" in the fight that
"ultimately" matters: against the myth of white supremacy.

So beautifully constructed is the sequence of images depicting
the fight between Butcherboy and Yusef the Turk that, from the
beginning, impetuous sympathies compel identification with the un-
derdog, Yusef who, though physically smaller, is no less vicious.
Subtle images, nuances of his physiognomy seize the reader, emotionally, unawares, like "He put his hand to his mouth and slipped
out his dentures"—his face becoming "thin and sunken" (83). And
by this simple gesture we are reminded of the manhood of the man,
the age and maturity of the man. Then, by the end of the fight, our
sympathies have shifted toward Butcherboy as "He lay big and

limp and still, and a tiny fountain of blood was just slackening off into a thin trickle out of the eye of the tattooed eagle" (88). The Casbah Kid, seizing the opportunity to revenge the beating Butcherboy had given him earlier, had stabbed him in the back with the sharpened key from a pilchard can when, during the fight, Butcherboy had stumbled backward into a crowd of prisoners. However, our sympathies for Butcherboy are blunted by what we know of his previous violent and intimidating behavior; and likewise dulled for The Casbah Kid, who acted and "spoke as if homicide was a normal activity, like going to the latrine or scratching an itch" (35); and for Yusef the Turk, whose unprincipled hubris allows him to decide "truculently that his mistress was a mean and inconsiderate bitch for not having brought him any clean laundry that week," and that he would "go and see her to give her something to remember him by when he got out" (78). The dehumanizing, debilitating effects of incestuous, introverted violence that characterizes intragroup relations, caused by an awesome, oppressive environment, could hardly be better illustrated.

Through his fiction, metaphorically, La Guma seals the Colored community of South Africa behind the stone walls of prison, thereby forcing that community and its detractors to witness the fratricidal tensions and violence that characterize their existence. It is a sharp and critical assessment and testing of that experience, and La Guma proceeds with a deep and courageous will down to the dark roots of Colored life in South Africa.

We come to realize that to account for the life of Yusef the Turk, George Adams, or any of the other characters is to account for the life of the author, if not the whole history of South Africa—and this is impossible. What we can know is that the history and culture that produced The Turk, The Kid, Butcherboy, and the other characters, contains no spiritual sustenance, no institutions that could hold and claim their loyalty and faith, has dehumanized them, sensitized them to violence and brutality, and left them isolated, stranded, alienated individuals free to roam the streets of Cape Town, Johannesburg, Oakland, San Francisco, Harlem, Sao Paulo, an angry, frustrated, volatile vortex of unchanneled impulses. The result, in the case of Yusef the Turk, is a man estranged from the society of which he is supposed to be a meaningful and productive participant. Yusef's tensity, like The Casbah Kid's, is in a nascent state, not yet articulate. His longing for self-identification and self-esteem is due to the effects of South African economic and racial oppression, which has not allowed for the forming of deep ideas of solidarity among Coloreds or Africans. He is still in a state of individual anger and hatred.

George Adams, on the other hand, holds within him the prophecy of the South African future, the outlines of action and feeling which will be encountered on a vast scale in years to come. It is through George that La Guma follows his own hopes and fears toward a resolution of the Colored predicament in particular and the South African dilemma in general. That resolution, the destiny of all the characters (except The Casbah Kid) remains unknown. Perhaps the bleak, unpredictable outcome of antagonistic social forces in South Africa weighs too heavily on the author, and the best assessment of the possible outcomes for Yusef, George, Solly, Gus, and the other prisoners can be obtained in the individual and collective consciousness of an alert and perceptive universal audience. In other words, what happens to the Georges, the Turks, the Butcherboys—in the real world—depends to a greater extent on outsiders who have been made aware of their plight than on the Georges/Turks/Butcherboys themselves.

Alex La Guma is a seer. He appears to derive great pleasure from the effort to invent the exact thing which is needed to express his ideas, feelings, and impressions. Use it. Break it down. Begin again. To see without limit and to invent the means, the iconography, for expressing that vision. For La Guma that vision includes the awareness that the images of character and environment must be seen in relationship to one another. His images of the prison environment are documents of the lives of the people living in South African prisons; communicating again and again the appeal of Eugene Debs: "While there is a soul in jail, I am not free" (*Stone Country*, 10). Each document is valid no matter how many times La Guma repeats the picture; his emotional and sensual memory of the prison environment remains consistent and universal. Thus, he could write in "Tattoo Marks and Nails":

> The heat was solid. As Ahmed the Turk remarked, you could reach out before your face, grab a handful of heat, fling it against the wall, and it would stick. *(Walk & Other*, 92)

Then, in *The Stone Country* La Guma embellishes the image, adds more description, more detail that contextualizes and gives a deeper indication of the meaning and effect of the oppressive heat on the prisoners:

> With over forty prisoners locked up in the middle of summer, the smell of sweat was heavy and cloying as the smell of death. The heat seemed packed in between the bodies of men, like layers of cotton wool; like a thick sauce which moistened a human salad of accused petty thieves, gangsters, rapists, burglars, thugs, brawlers, dope peddlers, few of them strangers to the cells, many already depraved, and several old and abandoned, sucking hopelessly at the bitter, disintegrating butt-end of life. (80-81)

In addition to the effective use of simile, this is an emotional portrait. It is like something thought, something remembered. La Guma reveals the spirit of the prison cell, not just its material aspects. In the original image, from "Tattoo Marks and Nails," we are given merely the skeleton of the image, and it was; perhaps, after a greater distance of the events from his own experience that La Guma could contemplate the material for adding flesh and feeling to this structure.

The development of the heat imagery in Part I of *The Stone Country* to a dominant motif, skillfully juxtaposed with the wind motif of Part II, could have been suggested to La Guma after its initial cursory use in "Tattoo Marks and Nails." In *The Stone Country*, La Guma masterfully invents the image of relentless heat simultaneous with that of scratching and itching, and the tortuous drip, drip, drip of a leaky pipe, developing them concurrently, and compelling attention to their parallel progress while relating them all the time to their common theme of adversity. The following are some examples of the repeated image of scratching and itching that, though not as elaborate as the heat and wind imagery, and not as subtle as the leaking pipe, nevertheless moves parallel with them and registers a non-obtrusive yet precise comment on the material conditions of the prison and provides a fitting analogy for the apartheid system.

> He dropped down on the bedding again, and scratched his armpits. (14)

He reached under his jacket and scratched his armpit. (24) And when the guard's hand pushed him into a cell, he saw four men seated on their bedding, scratching themselves and staring at him. (28)

He paused and scratched under his shirt, withdrew his hand and looked at what he had caught, and then crushed it against the wall. (40)

Yusef the Turk...scratching his ribs...found something under his shirt and looked at it...cracked the louse between his thumb-nails. (73)

George Adams...pulling up a leg of his trousers and scratching his shin.(90)

So Gus lay there on his blankets and scratched himself, wishing that time would pass quickly. (129)

Morgan...scratched himself and found a louse, cracked it between thumb-nails. (130)

Such images (like those of nausea in *A Walk in the Night*) are subtle and unobtrusive, and are barely noticeable unless the reader is looking for them. Their frequency, however, has the effect of raising them to a symbolic level. The meanings associated with the image—scratching and itching annoying parasites—have to do with the objective conditions of the prison, and can also be interpreted as a metaphor for the parasitic apartheid system that sucks the life-blood (the physical, mental, and emotional strength) of the people of color in South Africa, under the infantile and irritating notion of racial superiority. Every prisoner in the jail, like each man, woman and child of color in South Africa, is constantly being drained by the blood-sucking apartheid "louse." The engulfing and oppressive heat, the "beans and pap" (porridge), the over-crowded cells, the systematic humiliation by the guards, and the inequities imposed on prisoners by their fellow prisoners who enjoy a "privileged" position, have a far more deleterious effect on them than the overt presence of stone walls and iron bars. The added noxious community of lice—like the irritant of race (color) mystification (albeit now a fundamental variable in the oppressor/oppressed relationship in a decidedly class [economic] reality)—represents the "epidermitalization" of a problem: of skin-clinging, blood-sucking parasites, spawned not on the skin, to be scratched and "cracked between thumb-nails," but in the obscene ideology of apartheid—capitalism.

The metaphorical comparison of parasites and capitalism is imagistically and thematically appropriate and, because of La Guma's unique vision, is effective in capturing the imagination and enriching the experience of the novel. This noxious image, sprinkled throughout the text from beginning to end, becomes a recognizable motif that reflects the author's control and planned organization of his work. Because this image moves parallel with that of the wind and the dripping pipe, La Guma has invented three simultaneous image patterns and developed them concurrently while relating them all the time to the theme of the oppression in South Africa. In the examples which follow, are represented several ways in which the image of the dripping faucet appears:

> Somewhere outside, a leaking pipe dripped with infinite reluctance. (12)
> The voice had the expressionless sound of a dripping faucet. (61)
> The leaking pipe was dripping somewhere in the kitchen yard. (89)
> In the kitchen, pot-lids clanged and the leaking pipe still dribbled monotonously with its tantalising invitation to ice-cold water. (114)
> The Casbah Kid...half-listened to the dripping pipe. (129)
> ...Gus...scratched himself...The leaking pipe tapped away somewhere outside. (129)
> Doom advanced each passing second, with each drip of the leaky plumbing, the sucking sounds of the wind outside. (131)
> The guard unlocked the cell and The Casbah Kid let go of the other's hand, stepped past the guard. George Adams stood there in the cell, alone with the scribbled walls and the drip, drip-drip of the pipe that leaked somewhere. (165)

The two images—of men casually and incessantly scratching themselves to remove parasites, and the monotonous drip, drip-drip of a leaking faucet—move inexorably toward their common conclusion, the state-sponsored murder of The Casbah Kid. The prisoners, thereby, become a metaphor for people of color in South Africa and throughout the world, suffering both physically and psychologically. The parasites, then, a metaphor for capitalism and racism, are living at the expense of Africans and other peoples of color. Thus, the dripping faucet (a metaphor for the psychological torture the prisoners must endure) is both alluring (a "tantalising invitation to ice-cold water") and tortuous as "doom advanced...with each drip of the leaky plumbing." Again, it can be noted that the meta-phorical element is not superfluous or mere ornamentation; it is part of the very fabric of the book. From whatever angle one approaches it, literally or figuratively, the La Gumian image can be looked upon as an instrument, calculated and precise, for probing the implica-tions of simple everyday things: fixing a fleeting gesture, scratching , or expressing the ineffable by way of a dripping faucet.

In subtle and overt ways, La Guma establishes the allegorical meaning of prison and imprisonment as microcosms of the larger society; that South Africa is *"The Stone Country."* Taking every nuance and connotation of "stone," La Guma reconstructs through iconography, figuration, and imagery the microcosmic world of the prison, so as to leave no doubt about the hardness and harshness of the South African environment. The windows are barred, there is a con-crete gallery and concrete steps, a patch of asphalt for exercise, the walls are battleship gray; and "The prison overlooked the city and harbour, a squat, wide girdle of brownstone and grey-painted mortar and concrete enclosing a straining body of brickwork and more stone" (17). As La Guma squeezes every ounce of meaning from the novel's title and thematic palette, in it appears a deliberate and effective effort to reflect the hardness, insensitivity, stupidity and deadness of the myth of white supremacy in South Africa that George Adams con-templates, "was like a big stone prison, anyway" (58).

Thus, the image of stone, brick, mortar, concrete is noticeably present throughout the novel, sealing idea and meaning within the image. A particular corridor is "paved with worn flagstones in pink and white" (11); the eyes of The Casbah Kid are "hard and grey and cold as pebbles on a beach when the tide goes out" (20); and later, he is described as being "as unapproachable as a wave-washed rock" (25). Even the food is subject to this metaphor, as Yusef the Turk spat out a bean and exclaimed, "This - - - - stuff is hard as stones" (70). And the guards are described as not only hard but cold; their authority "enforced with the shock of ice" (76), maintaining "a sort of frigid superiority" (76). Finally, during the escape attempt by Gus, Morgan, and Koppe, Koppe is described as "shaking with fear that was like a stone in his belly" (150).

These images portray as well as comment on the atmosphere of the prison. They are not obvious to the casual reader, as they fit in so well with the subdued tone of their context. In this manner, the psychological and physical reality of prison life is described in a series of vivid metaphors. Although there is, in this imagery, an element of pathos which is motivated by the literal and figurative context, its primary purpose is to give an accurate analysis of some of the psychology, if not psychoses of imprisonment: fear, anger, disgust, impotence, indifference, hopelessness, fatalism, fratricide, infanticide, suicide, and so forth. Such images fix the principle themes and the allegorical implications of the story in marvelously memorable metaphors which become symbols, having complex associations and meanings. There is, therefore, a connected and sequential exposition of the theme that advances parallel with the plot and the action, commenting on and defining character, thought, and behavior.

It is easily observable that once Mr. La Guma has noticed an analogy, he likes to develop it, repeat it, and embroider upon it. That is, the recurrence of the same image, or slight variation on it, reappears in different parts of the novel of the cycle. Some images are remarkably persistent (for example, the wind, itching and scratching, the leaking faucet, stone), reappearing on consecutive pages, while another image will return after a long interval. It may be only a faint echo of the original, but it may also be an amplification or even consummation. The images of the "prison cat" provide a clear example of this process. La Guma's methodical and masterful creation of the symbolic image of the confrontation between the prison cat and a mouse, is undoubtedly one of the most brilliant, structurally and thematically, in all his works. It is not the originality or uniqueness of the image that gives it this quality, but rather the control and subtlety of its development to an intense and acute climax.

Early in *The Stone Country*, in Chapter 2, we are introduced to the prison cat, "fat and sleek under its tortoise-shell fur"; which immediately suggests that this "fat and sleek" animal is better cared for than the prisoners. In Chapter 9, in fact, the prison cat reappears "Around the drums...sleek and glistening with health...sniffing and purring, its shining tail raised like a flag-pole" (60). Somewhat later we see the cat undulating "across the concrete, its tortoiseshell pelt gleaming in the sunlight, its tail waving like an antenna." At this point, the images are mostly short and simple, adding a fleeting note to the narrative without holding it up or diverting attention from it. But, as the meaning and expressive force of the image gathers momentum, La Guma develops it into a little scene, still consistent and in harmony with the major thematic thrust of the novel:

> George Adams had been standing in a wedge of shade
> when the prison cat had stepped delicately over his feet,
> and he had stooped and picked up the cat, smiling at it and
> running his hand down the silky back, watching the fur rise
> as his hand passed. The cat had purred and had licked his
> wrist, the tongue warm and rough. (110)

This seemingly innocent gesture is suddenly transformed into a
major conflict, as Fatty, a guard, asks:

> "What business you got with that cat?"
> "Oh, I was just playing with it..."
> "Playing? You think you here to play?"
> "There's nothing wrong in picking up the cat..."
> "Still talking back, hey?..."
> "You asked me a question, so I answered...."
> "I've had enough of your cheek...Now put that cat down
> and come with me." (110-111)

As a result of this encounter, George Adams is put into the Isolation Block along with The Casbah Kid, Gus, Morgan, and Koppe.
The prison cat, therefore, in this incident, has become the pivotal
point in the novel: allowing the action of the second half of the
novel to advance in a logically connected way from the first part:
since the second half deals primarily with the escape attempt and
The Kid's approaching execution. In addition to illuminating
George's sensitivity, this image of him gently stroking the cat serves
as a structural bridge between the two parts of the novel.

Having established this essential structural role of the prison
cat, and very shrewdly placing George (the vehicle through whom
the action of the novel is seen and interpreted) in the "advanta-
geous" environment of the action of this part of the novel—the
Isolation Block—La Guma then masterfully joins to this structure
the thematic flesh of the image. In the incident involving the cat
and a mouse, the general state of prisoners (both literal and metaphorical) and their relationship to the myth and power of white
supremacy is conveyed. In the image-sequence of the prison cat
sadistically chasing and teasing the mouse, La Guma captures the
essence of the life of haunted people of color as they live their

tragic lives against the harsh, insensitive, and brutal background of the "stone countries" around the world:

> The cat was watching the mouse crouched between its paws. It lay on its belly again, breathing on the dusty-grey creature with the bright beady eyes and tiny panting jaws. The mouse had its body drawn taught into a ball of tensed muscle, waiting for another opening, refusing to give up hope. A clubbed paw reached out and nudged it. To the mouse it was like the charge of a rhinoceros. Pain quivered through the bunched muscles and the hide rippled, but it remained balled up, waiting with tiny, beating heart for another chance to escape the doom that waited for it with horrid patience.
>
> Then the cat made a mistake. It rose up on all fours. Without hesitation the mouse streaked straight forward, under the long belly and out past the swishing tail. There was a vast roaring sound in its ears. It was the laughter of the onlookers. The cat spun round; too late. The time taken to turn by the cat gave the mouse a few seconds headway and it was off, hurtling across the square again. Something huge and shiny— it was the boot of a guard—tried to block its passage, but it swerved skillfully, and its tiny muscles worked desperately, and it headed into the shade.
>
> The cat was a few inches behind it, but it swerved again and then the blurred dark hole of a drain-pipe loomed somewhere to its right, seen out of the corner of one pain-wracked eye. The mouse dodged a slashing, sabred paw by a hair's breadth, and gained the entrance to the hole.
>
> The paw struck again, just as the mouse dashed in, raking the slender tail, but the mouse was gone, and outside the spectators were chuckling over the disappointment of the cat as it crouched waiting at the hole. Inside, in the cool, familiar darkness, the mouse lay panting to regain its breath. (126-127)

La Guma's main success in this passage lies in the sympathetic relationship established between the imprisoned and the mouse in this symbolic confrontation with the cat. He develops this analogy to the point of its becoming an autonomous allegory. The image acquires its own momentum, and the initial analogy is embellished in a series of metaphors closely related to the central motif: the paw of the cat, when it nudges the mouse, "was like the charge of a rhinoceros"—a simile that expresses the anomalous relationship between the awesome physical, military power of white South Africa (the cat as rhinoceros) and the virtual powerlessness of Africans and other people of color in South Africa (the mouse as mouse).

"Then the cat made a mistake. It rose up on all fours." This is a very interesting image, as it tends to suggest, for example, that white South Africa losing all humanity ("rising up on all fours," militarily, politically, economically, socially, religiously, ideologically) its atavistic dependence on brute force, may finally be the undoing of the system, the point when the mouse gets away. George Adams, reflecting on the symbolic value of the event, provides perhaps the best explanation of its meaning:

> You were on the side of the mouse, of all the mice, George Adams thought. The little men who get kicked in the backside all the time. You got punched and beaten like that mouse, and you had to duck and dodge to avoid the claws and fangs. Even a mouse turns, someday. No, not mouse, it's a worm that turns. Okay. But he was glad the mouse had won out eventually, had managed to escape the slashing claws. You were on the side of the little animals, the weak and the timid who spent their lives dodging and ducking.
>
> Well, that mouse must have been bloody punch-drunk, slap-happy, after that mauling it received. People got knocked slap-happy by life, too, and did funny things. (127-128)

This metaphor seems to have so engrossed the author that he works it out in great detail, seeming to have forgotten that it is merely meant to illustrate a point, e.g., brain (or instinct) over brawn; or might does not make right; or ends do not, ipso facto, justify means; or even the Biblical notion that the meek shall inherit the earth. Instead, La Guma goes deeper and, through the perceptive interior monologue of George Adams ("You were on the side of ...all the mice...The little men"), wonderfully embracing the universal and organic nature ("Even a mouse turns, someday...a worm"), conveys a latent revolutionary impulse. Or one can glean from this the simple notion of the meek inheriting the earth, or victory for the universal working class, or that people of color will overcome their oppressors, will escape annihilation, will survive.

Arching over this action, however, is the planned escape of Gus, Morgan, and Koppe. This is a very teasing sort of action. It is parallel with the incident involving the cat and mouse; yet, this parallel goes along only so far, and seems to contradict the suggestion of "escape" or "liberation" implied in this extended metaphor. In fact, it seems to suggest failure, since the prisoners, Gus and Morgan, fail in their escape attempt. Koppe miraculously gets away, but he is the most unlikely candidate for perpetuating any kind of revolutionary ideology or posture, since he did not want to go in the first place, and was forced, coerced by circumstance and the other two men. Following the pattern of the two images, one conclusion is simply that La Guma's vacillation, in terms of a consistent idea and theme in these two images, obfuscates a major premise of the work. That premise is that it is the assertive and courageous who are needed to resist and eventually overthrow systems supporting the myth of white superiority; yet, it is the "weak and timid" mouse and the "weak and timid" Koppe who escape, and we're on the side of the weak and timid. There is suggestive power, irony, contradiction in these two images.

The irony is unconscious on Koppe's part, since he does not realize his own potential or the absurd situation he is in, being the only successful escapee. The effect of the irony, however, is seriously diminished, if not lost entirely, in relation to one of the major themes of the work, namely, the building up of the self-assertiveness, and self-awareness of these characters as a means of establishing the basis for a radical ideological principle. Koppe is totally inadequate to the task of establishing such a principle. Koppe's desecration is evident at the psychological or mental level. For example, when asked by Gus why he rushed the guard with him and Morgan, Koppe answers:

> Hell, I didn't mean to, mos. It just happened, likely. Something made me to do it. I am going to tell that in court. I just saw you johns charge that special, and the next thing I was

in it, too. I didn't mean to, hey. It was just something."
(100)

Koppe is similarly surprised with himself when, during the escape attempt, he reaches the outer wall of the prison, he never thought or believed he would make it. He is surely not the one who will promulgate and disseminate revolutionary values.

It is doubtless easier to run a prison, or a country, populated by meek and broken pets or domesticated animals than one with men like George Adams, who proclaim their rights and stand up to injustice. Adams maintains the primacy of basic human values in the struggle against his own annihilation. He considers the ethical standards of the other prisoners, succumbing to the brutality and intimidation of the guards, an unacceptable price to pay for survival. Yet, unlike Koppe, Adams is astute enough to realize that the problems facing the imprisoned, both behind and outside prison walls, are too serious to sacrifice oneself for a momentary victory or the temporary satisfaction of letting off steam. *The Stone Country*, obviously, is not just about George Adams, but about all the other characters too, and the variety of responses each manifests in trying to retain their dignity and self-respect against powers which would dehumanize and desecrate them to such an extent that their resistance and vitality break down.

Solly, for example, is the antithesis of George Adams; he clowns and dances the jig for the guards and for the brute Butcherboy; La Guma describes him as a "crumpled memo-sized, yellow duplicate of a man" (30). Later, however, from behind the mask Solly dons as the perfect prisoner, or slave, there emerges a free man struggling to preserve his honor and dignity. He, at tremendous personal risk to himself, smuggles the blades into the prison that Gus and the others use to saw through the bars; nor did the prisoners "bully the little man; he had assumed the position of court jester" (122). Solly's desecration, his scars, are all internal but, unlike Koppe his reaction, his antidote against his dehumanization is self-imposed. For reasons of survival he "chooses" to act the role of court jester, this self-effacing role of clowning, giggling, dancing the jig, and after having his thumb-prints taken "He rubbed the black ink casually into his hair," all in a desperate attempt to affirm some control of his life, even if it must be in this terribly minimal, self-deprecating way. It is, of course, superfluous to have such a man living according to certain prescribed revolutionary principles, a man whose very survival under the conditions described in this novel is already a miracle in itself.

In addition to internal, subjective violations of characters, the reader of *The Stone Country* will also be struck by the frequency of the image of the desecration of physical bodies as a metaphor for the South African reality. For example, in the sequence of images in the flashback summarizing Adams' and Jefferson Mpolo's arrest, the scene shifts to the "outside" world, and La Guma makes quick use of the desecration of physical bodies as he describes a row of "dark stores...and scarred and broken walls on which the exposed brick-work showed like scabless sores" (46). Such a depiction is a human document of the lives of the people living in this community. Such an image will carry into future time the feel and objective conditions—scarred, broken, exposed—as they were seen and understood by the artist. It is because of La Guma's attitude that this image assumes the meaning and impact that it does. It is because he feels deeply and respects what he sees that the most casual image can expose the sick and torturous circumstances overwhelming the African majority in South Africa.

Such fleeting images tell us of the conditions, not just of the buildings, but the conditions of a significant segment of humanity whose lives, like the building, are scarred, broken and exposed. The details about the building mean nothing to us if they do not express some mood, some emotional and psychic reaction as felt by the artist. Again, it is not just the object (the building), but the sensations connecting La Guma with the object; that is, both the facts and the tone of the experience. The physical abuse of buildings becomes associated, in La Guma's mind, with the ruin and abuse of the human body, of human beings.

In fact, far more than in any other of his novels, *The Stone Country* depicts the desecration of the human body as an essential metaphor for the South African situation. As stated earlier, the human body should be, in itself, an object upon which the eye dwells with pleasure and which we are glad to see depicted: "The Word was made flesh, and dwelt among us...full of grace and truth" (John 1:14). Yet, from the first chapter of this novel, we are given an image of The Casbah Kid with a "raw and swollen lip" and his "fingers with bitten nails," which become synonymous with his identity throughout the work. The sustained repetition of the image of the "swollen lip and bitten nails" assumes symbolic proportions, like a sculptor transforming details of the human anatomy into an instrument of autonomous expression.

One detects early the important role this kind of metaphorical iconography is going to play throughout the novel. As George is being transported to the prison, in Chapter 2, standing, packed in the prison van, "A face grinned at him, showing greenish, carious teeth.... The face yelled at him, sending a horrid blast of breath into his" (16). Such an image is an undisguised portrait of physical abuse and neglect, and an essential element in La Guma's whole philosophy. Whether such abuse is self-imposed and an expression of self-hate, as when Solly rubbed black ink into his hair; or more masochistic forms, such as that of Butcherboy's "ape-like torso covered with tattooed decorations—hands holding hands, a skull-and-crossbones, a Union Jack, a dripping dagger, and various other emblems" (31); or whether such self-mutilation and abuse is a result of the violent and indifferent environment saturating and engulfing their lives, like Gus, who "had a knife-scar down the left side of his face from eyebrow to chin, and it gave him a lopsided look, as if his face had been hastily stuffed and sewn up" (28); or like Brakes Peterson,

> ...who had only one good side to his face. The other was a
> hideous mapwork of wrinkles and folds caused by a care-
> lessly treated burn received when his mistress, tired of a life
> of brutality, had held a hot flat-iron to his cheek in revenge,
> one night when he lay asleep. (34) All such images express
> Alex La Guma's sense of the lack of human wholeness. In
> each case, the divine element in the human body is sum-
> marily vulgarized. The moving quality of these portraits
> depends directly on the distress of the body, on a condi-
> tion that is exactly the opposite of physical beauty.

The curious thing is that, for our purposes, La Guma chose to communicate specific ideas through the physical anguish and physical abuse of his characters. He has done so, it seems to me, precisely because it gives him the most pain. It has hurt him to see so much suffering, so much anguish and pain, so many torn and mangled bodies and lives around him, and he is determined that it will hurt us, too. And if it hurt him, that's really not what is important, everybody gets hurt. What is important is that he must use this pain to connect him with everyone else alive, and his writing, his art, is all he has to do it with.

All those delicate feelings which come together in our joy at the sight of an idealized human body are shattered and desecrated through La Guma's imagery, just as they are shattered and violated in life. The dream of a perfectible humanity is broken by his relentless reminders of what African humanity (mixed and unmixed) must endure form cradle to grave as a result of the iniquitous and defiling myth of white supremacy. No perfection, no health (spiritual or physical) is possible in a system under such a myth. For instance, Yusef the Turk looks "like a discarded folding ruler" (38) and wears dentures; Casim, George Adams' underground accomplice, has "pock-mark cheeks"; the girl with the reddish hair running the duplicating machine has "a smudge of ink on her chin" (44); one of the background characters, "A nude boy with curly hair," has "a line drawing of 'The Saint' tattooed on his right arm" (58); and a close-up of Butcherboy reveals "blood-flecked, gorilla eyes and the heavy, red, rubbery lips pealed back to reveal broken, stained and mossy teeth like desecrated tombstones grinning out of the bludgeoned and badly-repaired, stubbly face" (65); and Major Planks, one of the white warders, has "a dry, brittle face like crumpled pink tissue-paper with holes torn out for eyes, and a horizontal crease left for a mouth" (68); a final example is Morgan, one of the would-be escapees, who "had a very dark, flat, round face, like the bottom of a frying-pan on which somebody had, with a blunt finger-tip, hurriedly drawn eyes, nostrils and a heavy mouth in the layer of soot, burnt oil and congealed fat" (99). Several other examples could have been noted, but I think the point is made.

The sense of a healthy structure, physical attractiveness, desirable, flawless figure and skin, has been rejected, and must be rejected in this context, in favor of raw and swollen lips, cut and burnt faces, emaciated and tattooed bodies, all symbols of tortured flesh, profaned humanity. La Guma has shown how the human body has been defiled and desecrated in order to communicate specific ideas and states of being and feeling inherent in and a consequence of apartheid. It may prove worthwhile to cite one of Daniel J. Goldhagen's (1996) observations concerning "Ordinary Germans and the Holocaust":

By denying the camp system's populace adequate nutri-
tion, indeed by subjecting many to starvation... by providing them with grossly inadequate clothing and shelter, not
to mention medical care, and by perpetrating steady violence
on their bodies and minds, the Germans succeeded in making
many of the camp system's inhabitants take on the appearance—including festering, open wounds, and the marks of
disease and illness—and the behavioral attributes of the
"subhumans" that the Germans imagined them to be. (176).

Similar insight has been proffered by Albert Memmi concerning
slavery and colonialism, and helps us better understand The Casbah
Kid, Ronny Pauls, and Michael Adonis:

Thus oppression justifies itself through oppression: the oppressors produce and maintain by force the evils that render the oppressed, in their eyes, more and more like what
they would have to be like to deserve their fate. (1967:
xxvi).

Hence, the white attitudes towards people of color, and the latter's
attitudes toward themselves is a direct result of the ideology and
practice of white supremacy. An ideology that has at its roots and
in its very fibers a conception in which the black body, the colored
body, ceases to be the mirror of divine perfection and becomes an
object of capital value, humiliation and shame.

It is through this conception of the human body, that we can
become more acutely aware of a universal order, characterized by
a white hegemony that defines the quality and dignity of human
beings on the basis of color and race and their value to society as
units of labor only. A universal white hegemony that desecrates
the very essence of scriptural theology that "God created man in
His image...In the image of God created He him, male and female
created He them." And whether we follow a creationist or evolu-
tionist epistemology, we must come to terms with the black, the
brown, the African man and woman as the object and subject of
creation.

A creation cycle, if we follow the creationists' view, in which
man was not created from the clouds, or from snowflakes, or from
the snow, but man, human beings, Homo sapien was created from

the dust of the earth. The very ground that you and I walk on and observe to be black and brown and related shades of the full color, black. And if one follows the evolutionists, then according to Dr. Louis Leaky and other eminent anthropologists, it was in East Africa, somewhere in perhaps Kenya or Uganda, man first walked upright; then spread north, east, west, and south.

How then can the original man be last? How is that so? What makes this reality real, economically, politically, materially? And particularly, why is this true, with the very people that God has blessed with the color black? Africans, I read somewhere, are the "children of the sun," God's original creation. Their very blackness is religious, a blessing and honor. We must, then, deal with the tyranny of color on human consciousness. Now, not only the white world, but millions of African people themselves have tragically internalized their color as ugly and despicable; and this is tragedy, the ultimate desecration. Dr. Frantz Fanon writes that:

> In the colonial context, the settler only ends his work of breaking in the native when the latter admits loudly and intelligibly the supremacy of the white man's values. (1981:43)

An important thematic focus of *The Stone Country* is this very process of "breaking in the native." There is a tenacious resolve in George Adams, much more so than in Michael Adonis or Charlie Pauls, a resolve that refuses to be broken, even by the intense, awesome power of prison guards: who retains hope and belief in the eventual overthrow of the entire oppressive South African regime. By building up the level of consciousness, of self-assurance and self-assertiveness in his major characters, La Guma establishes the basis for a radical, ideologically committed principle of revolutionary action. The task of preparing and convincing the entire people—African, Coloured, Asian—is an extremely difficult one; it is begun in this work and becomes the dominant theme of *In the Fog of the Seasons' End*.

Chapter 4

In the Fog of the Seasons' End:
Image and Idea

After the Age of Pain
Other great pains may follow.
The season of the locust passes;
Then enters the age of the sterile ones,
Fools that rule from gigantic thrones
Deriving their joy from the words of dry leaves,
The leaves that spread their emptiness on the dry sand.
The earth will become fertile one day
And the islands will stretch to the horizons
Overgrown with fruits from the weeds.

—Mazisi Kunene

In the Fog of the Seasons' End is Alex La Guma's fourth novel. It may, perhaps, best be defined as a novella, for it is merely 181 pages and confines itself almost entirely to one character. This is "Buke" or Beukes, a full-time underground organizer in a movement dedicated to the overthrown of the white-minority-ruled South African apartheid system, based in Cape Town, where the statue of Cecil Rhodes points "north towards the segregated lavatories" (*In the Fog*, 12). Again, our concern is with La Guma's imagery and the ideas about man and society they imply. Our first concern will be with those images that play a vital part in development of the themes in this novel. As with his other protagonists—Michael Adonis, Charlie Pauls, George Adams—La Guma does not pay much attention to exploring the psyche of Beukes, the lonely, hunted, determined protagonist of *In the Fog of the Seasons' End*; rather, he is defined largely by his actions. Although a man of great integrity and real courage, he is a type. In fact, Lewis Nkosi has remarked, "He is not an original creation who can be said to take a hold upon our consciousness; nor is he...a man bristling with ideas" (1981:85). Still, it is through the words, the thoughts, the actions of Beukes that some of the dominant themes of the novel and the concerns and consciousness of the author—and with him those of the Coloured community—are revealed.

Pursuant, therefore, to the revelation of one major theme of this novel—the convincing and preparing of the entire people for armed struggle—it should be noticed that the book is dedicated to "the memory of Basil February and others killed in action, Zimbabwe, 1967." And its title is taken from the poem "Martyrs" by Conte Saidon Tidiany, of Guinea:

> Banquets of black entrails of the Black,
> Armour of parchment of wax,
> Fragile and fugitive when facing the burning stone,
> Will be shattered like the spider's web,
> *In the Fog of the Seasons' End.*

Obviously, this poem spoke to Mr. La Guma; for through its surreal imagery it speaks of the struggle and travail African people must endure; the brittle and fleeting "Armour," prehaps, of racists' mystification, feasting on the "entrails of the Black...will be shattered like the spider web," as all things, all life passes into mystery. *"In the Fog of the Seasons' End,"* suggests that, even as African people struggle for true independence and their humanity, in these "final days" of the hegemony of colorism and racism, the end may appear cloudy and often obscure; still, at the "end" of the "seasons," in the words of Dr. Martin Luther King, "We as a people will get to the promised land." This is a very functional and optimistic image, one that plays a wonderful role in the thematic development of this novel. Elias Tekwane, one of the major characters in this work, could in fact be a fictionalized recreation of Basil February, to whom the novel is dedicated. Tekwane's torture and death, even like that of Steve Biko, at the hands of sadistic South African police, exposes the punishment reserved for African patriots who have decided to fight; it is vividly portrayed in the opening "Prologue":

> You are going to torture me, maybe kill me. But that is the only way you and your people can rule us. You shoot and kill and torture because you cannot rule any other way a people who reject you. You are reaching the end of the road and going downhill towards a great darkness, so you must take a lot of people with you, because you are selfish and greedy and afraid of the coming darkness....(6)

This opening image of the intellectual posture of Elias Tekwane extols the virtues of courage and determination, a couple of the thematic building blocks of this work.

Tekwane and Beukes are organizing their cadre in the activities possible in the South African police state: distributing agitational leaflets as part of an underground political organization, and helping to smuggle out of the country women and men prepared to topple the government by force.

The "Prologue" opens with the scene of a police raid on the the shanty-town, meeting-place of Beukes and Tekwane. This event, in the narrative sequence of the story, is picked up in Chapter Fourteen. Beukes is wounded by a police bullet, but manages to escape, while Tekwane is captured (Chapter Seventeen). Structurally, therefore, Chapters Fourteen and Fifteen are a continuation of the "Prologue." And thematically, the "Prologue" and these two chapters clearly and firmly establish that the task of preparing and convincing the whole people of the necessity of an armed national liberation movement seems to be the primary theme of the novel. Defining the "whole people," even after the 1990 release of Nelson Mandela, may still be ambiguous to some. Here Njabulo Ndebele, writing from Johannesburg in 1991 observes:

> ...whites are still in government; they control the army and the police; they still enjoy what must be one of the highest standards of living in the world; they still manage the economy, although they will grudgingly let in competent blacks; they own practically all the means of production that matter; they dominate the privileged universities and research institutes. Their overall power is still pervasive. (1994:viii)

On the other hand, Ndebele observes that the overwhelming majority of Africans and other people of color, "the vast masses of this country are poor. There is massive unemployment, an acute housing shortage, a tottering educational system, and an inadequate public health system" (viii). Convincing and preparing the "vast masses," the "whole people" to use "any means necessary" to change these wretched conditions is, La Guma wants us to know, fraught with danger and the possibility of an early death. Beukes understands and accepts this inevitable next stage in his peoples' struggle, and says to Elias Tekwane during their surreptitious rendezvous:

> It is a good thing that we are now working for armed struggle. It gives people confidence to think that soon they might combine mass activity with military force. One does not like facing the fascist guns like sheep. (143)

And Tekwane's response sums up this major theme of the novel in a clearly expressed intellectual image:

> Well, we have started,...We are beginning to recover from earlier setbacks. Step by step our people must acquire both the techniques of war and the means for fighting such a war. It is not only the advanced ones, but the entire people that must be prepared, convinced. (143)

It is because of La Guma's personal interests, context, and preferences that he creates this kind of intellectual, ideologically laden theme-image. One of the principal social and political objectives of the image is achieved—to endow the masses of exploited people of color in South Africa with the consciousness that a new stage has been reached in their struggle for liberation. The artistic objective is likewise achieved because it is an enjoyable story. The image is sadly prophetic, in that it anticipates the effectiveness of this position in creating the national liberation movements of Mozambique, FRELIMO and MPLA: Zimbabwe's ZANU and ZAPU: Namibia's SWAPO, and South Africa's own ANC and PAC.

The main function of this kind of character figuration—intellectual rather than descriptive, because it compares ideas rather than concrete objects—is to elucidate certain themes: the theme of courage, or unity, or preparation and participation in armed struggle. However, the "entire people" is not a monolithic singular essence, but complex, variegated. There are the "advanced" leading fighters in the movement like Beukes, Isaac, and Elias Tekwane. There are also those on the fringes of the action like Tommy and Henny April and high-school teacher Authur Bennet, who still perform vital tasks; and still others like Red Braces, who are completely demoralized and have surrendered to the status quo: and Tommy, the dancer, who wants nothing to do with anything serious. All these characters represent specific responses, intellectual or ideological perspectives, to the same reality, to the same struggle.

Figurations and iconography of Beukes, Isaac, and Tekwane reveal that not only do they refuse to surrender, but even while under arrest and torture courageously refuse even to cooperate. Tekwane says to his captors:

> You want me to co-operate. You have shot my people when they have protested against unjust treatment; you have torn people from their homes, imprisoned them, not for stealing or murder, but for not having your permission to live. Our children live in rags and die of hunger. And you want me to co-operate with you? It is impossible." (5-6)

The idea presented in this image of Elias Tekwane is one of uncompromising defiance and courage: virtues that, in the "waarheid kamers" (truth rooms) of South African police stations, are put to the test. In these torture chambers, individuals are tortured mercilessly until they "speak the truth," which simply means until they answer questions to the satisfaction of their inquisitors.

The verisimilitude of La Guma's account is authenticated by Gordon Winters, an ex-BOSS secret agent, in his book *Inside BOSS.* Winters discloses several methods used by the South African Security Police when they "interrogate" detainees. There is the "Portuguese Statue," where the victim is made to stand for many hours in a corner; and the "Portuguese Bookshelf," where the victim is made to hold a cardboard box full of books above the head for two or three hours. Then there is the "Tower of Pisa," where the victim is made to stand on tiptoe with both feet tied together four feet from a wall; the "Cliff Edge," where the victim is forced to stand barefoot half-on and half-off two house bricks; the "Sleep Walker," where the victim is made to sit on a wooden chair in the same position for two or three days; the "Monkey Man," where the victim is suspended from water pipes by ropes or pieces of cloth, with the feet left dangling a few inches from the floor; "The Parachute," which involves threatening to hold or throw the victim out of a window; and "The Tokoloshe," a homemade electric-shock machine made from batteries with two wire leads and winding apparatus. The leads may be applied to any part of the body, including the lips, private parts, or stomach. A few spots of water sprinkled beforehand intensify the pain (Winters 1981: 600-601). It is because of "The Tokoloshe" that Beukes "remembered the electrode burns on the hands of prisoners" (25). And there are, of course, other variations on the sadistic, "civilized" methods just noted. For example, during the "Monkey Man" technique, the "civilized" police will repeatedly apply burning cigarette ends to the victim's naked body. While yet another common method is to take the prisoner to a river, put him into a sack and throw him into the water for a couple of minutes; this may be done repeatedly. For really stubborn prisoners, there is "The Cracker," where the testicles of the victim are squeezed with a pair of ordinary nut-crackers until he loses consciousness (601).

These examples of the torture methods of the South African Security Police, taken from the personal, factual account of Gordon Winters, confirm the veracity and rock-hard realism of La Guma's "fiction"; so it is perfectly believable when he writes:

> A uniformed man opened the door at the top of the steps to a basement room. The two security men let the prisoner go and the young man kicked him so that he rolled over and over down the stone steps, crying out, "we don't want to kill him yet." He unzipped his fly and urinated off the steps into the prisoner's face.
> ...Manacled to the staple by his wrists, his arms aloft, the prisoner choked and heaved.
> The two detectives removed their jackets and the sportsman hit him in the stomach and then began to batter him mercilessly with his fists...The young one drew his revolver and struck at the prisoner's writhing shins with the barrel. (7)

The thoroughness and meticulousness of La Guma's description easily convinces the reader of the reality of the world it creates. It is those who believe that "civilization" is in their hands who "urinate into the prisoner's face." Contemplating such an image and the emotions it produces should help us to see what it is about life in South Africa that leads to the expression of anguish and despair, but also what gives rise to courage and defiance. Granted, the feelings and emotions come chiefly from the reader, but the feelings are given form, they are organized by the work of art.

In *In the For of the Seasons' End*, the image of the torture and subsequent death of Elias Tekwane is the opening and penultimate image of the novel. It is, therefore, from this image back to this image that the movement of the narrative progresses. The intervening sixteen chapters can, in a sense, be seen as a kind of explanation of this beginning, which is also the end, where again, like a Christ-figure, we confront the agonizing portrait of Tekwane:

> Pain was like a devil which had usurped his body. It was wrenching in his wrists and hands and the sockets of his shoulders as he dangled with all his weight on the handcuffs that shackled him to the staple in the wall. It was his body, battered and bruised by the pistol barrel, and in his legs, his skinned shins, which would not hold his weight... His whole body was held together on a framework of pain and he was thirsty. His head dangled on his chest...he knew vaguely that he was alive. (169)

One of the most remarkable features of this image, in addition to its resemblance to Christ on the cross and the multiple themes of suffering humanity, of courage and endurance, is its functional character, the dynamic role it plays in the structure of the novel. The completed image is not fixed and ready made, but arises, is born from the body of an emotionally exciting and moving story. This approach does not convey mere documentary information, but rather imbues the image with facts of South African existence raised by means of art to a created, exciting force and emotional effect. In this way, La Guma (consciously, by means of selected images) hands on to others feelings he has lived through and that attach him to the image; we, in turn, are infected by these feelings and also experience them. The catharsis is good. Such images comment on and criticize the social and political realities that form and condition the lives of human beings in South Africa. La Guma's preference for the material and metaphorical essence of his environment, and his obvious sincerity, characterizes not only the manner in which he writes, but also the themes he selects. His dominant themes, to my knowledge, do not involve homosexuality, slapstick comedy, science fiction, the search for nirvana, or the infantile fantasies of the Ian Fleming variety; rather, "The torture chambers and the third degree had been transferred from celluoid strips in segregated cinemas to the real world" (25). For Beukes, Elias Tekwane, and others like them, who are determined not just to resist but to attack and overthrow the oppressive white supremacist myth, their very worst fantasies become reality:

> Now there was another darkness as a sack was dragged over his head. They pulled off his trousers and underpants. He was suspended grotesquely, with his arms about his drawn-up legs and a broom handle above his elbows and below his knees. The sportsman had fixed certain electrical apparatus into a wall plug...He screamed inside the sack.
>
> The glossy-haired one cranked the handle of the magneto while the sportsman ran the electrodes against bare legs, genitals. Elias screamed. He had anticipated violence, but not this, not this....His flesh burned and scorched and his limbs jerked and twitched and fell away from him, jolting and leaping in some fantastic dance which only horror linked to him.
>
> ...the ghosts waited for him on some far horizon. No words came, only the screaming of many crows circling the battlefield. Wahlulu amakosi! Thou hast conquered the Kings! The figures moved along the horizon. He! Uya kuhlasela—pina? Yes, where wilt thou now wage war? Far, far, his ancestors gathered on the misty horizon, their spears sparkling like diamonds in the exploding sun. Somebody came out of the bright haze and touched him with a hand. His mind called out "Mother". From afar came the rushing sound of trampling feet. (172-175)

Elias Tekwane, like Steve Biko, pays the ultimate price. He gives his life in the effort to "prepare and convince" the "vast masses" to do whatever is necessary to regain their dignity, their nobility, and their land. There is certainly no reason for La Guma to go into the legal ramifications of this "officially sanctioned" torture, "The Tokoloshe" and murder, as this would be a rather obvious distortion of reality; since, in most such cases—and there are literally hundreds of them every year in South Africa—the police are absolved of any blame. In contemplating such an image, it is not merely a question of whether we like or dislike such images as police brutality and torture of victims as themes in a novel. Rather, it is a matter of analysis and examination to at least make an effort to gain some insight into the kind of world we yet live in. If such images and themes reflect truthfully the times and circumstances as well as the deep concerns of the artist, they are worth serious attention whether we enjoy them or not.

Alex La Guma finds nothing redeeming in the contemporary image of South African police and he endeavors to terrify us to the very marrow of our bones via the luxury of experiencing vicariously what far too many African men and women must actually endure on a daily basis in pursuit of basic human rights.

In examining the iconography of Elias Tekwane's torture and death, apart from the rather unrealistic translation of the African phrase "Wahlulu amakosi," into English as "Thou hast conquered the Kings!" we grasp the horror of such iconography along with its suggestions of the "granite" resolve and bravery of Tekwane. The iconography itself exposes and accuses the South African police state of its crimes against humanity; while it extols the fortitude and courage of African freedom fighters. There is very little subtlety in La Guma's narrative technique, and consequently this tense and dramatic portrayal seems appropriate to the moral scale of the crime and the character of an actual account. This iconography, alone, is a terrifying document of the devastation of human values; and, ironically, it is also a document of a life free of the fear of death.

La Guma's iconography portraying Tekwane's torture and death suggests that a major stride toward African freedom can be accomplished only when Africans as an "entire people" conquer the fear of death. Indeed, the centrality of the image in the structural and thematic design of the novel suggests that La Guma views the fear of death as one of, if not the most important impediment to the achievement of freedom for Africans in our time. In that connection, whether one believes in life after death or not, death itself is inevitable. All men and women, African, Coloured, Asian, and white, rich and poor, Christian, Jew, or Muslim are affected by a common destiny—physical death. Tekwane's death reminds us again of this inevitability; and to fear the inevitable is to abandon rationality and to waste precious amounts of psychic energy in contemplation of an event over which one is powerless to exert influence or control.

Rather than fear or deplore the fact of death, Tekwane understands and even rejoices in the awareness that it is the inevitability of death that makes possible his freedom in life. He does not cower or tremble before the prospect of death, but seems to see it as a completion of the cycle of life, a return, a going to join the ancestors, "ancestors gathered on the misty horizon." He teaches us that since death is inevitable, one is ultimately free to do with one's life what one wills. It is Tekwane's acceptance of the inevitability of death that frees his mind, his body and his spirit to do the courageous and memorable things in life.

La Guma created him quintessentially free: committed to a goal for the achievement of which he is prepared to die. La Guma's achievement in the iconography evoking Tekwane's life and death is the preparation, among his African audience, of a mind-set that removes the individual mind from the confines of petty quotidian concerns to a point from which one sees oneself as a free agent operating in a free environment where all things are possible. Certainly our study of images and the themes they produce should help us to see what it is about life in South Africa, in particular, which leads to images of anguish and savagery on the one hand, and hope and courage on the other. For it becomes clear, from the beginning to the end of *In the Fog of the Seasons' End*, that one of the primary virtues demanded of the revolutionary is the "granite resolve" exemplified in the life and death of Elias Tekwane. There is a kind of "meek inherit the earth" idea here, but not by the force of faith alone. Thinking to himself, and by implication saying to all those who would take up the mantle of resistance and revolution, Elias thinks:

> These days one could not depend only on faith: the apparatus of the Security Police scraped away faith like strata of soil until they came to what was below. If they reached crumbly sandstone, it was spendid for them. It was the hard granite on which they foundered. (13)

Tekwane finds fortitude and solace in the long history of African resistance: "remembering Mdlaka and Tsatsu the old man again he had no regrets, and knew that he would have done everything over again, given the opportunity" (156). Then, at the limits of endurance under torture, he finds strength in hallucinated historical visions:

> Far away the tramp of thousands of feet drummed on the crackling earth, the rattle of spears and shields came across the lon, hazy distance with the cries...The ghosts of his ancestors beckoned from afar...He! Uya kuhlasela-pina?
> (172-175)

Beukes too is fortified in a similar way: when passing a cast of a Bushman in an ethnographic museum, he thinks sentimentally: "they were the first to fight" (14). This is a significant image for Buekes, and surely for La Guma, for, as Edward Said has noted, "To become aware of one's self as belonging to a subject people is the founding insight of anti-imperialist nationalism" (1993:214). Such an observation helps to redefine the "colored" population as fellow Africans, a very important consciousness. Tekwane and Beukes have decided to take full responsibility for their actions. They have no intention of succumbing to remorse or despair. As revolutionaries, conscious of their past, they can envision a future which promises hope and ultimate liberation, in spite of the "fog" of their present circumstance. But it is a struggle that is collective and not individualistic: the entire people must be involved. Tekwane, Beukes, and Isaac must try to reach out to the democratic majority and make their message known to them. The handbills that Tommy procures for Beukes is, in this context, a meaningful contribution, as the handbill itself makes perfectly clear:

> We bring a message...you will wonder that men and women would risk long terms of imprisonment to bring you this message. What kind of people do these things? The answer is simple. They are ordinary people who want freedom in this country...From underground we launched the new fighting corps...sent youth abroad to train as people's soldiers, technicians, administrators... We will fight back...To men who are oppressed freedom means many

things... Give us back our country to rule for ourselves as we choose...Many ways to fight for freedom. (58)

One of the themes implicit in this intellectual image is that those who have taken up the struggle for liberation are not extraordinary men and women engaged in heroic actions which only a few daredevils can undertake. For example, "Beukes," notes Vernon February, "is not a superman, but an ordinary person with ordinary desires" (1981:159). February also seems particularly pleased that, "La Guma at least refrains from creating a super-educated hero, who can only find salvation in the arms of a white liberal woman" (159). Rather, these "revolutionaries" are ordinary men and women "who want freedom"—industrial workers, domestic workers, miners, farmers, taxi-drivers, middle-class professionals, unemployed seasonal workers, even some doctors who have decided to put up a fight, utilizing all the means available to them, making the contributions they can make; men and women who fully recognize that they are brothers and sisters in the trench together, and they must do what has to be done for each other without the raising of questions.

The theme/task of preparing and convincing the entire people that the time of taking up arms against their oppressors has come is a constant preoccupation of Beukes, Elias, and their cadre; and this task pervades their most incidental contacts. For example, when the African domestic worker, Beatie Adams, unintentionally arouses Beukes when he is sleeping on one of the "Non-White" benches in the municipal park, he tries, and to some extent succeeds, at convincing her of another perspective of their common plight as Africans in white-minority-ruled South Africa.

Their dialogue is instructive:

"We all good enough to be servants. Because we're black they think we good enough to change their nappies."

She said..."That's life, isn't it?"

...he said, "Life? Why should it be our life? We're as good or bad as they are."

"Yes, I reckon so. But what can us people do?"

... "There are things people can do...I'm not saying a person can change it tomorrow or next year. But even if you don't get what you want today, soon, it's a matter of pride, dignity. You follow me?" (11)

Another important theme in La Guma's oeuvre is the heroism of ordinary people. Beatie Adams is an "ordinary" woman, a domestic, a nanny; still, she must be convinced, her consciousness raised, and Beukes is patient with and sensitive to her apprehension and dubiety. He listens to her, carefully, and responds politely and insightfully, without hostility or bitterness. Beukes and the other leaders of the movement realize that to be effective they cannot afford to alienate anyone; "The factory bloke got to take some (leaflets) in. Leave them around the machines, in the canteen" (16) and people in the various districts must be "ready to have meetings in their houses" (16). Even members of the professional class, like Authur Bennett, living in comfortable homes, tastefully decorated with "low stuffed settee and heavy armchairs with circular, gleaming wooden armrests...starched, crocheted table centres and a display cabinet full of miniature bottles which had once contained sample liquers and soft drinks" (19); the Bennetts, literal and metaphorical, must provide the friendly waters in which the underground movement must swim (Mao Zedong).

In politicizing and preparing the "vast masses" for armed struggle, the Marxian precept that "condition determines consciousness" is not lost on the author, La Guma, nor his characters. Beukes, for instance, takes each of his contacts where she or he is without raising unnecessary questions: even Arthur Bennett, who fails to live up to his part of their agreement to permit Beukes to stay in his home while he and his wife, Nelly, are away for the weekend; a failure that forces Beukes to have to spend "two nervous nights in a pretty gully, among pines and perfumed undergrowth" (23); still Beukes does not alienate him. Instead, he takes Bennett, like Beatie Adams, right where he is in order to fulfill certain basic needs of the moment. Instead of showering him with verbal abuse, Beukes quickly perceives the entire family context: the Bennetts' sleeping child, the apathetic wife, Nelly, of whom he thinks somewhat later, "His nagging wife (who) had undermined his shaky enthusiasm, like a tide washing away sandy foundations"—and taking it all in, he simply "looked at him (Bennett) feeling a little sorry for the harassed fellow" (137). Knowing what he wants and how much he can expect from Bennett, Beukes asks that he simply be allowed to brush his teeth and shave. Then, predicated on this same knowledge, he refuses the "ten bob...donation" Bennett offers to assuage his conscience, "sorry he had to hurt the small, bald man," but at the same time convincing him, by example, of the integrity of their cause, he says to Bennett, "Keep it. You don't have to buy your way out," (22) smiles and leaves.

In some cases, it is the perpetual pattern of prejudice and powerlessness that convinces an individual that preparation for a protracted military struggle is the only solution to their malaise. In contrast to the bourgeois Bennetts, there is, of course, the proletarian masses, like the taxi-driver "wearing dark green sunglasses which gave the impression of two holes cut out of his face" (24). His rather spontaneous, unquestioning willingness to play his small part as a courier for the movement is indicative of his personal anger and perpetual alienation from the apartheid system. One quickly understands and accepts the basis of his personal rebellion when, en route to Tommy's flat, he relates to Beukes the incident of his goose, who had worked in a certain factory for twelve years, and now has to "give up her place as a supervisor of the conveyor belt to some white bitch to take over" (25). Such a story becomes a symbolic image of human abuse and misuse; it also convinces the reader of the moral premises on which the new movement for change in South Africa is based. The taxi-driver's statement and the tone by which it is conveyed is in keeping with the logic of La Guma's developing theme.

It should have been established in the foregoing discussion that the images that convey theme cohere, inevitably, in the portraits of individual characters. And, undoubtedly, one of the most precise and thorough theme/images comes through the perception of Beukes, as he considers the present status of the underground movement using the sport of boxing as a metaphor:

> The movement writhed under the terror, bleeding. It had not been defeated, but it had been beaten down. It crouched like a slugged boxer, shaking his spinning head to clear it, while he took the count, waiting to rise befor the final ten. Life still throbbed in its aching arms and fingers; wholesale arrests had battered it. The leaders and the cadres filled the

prisons or retreated into exile. Behind them, all over the country, tiny groups and individuals who had escaped the net still moved like moles underground, trying to link up in the darkness of lost communications, and broken contacts. Some of them knew each other and wrestled to patch up the body. They burrowed underground, changing their nests and their lairs frequently. Those who were known to the police walked in fear, shaken, hoping that they might be able to disappear before the police decided that their time had come. Little by little the raw nerve fibers and tired muscles of the movement established shaky communication with centres abroad. (48-49)

This metaphor aptly summarizes the relentless determination of the fighters. It is, therefore, through the thought, the interior monologue of Beukes that the positive message of the book is summed up. La Guma doesn't simply note an analogy but enlarges on it in careful detail. The image elucidates one of the dominant themes of the work; that is, what it takes to prepare and convince the entire people for armed struggle.

Using the sport of boxing as a metaphor for the political combatants in South Africa is thematically and structurally effective. Structurally, it follows the pattern of events (the plot), the successes and setbacks of the underground movement, thereby fulfilling synchronically what characterizes the diachronic pattern as a whole. La Guma sees the analogy and translates it into an image of compelling interest. Such awareness of analogies and equivalencies is at the root of aesthetic enjoyment. Thematically, the analogy conveys the vicissitudes of the human experience and capsulizes the major theme of the novel through the thoughts of just one character. The logical outcome, however, of the theme is that there are alternative responses to the same political and social reality.

As such, La Guma illustrates some of the specific attitudes and actions of those who acquiesce and work for the oppressive system—Beatie Adams, Authur Bennett, Tommy, Red Braces, on the one hand; and those who resist and oppose the system, like Beukes, Tekwane, and Isaac on the other. And, in each case, the character is individualized by the particularity of their response to this common reality.

The preparation being made by Isaac, for example, is on yet another level from that of Beukes and Tekwane. Beukes and

Tekwane are primarily concerned with the mental preparation of the masses; Isaac, however, is strictly preoccupied with military preparations. Every nuance of his environment is permeated with military imagery. While walking through the area of the secretarial typing-pool in the American firm where he is a "messenger boy," he thinks of being "ambushed by the telephonist," (110) and "The chatter of typewriters met him like rifle fire" (111). And a few minutes later, "He drew a rifle on the soiled sheet of paper before him, while he sipped his tea...(he) added a long magazine and a forward grip to the rifle and turned it into a submachine gun" (115). Isaac's whole world is charged with images of warfare and modern weapons, "the clattering of typewriters died away like the observance of a cease-fire" (115) and before long, he had "completed a whole array of weapons, some of it improbable, on the sheet of paper before him...he scored out a weapon which looked like a cross between an old-time blunderbuss and a ray-gun" (117).

Isaac's "preparation" seems to be indicative of an awareness, by him and the underground movement, of the systematic militarization of South African fascism, and the fact that, today, the Republic possesses a strike potential in terms of arms, military equipment, and men which far exceeds the combined strength of all the independent African states south of the Sahara. The task of preparing the people mentally is arduous enough and, when added to that of the military preparation, it is easy to see how Isaac and the others must constantly try to steer a middle course between hope and despair. The task is awesome:

> Far overhead a jet fighter whined, leaving vapour trails in its wake like white scars on the blue skin of the sky. Isaac looked up and watched the plane disappear. They are very strong, he thought. Mirage fighters from France—how long would it take to defeat them. (118)

La Guma, in using the simile of "a jet fighter...leaving vapour trails...like white scars on the blue skin of the sky," gives this image a sensuous, almost tangible quality; whereas, the idea imbued in the image serves to substantiate the fact that behind the forces of South Africa's military machine stands the might of the western imperialist powers: France, Great Britain, West Germany, Japan, and America. The image also indicates that Isaac, and his cadre, know what they are up against, that they are neither romantic, ide-alistic, nor naive. Isaac, Beukes, and Elias realize that with "the whole organization of the authoritarian state ranged against you" (23), they must become as well-prepared as the enemy. Such prepa-ration, the image of Isaac and the images created by Isaac suggest, must be not just theoretical and mental, but also practical and mili-taristic.

Consequently, Isaac had taken it upon himself to educate him-self about regular and irregular military warfare:

> He had read history books and the smuggled handbooks on
> guerilla fighting, he had examined pictures and drawings
> of small arms of every sort. Theoretically he knew much
> about Magnums, and about Uzi submachine guns manu-
> factured in Israel. (119)

In addition, he knew about the small arms made in South Africa "the 7.62 mm RI automatic rifles, an improved version of the FN standard NATO rifle and produced under license from the Fabrique Nationale of Belgium" (119). And he knew about "guns which could fire a thousand rounds a minute...about link-belt feeding, 82 mm mortars, grenade launchers and bazookas" (119).

From this perspective, familiarity with military hardware, Isaac can be considered a step ahead of Beukes, who, in addition to his essentially intellectual role, seems to be always nostalgic for the "good old days" of speeches and rallies and is in constant doubt, even as to the efficiency and outcome of their theoretical, leafleting efforts, thinking at one point that those given leaflets to distribute would dump them in the nearest sewer. Isaac, on the other hand, "longed like a lover for the time when he would be able to turn from theory to practice" (119). Isaac's confidence, his "cockiness" rests on the assurance that he is preparing for war, and not more leafleting.

La Guma, it should be noted, stresses the collective responsibil-ity of this characters. Isaac is not an isolated individual whose acts would affect him alone. He cannot afford to act spontaneously or irresponsibly. Rather, he must wait for the collective decision of the underground movement before "he would be able to turn from theory to practice." Even though Isaac is, or certainly thinks he is, ready militarily, La Guma skillfully and thoughtfully places the emphasis on the collectivity and the wise leadership the movement is expected to exhibit. Isaac accepts this, that he must act in concert with the underground movement, that he cannot and should not attempt to legitimize his own, private interests at the expense of the whole. Without such an ideology the movement would soon collapse. Isaac, like La Guma himself, realizes that no movement can function without ideological legitimization, that when one acts, it must not be for one's self; thus, like a lover, one must wait for the right time.

In a similar way, most of La Guma's characters are simply and artistically portrayed. La Guma does not judge them. He does not hover over their destinies; they all appear to exercise free choice in the decisions they make, so that what they do seems psychologically necessary. Even though an individual character's notion of the prerequisites for change and the role he or she should, or might, play in an armed struggle, in the La Gumian sense, is somewhat illusory: illusory, because history and the given South African sociopolitical reality often predisposes individuals to act in certain predictable ways; predictable because La Guma creates the impression, which is the quintessence of realism, that somehow the characters are telling their own stories, are responding to their environment in ways consistent with their intellectual, social (class), and ethnic physiognomies, without conspicuous and laden authorial intrusion, except as an occasional commentator.

Beatie Adams, Authur and Nelly Bennett, the Taxi driver, Elias Tekwane, Tommy, Isaac, Beukes, Frances, Henny April—the major characters in *In the Fog of the Seasons' End*, each have a life of her or his own, often behaving quite differently from the way the author, La Guma, a committed revolutionary, would want. Their responses to the very same reality range from naivete, vacillation, and apathy to superficial, mediocre, and total commitment; while the life and death of Elias Tekwane remains the ultimate standard against which they are all measured: "Greater love has no man than this, that he lay down his life for a friend" (Bible).

There are, for instance, some significant differences in the backgrounds of Beukes and Tekwane that condition their responses in unique but predictable ways. Beukes, as suggested earlier, tends to look backward to the old politics of demonstrations and speeches and strikes against the pass laws, protests against the rise in bus fares, speeches against racist tyranny and for freeing political leaders: "He remembered the rallies, the blaring loudspeakers, the banners sagging between their poles, the applause" (56). Even his memories of his childhood differ from those of Tekwane, for example, and further delineate the more "intellectual" (as opposed to militaristic) role that Beukes performs for the underground movement. He remembers trips to the circus, albeit in segregated seats, and attending "a school for Coloureds...The monotonous chanting of multiplication tables...the years of primary readers, the fables of Aesop, the Cruel Queen and long division, the rehearsal for the annual concert" (83).

Elias Tekwane, an African (as the name implies) only went to classes at the mission down the track from his village "when he was not driving the family's two cows out to graze" (72). Whereas Beukes, a Colored, remembers:

> Once upon a time he had worn a little blue cap and had carried a slate in one hand while his father had held the other, escorting him into the grounds of the] school, red brick and tiled roof, on the hillside above the city. There had been many windows and they made the school look vast. (83)

Tekwane, the African, remembers going to school in a "little corrugated iron classroom," and the only books available for him to read were "an upset pile of damp and mouldy books" he found in an abandoned stable behind Wasserman's dry-goods shop where he used to work sweeping floors and running errands. There was no "little blue cap" or Dad to walk him to school; his father had been killed in a mining accident near Johannesburg (76). The mine had awarded his mother two pounds a month for the rest of their lives (74). Tekwane remembers, not the circus or trips to the City Hall to listen to the municipal orchestra, but the train as it went whistling past their village and the "packets of half-eaten food tossed out to the shrieking children...partly-bitten sandwiches, broken biscuits, some chicken bones with a little meat left on them sticky with jam from crumble cakes, burst oranges and chipped candy" (74).

Such meticulous character delineation is the author's skill. La Guma, by relating these images of character background, individualizes their character and personality. At the same time, the iconography as a whole exposes social realities that are characteristic of South African society. For example, the mining accident that killed Tekwane's father underscores one of the most common tragedies of South African labor relationships. It is not unique, but part of a social tragedy that many more, like Tekwane, have to contend with. For not only are white miners paid more than African miners; but, in a rather ironic way, the scene gives rise to the illogic Bantustan fraud. That is, where once Africans had been driven from their land to labor in the mines and factories owned by Europeans, now the white supremacist, capitalist system is driving them from such labor back again to the land; like the old man Mdlaka, Elias Tekwane remembers, who is considered to be "no longer of value in the big city...(and) had been dumped...like broken and useless machinery" (155).

For Tekwane, the death of his father meant, among other things, that: "He and his mother lived on the anemic ears of corn which the land yielded, on a sinewy chicken now and then, on the remains of meals begged in the town and on the kindness of the village community" (79). The author does not dwell on the iconography of Tekwane's father's death, but simply uses it as further background in delineating the relative stances each character assumes while confronting a common problem—the international myth of white superiority. This is in keeping with what seems to be one of La Guma's primary aims—to wit, to dramatize, through poignant imagery, the evils of racism, and then examine the manner in which this aim is sustained in individual characterizations.

In *In the Fog of the Seasons' End*, much more so than in the earlier novels, La Guma seeks to describe and differentiate the cancerous scope of racism in South African life and the varied levels of response each individual character is capable of; indeed, there is, throughout the novel, an echo of the Marxiang dictum, "From each according to his ability." As such, the background and childhood experiences, even the casual references to clothing of the characters, reveal something of their social status, identity, and perspective on the meaning of struggle in South Africa. So, while Beukes the "Coloured," in conversation with Tommy, can make references to "Dorsey playing Rimsky-Korsakov's 'Song of India'...Caruso...Schhwartzkopf or Victoria De Los Angeles" (56-57); Elias Tekwane has memories of the humiliation of having to let down his pants at the insistence of the Native Commissioner and his black lackey, Red-braces, in order to prove his age so that he can get his first Pass.

It is, therefore, not surprising that the African Tekwane's granite-like resolve and commitment to revolution is unshakeable: it is rooted in his personal history, just as Beukes' constant doubt and uncertainty is rooted in his. Rather than dreams of victory, Beukes has nightmares of defeat, in which his pregnant wife, Frances, is disemboweled:

> In the dark he saw Frances and their child. He was glad there was a child, in spite of everything. He remembered the fearful dreams he had while Frances had been pregnant. He had dreamed of Frances pregnant and shot in the belly, or with her abdomen torn open by wild dogs, bayonets, spears: Frances writhing in pain and blood and horror. (135)

The mention of "their child" in this ghastly image should again remind us that children in La Guma's works usually symbolize the future: this novel, for example, closes with an image of "children... gathered in the sunlit yard" (181). Yet, in the heart of the novel, there is this constant, nagging doubt of Beukes: "It's a gamble , he thought. You did this work, taking a chance all the time, hoping the bugger behind you or the one ahead of you would play the game" (50). He doubts if the leaflets will be distributed: "Perhaps one or two would dump their allocations in the nearest sewer and sneak off home with their hearts in their mouths and a sense of relief" (51). He questions directives, wondering if "they bladdy knew what they were doing...His mind was nervous...worrying again... worrying because you're never sure that everybody will do his part...wondering whether they'll do the _____ing job properly" (52).

Beukes is fortified by his relationship with the granite confidence and defiance of Elias Tekwane. He worries, yes, but not to the point of being immobilized. He is further fortified by the organization, the collective history he identifies with, and his own keen intellect. In spite of his misgivings and nagging doubts, he realizes he must risk at least talking to people, that if he worries too much about spies and traitors he would get nothing done; that in strengthening others, like the Asian, Abdullah, he strengthens himself. "Once the workers have seen that they should make a stand," Beukes says to Abdullah, "no silly official is going to get in their way" (96). When Abdullah, the olive-skinned man, is on the edge of despair because the police shoot down people who "only want our rights...to give the order to shoot, just like that," Beukes strengthens him, renews his hope, saying: "It shows that they are becoming incapable of governing any longer. That is why we must press on...That is why every little thing we do helps" (96).

Perhaps by exhibiting such fundamental qualities as doubt, fear, courage, and confidence, Beukes becomes even more real, more believable as a character. He suffers and he is defiant. He, like the other characters, show both individual and class characteristics which distinguish perception, relation, and fulfillment of a major theme of the work: something like "condition determines consciousness."

Class-consciousness is very important to La Guma's own ideological persuasion and is reflected in the interior monologue and behavior of his major character, Beukes. Beukes is constantly concerned about being well-groomed, clean-shaven, and informed. he is easily recognized, and distinguished from the other characters, by his inevitable brown suit, dress-shirt, and tie; "The brown suit was cheap, but not so cheap that it wrinkled permanently, and he wore a lighter brown shirt, the collar gone limp, and a maroon patterned necktie. There was reddish-brown dust from the graveled pathway on his tan brogues" (10). And in most cases he is carrying a newspaper under his arm, reading one or discarding one. This, perhaps, may have something to do with La Guma's journalistic career, and the close physical and ideological affinity of Beukes and the author.

So, when Beukes meets Beatie Adams in the municipal park, "He was holding a parcel wrapped in brown paper on his lap, and a rolled newspaper" (10). Later, when he is leaving Tommy's apartment to deliver the leaflets hidden away in a record-album case, "On the main road he bought a late evening newspaper from a youth with the face of a young wolf and a set of overalls three sizes too large" (62). In fact, the newspaper itself represents a sort of "bourgeois" preoccupation, a symbol of the "informed" vis-`a-vis the "uninformed." Thus, when an argument breaks out on the seg-regated bus Beukes is riding, concerning why Ali was grabbed by the Security Police (because he was a communist or because the government was "just making money out of fines"), an anonymous character shouts, "Man, don't be so blerry stupid, mos man. Don't you read the koerant then?" "What papers?"—the advisory re-plies, giving the former a chance to put on airs, "I don't talk about it here, hey, political stuff. You can't open your jaw too much, according that walls got ears, mos" (70). La Guma's possible in-tent here, and in several other thematically and structurally signifi-cant images—of journalists, and of secretaries and messenger "boys" reading aloud from the morning newspaper in the Ameri-can firm where Isaac works—may be to indicate, by way of the recurrent image, the newspaper as power, as opinion, and as a cru-cial means of information.

Thematically, the newspaper, as an image, provides informa-tion for the members of the underground: on what reactions the government is making toward their leafleting and other political activities; where they're cracking down; who or how many have been arrested or escaped; the most recent police raids. Invariably, however, the newspaper story that is being followed by Beatie Adams, the white secretaries, and the Coloured messenger "boys" in the American firm is the story of the "Bainsburg Murder"; the story of a white, middle-class woman who poisoned her husband, little by little, by putting a tiny bit of white powder containing arsenic in his coffee each day. "Since he took milk, she would put the deadly white powder in the cup first and then pour in the steam-ing coffee" (62). Much later in the novel, we pick-up the thread of this story again when the murderess, becoming impatient with this technique, "Putting her hands on the weakened man's chest, she pushed him and he sat down abruptly on the bed. She drew the cord around his neck and started pulling it with both hands, forc-ing him back to a position sideways on the bed" (115-116).

The sequence of images on the "Bainsburg Murder" reveal yet another side of the author's technique, namely, satire. La Guma was a journalist, master in the art of parody and anecdote, and this skill stands him in good stead when he wants to ridicule a charac-ter by means of physical characteristics or observable behavior.

Therefore, as in his portraiture of African women, it is necessary to interpret this dimension of La Guma's technique in light of the South African socio-economic context and its function in *In the Fog of the Seasons' End*.

The imagery depicting Mrs. Bainsburg, a name and a "criminal method" with clearly white bourgeois trappings, is painfully humorous: as she pushes her weakened husband, forcing him down on a bed, then drawing a cord around his neck and pulls it with both hands until he is sideways on the bed, the scene actually comes to life. The humor comes, not from any perverted knowledge that "whites are killing whites," but from the more obvious realization of how out of character it is for a woman to use such an extreme "masculine" method to kill, as well as from the awkward, clumsy struggle the reader can imagine it takes for her to complete the task. One can see Mrs. Bainsburg, maybe in designer dress or pants, bracing a high-heel adorned foot against the bed, her face grimaced and contorted, gritting her teeth as she pulls the cord choking her husband to death. The reader can imagine all this and more, although it is quite enough for the author to offer the suggestion of the completed image as it appears in the newspaper. A possible interpretation of the image is that when rather "feminine" or "polite" forms of murder are not adequate—that is, if there is resistance—more "masculine" or brutal methods will follow. It certainly confirms that evil is not gender-biased.

Also, the visual aspect of this satirical image, focusing as it does on white society, is used to caricature and exaggerate the moral shortcomings of white South African society. To have one's (group) imperfections magnified and made to symbolize attitudes and behavior which another community finds repulsive can be very painful, especially if one's psychic defenses are weak, as white South Africa's psychic defenses surely are.

In addition, such visual, imagistic forms of satire admittedly employ caricature, and are intentionally malicious. The malice, however, is not a moral fault, but a kind of civic virtue; since satire serves society by acting as a check on the excesses and misapplication of power and the erroneous notion of cultural or racial superiority. It is fitting, therefore, that La Guma should develop a visual formula, like the newspaper cartoonist he once was, to portray a white middle-class South African murderess; a formula which quickly identifies a personality, physically, and also endows her with traits such as cruelty, vindictiveness and courage, if not madness.

Then, when Isaac is thinking about the Bainsburg Murder, he puts the event in the context of the general South African milieu:

> Now, sitting there in the hot, steamy kitchen, he thought that all this kow-towing to stupid idiots who cherished the idea that they were God's chosen just because they had white skins, had to come to an end. The silly bastards, he thought, they had been stupefied into supporting a system which had to bust one day and take them all down with it; instead of permanent security and justice, they had chosen to preserve a tyranny that could only feed them temporarily on the crumbs of power and privilege. Now that the writing had started to appear on the wall, they either scrambled to shore it up with blood and bullets and the electric torture apparatus or hid their head in the sand and pretended that nothing was happening. They would have to pay for their stupidity the hard way. Isaac felt almost sorry for these people who believed themselves to be the Master Race, to have the monopoly of brains, yet who were vindictive, selfish and cruel. (114-115)

Isaac's thoughts are, *inter alia*, in response to the routine he must personally endure as a messenger and handyman in the office of an American petroleum company where African workers must "kow-tow" to the white employees and are treated as "boys" in the worst sense of the word. The white women in the typing pool constantly harass and belittle them, asking them for tea, muffins, a little more sugar for the tea, aspirin, or anything that comes to mind. "The 'boys' were only noticeable," La Guma writes, "when an order had to be given or when a favor was required, otherwise they were part of the furniture, like the grey typewriter covers, the coat rack, the tin bottles of liquid eraser, copies of memos" (113).

It is most appropriate and effective that La Guma contrast this image of assumed superiority with the tragic-comic figure of the murderess, Mrs. Bainsburg, especially when we remember that the social purpose of satire is to ridicule people and institutions so that they change. It is aggressive in intent. It makes fun of its object, bitter and derisive fun. But although laughter is involved, the purpose is quite serious, serving to puncture the inflated ego, to cut the "mighty" down to size, to dramatize the gap between official rhetoric/propaganda and actual performance. Just as humor plays an important role in the psychological health of the individual, satire is vital for the healthy functioning of society. And if a society as a whole cannot accept satirical comment and criticism, then its institutions and customs are fragile indeed: "feeding them temporarily on the crumbs of power and privilege." Satire can only thrive in a society where there is freedom from political or social repression.

La Guma's satire falls on the "just" and the "unjust." Tommy, for example, an otherwise "just" individual, is also a target for La Guma's sardonic imagery. He too is a caricature, an exaggerated type. And Beukes' relationship with him is instructive. This ordinary, commonplace relationship is not, however, just thrown in for good measure. Rather, it appears to be further presentation of the problem of preparing and convincing the people; some, who, like Tommy, are either demoralized or brutalized and have insulated themselves in their own little world. He represents a type and an attitude that can be more difficult to deal with than those who are still questioning and seeking answers and direction. Tommy, as La Guma depicts him, has found his answer, but one which is widespread among the working population, in varying degrees, wherever capitalist exploitation and racial oppression exist:

> ...Tommy had substituted the workshop of dance-music for religion. The radiogram stood like an altar in the gloom and the wafers of stacked records waited for communication with the faithful. He'll never grow up, Beukes thought; the bloody clown's mental development must have stopped in his teens. (48)

Tommy, for his part, thinks Beukes is crazy for worrying about governments and speeches "instead of enjoying life." And whatever he does to help Beukes is because of his personal friendship and respect for him, and has nothing to do with any larger issues:

> For Tommy reality, life, could be shut out by the blare of dance-bands and the voices of crooners. From this cocoon he emerged only to find the means of subsistence, food

and drink. Politics meant nothing to him. He found it easier
to live under the regime than to oppose it. (53)

Tommy's self-depreciation is another characteristic of the oppressed,
which comes from their having internalized the opinion their oppressors hold of them. Tommy, and those whom his image represents, have heard so often that they are good for nothing—except,
perhaps, dancing and playing one sport or another—that they know
nothing and are incapable of learning anything; that they are sick,
lazy, unproductive, and happy-go-lucky; so that in the end they become convinced of their own unfitness and so-called inferiority.
As such, the images of Tommy are not invariably humorous or
ironic, but involve metaphors depicting moods and emotions that
are also serious and filled with pathos.

Dealing with perspectives and attitudes like those of Tommy is
a major political problem, and the way Beukes handles Tommy
shows that he understands this. Tommy's life-style and outlook are
objectionable to Beukes, but he does not alienate him or adopt an
"holier than thou" attitude. He does not make an enemy of Tommy,
but manages to get his assistance in performance of certain small
tasks—"From each according to his ability." For example, Tommy
procures for Beukes a package of handbills to be distributed throughout the city—not out of any political conviction, but because he is a
friend. He says to Beukes:

> Ou Buke, I don't mos mind doing stuff and things for you
> now and then, but I don't want to get into trouble, hey. I
> mean likely, I do it because you an ol' pal of mine, not for
> politics and stuff. (55)

Such a relationship, by its very nature, is unstable and dangerous
in the context of the tasks to be performed. Beukes, as indicated
through his own interior monologue, understands this:

> You had to make do with the material you found at hand.
> Nowadays you could hardly pick and choose; you could
> not be too fussy. It was like a bride unable to afford the
> expensive gown seen in a glossy magazine: she had to make
> do with a copy. (48)

La Guma, in this way, takes a personal relationship, anchors it firmly in the social and political context of South Africa of the 1960s, yet, never loses sight of the aesthetic demands of his medium: by reasoned and careful use of analogy and simile to heighten the artistic effect.

The relationship between Beukes and Tommy, therefore, gives rise to another major theme of *In the Fog of the Seasons' End*: self cannot liberate self, but neither is self liberated by others; obviously, self can only need "liberating" in relation to another or others. Jean-Paul Sartre, in the Preface to Fanon's *The Wretched of the Earth*, puts the matter this way:

> ...when one day our human kind becomes full-grown, it will not define itself as the sum total of the whole world's inhabitants, but as the infinite unity of their mutual needs. (22)

Deconstructing, to some extent, Beukes and Tommy suggests that the meaning and significance of their relationship is related to broader social and political issues about which the work is ultimately concerned. Such delineation of characters further indicates that, under conditions of extreme repression, only the best emerge to lead the movement and can see through "the fog of the seasons' end."

One final example—the school teacher, Flotman—will serve to illustrate how La Guma has selected diverse, yet typical characters to represent both psychological and sociological types. That is, their intellectual and behavioral responses to the same environment is conditioned by their individuality, racial identity, and class. Just as Beukes, Tekwane, Isaac, and Tommy represent both specific and general human qualities, so does Flotman. He too is distinguished by his thought and observed action. When he says, "I'm scared...I don't want to go to jail and eat pap and lose my stupid job or get bashed up by the law," he is giving us, through his inward life, simply and directly the keys to his character. All of Flotman's later actions, or lack of them, are derived from these two principles of "fear" and "self-preservation."

Even though his is one of the lesser characters in the novel, La Guma provides brief descriptive passages of Flotman's attitudes, prejudices, morals, and preferences. In addition to his fear, and all that that implies, Flotman fully realizes that he has a "stupid job" as a teacher who must teach what he does not believe:

...to teach that everything that happens is ordained by God and that it's no use, even sinful, trying to change the order of things. The Boer War was a sort of holy crusade, evolution is heresy and nobody existed in this country before Jan Van Riebeck arrived. In our segregated, so-called universities, modern psychology is a cardinal sin. (86)

"Befogging the mind," Beukes responded, "It helps them. Unfortunately, our teachers have to participate in this indoctrination" (86). Beukes and Flotman mock and rebuke the revisionists' interpretation that the oppressed condition of Africans, in South Africa and the world, is somehow ordained by God. That Europeans must keep oppressing or ruling Africans and other people of color until they learn "Civilization," until they learn "Democracy." And since, if I understand it correctly, people who call themselves "White" are a minority in the world, the ruling logic and practice is itself undemocratic.

There is no question in Flotman's mind about integrating into this educational system or reforming it: "that," he says, "is like banging your head against a wall" (86). And he intensely questions himself: "Why do I stay? I could be teaching in Canada" (87). Yet he stays. While hundreds of other teachers have gone overseas in the last few years, he stays on. Flotman, to be sure, does not share the same political commitment or analysis as Beukes; but, more like Tommy, assists Beukes out of personal motives "to ease (his) conscience" (87). Unlike Tommy, however, Flotman understands and willingly accepts the broader implications of his involvement: "If I can't teach history to my young students," he says to Beukes, "at least I can get them to help make it in some small way" (87). Because some of his young students are inclined to be rather romantic about revolution, Flotman's consciousness is strengthened and noticeably elevated by the valuable dialogue and example of Beukes and the other "revolutionaries" until, by the time Beukes is about to leave his home, Flotman can say to him:

> "We bloody teachers need to help. We have talked about the revolution among ourselves too long. All very intellectual." (90)

Flotman, it would appear, has come to realize that the oppressed must be their own example in the struggle for their liberation: that he is no longer merely the one who teaches, but one who is himself taught in dialogue and by the example of others, and who in turn while being taught should also teach in both word and deed. Flotman's rhetoric, however, presupposes action, and if Beukes' behavior, as he walks slowly away from Flotman's house, is any indication ("he turned back towards the house, feeling a little sad") the content of Flotman's comments must also be viewed as another way for him to "ease his conscience."

Such a scene is an important socio-political event; it reveals a particular level of commitment, a contrasting attitude with patterns of juxtaposition and antithesis that serve to distinguish and illuminate all the major characters. Such individuation of character creates the appearance of perpetual movement involving a variety of action, people, moods, and thought—a rich variety of types and of life. Beukes' encounter with Flotman is important in advancing the action and adding something to the theme and characterization of the major participants. Because of Flotman we think of Tommy at one extreme, and Elias Tekwane at the other—with Flotman, floating like flotsam somewhere between these diametrically opposing levels of commitment.

It is precisely because of the unique portraits, especially the mental attitude of Tekwane, Beukes, Isaac, Tommy, Red-Braces, and Flotman, that we become acquainted with them as we would become acquainted with real people whom we meet for the first time and about whom our knowledge and understanding increases as our intimacy increases over time and exposure to La Guma's characters and their environment.

At the risk of being redundant, it needs to be repeated that there are no overtly psychopathic cases in La Guma's writings—no erotica, no homosexuality, no pornography, no obscure esoteric existentialist search for personal identity or Karma, no slap-stick Negro comedy. rather, there are common, ordinary people living and dying—meaninglessly and nobly—in one of the most oppressive systems in the annals of history, and certainly the most overtly racist and oppressive in the modern world. The effect of this oppression take their toll in the mental, emotional, and spiritual well-being of the peoples of South Africa, but, even more noticeably, in the physical environment itself.

It is, in fact, in the quality of the imagery of the setting or physical environment rather than in its frequency that *In the Fog of the*

Seasons' End marks very real progress and shows Alex La Guma at the peak of his image-making power. Here the images are remarkably wide in range and varied in tone. The earlier works formed a closed stylistic universe, and the imagery in each was fairly homogeneous, although it differed greatly from one book to another. Here we have a multiplicity of styles and corresponding diversity of images within one novel. In a matter of three pages, for instance, there are the following radically contrasting images of residential patterns:

> At the foot of the main street traffic splashed in from the seafront suburbs and purled away among the mixture of Victorian and modern buildings of the city centre, then retreated again in all directions, back towards Sea Point, Camps Bay, or inland. (23)

And then Beukes, en route to Tommy's apartment,

> ...left the waterfront, climbed a fly-over bridge and entered a cramped, oily district full of factories, warehouses and garages...into the back of the slum area. The sector had the look of a town cleared after battle. Whole blocks had disappeared, leaving empty, flattened lots surrounded by battered survivors. (26)

The extraordinary impact and density of these passages is due to the structure of the image-pattern. By opposing, diametrically, the opulence of the "white" city-center and the suburb with the slum area (reserved, temporarily, for Africans) La Guma unobtrusively exposes the unnatural and dehumanizing relationship between whites and people of color in South Africa. And to further twist the knife, the "whole blocks (that) had disappeared" represent areas, like District Six, which are to be remodeled for white occupancy.

Again, La Guma's descriptions include both the object of his perception and the feelings connecting him with the object; that is, both the objective facts and the tone of the experience. The latter image, for example, calls forth military analogies, "The sector had the look of a town cleared after battle...leaving...battered survivors." The picture is not just one of slum conditions but of "military" combatants, which is consistent with one of the major themes of the work—again, something like "condition determines consciousness"—whereas, the earlier city-center image seems to compel the author to even more pretentious, artificially genteel images as he conveys the sight and feeling of auto traffic that "purled away among the mixture of Victorian and modern buildings."

The contrasting environments are not merely objects of perception alone, but images, iconography in the context of an experience; therefore, an image with meaning and part of a relationship; an emotional and psychic relationship that accompanies the author's and the reader's perception, whether the images are viewed separately or together. It is by way of metaphor that La Guma establishes an affinity between these two concrete realities. It is clear, and important to the theoretical premise of *In the Fog of the Seasons' End*, that such image patterns are deliberate—and indeed, patterns, and not just random assemblages of word pictures. Perhaps another example will serve to verify this premise.

While Beukes is in the city centre to make contact with the Taxi-driver, he observes, at a hotel, "the clink of glasses...(and) soft music from the dim futuristic cocktail lounge...the tourist bureau (where) a sleek, streamlined coach was taking on a line of White passengers in front of the gay posters of lions, golf courses and sunny beaches" (24). And this image stands in stark contrast to one a couple of pages later, where "A pile of banana crates stood against a wall with a scabby sign that said 'Bombay Fruit Produce', and two children in ragged clothes searched the gutters" (26).

The principle that organizes this image is a concord between image and theme—in this case, images of the environment, lighting the way for the theme and helping to reveal it. That is, to prepare and convince the entire people of the absolute necessity for revolutionary change, it is necessary to objectify the dialectical relationship that exists between European and African environments; for the actions of all the characters, especially Tekwane, Beukes, and Isaac, evolve from this environment and its implications.

The range of imagery in this work also embraces the rural environment. Here La Guma indulges his nostalgia, not in any escapist sense, but, it seems, to give some pictorial sense of more tranquil and harmonious times as enjoyed by the rural populations of South Africa on the precipice of change. For he seems intent on demonstrating, in a series of images, the ubiquitous tentacles of white penetration even into this environment and its effects.

Thus, in a lengthy flashback involving the childhood of Elias Tekwane, Elias remembers "driving the family's two cows out to graze on the scrubby hillside behind their house" (72). He also remembers the spring ploughing season when: the sun began to rise early and the yellow light lay on the land like a bright, wrinkled sheet in the mornings. The sounds of life emerged with the early sunlight: the shrilling of the wheels of the ox-drawn ploughs, the pop of a whip, bird songs and the songs of children, the hallooing of many voices. (72) The narrator seems haunted by a deep feeling of nostalgia, of love for a way of life and an environment that was satisfying and worthwhile, but also a "scrubby hillside" in need of development. Yet the mere thought of his rural home compels Tekwane to poetic imagery:

> When the sun set in that part of the country, the sky in the west turned yellow and orange and green, and the straggling clouds hung lie tattered tinsel from the rafters of the sky. The houses of the village lay on the hillsides like discarded toys on a rumpled carpet of brown ochre. The scene looked as pretty as a postcard to any newcomer or passer-by. (73)

This is, of course, before the labor-recruiting teams came into the area to contract workers to work on white farms and in factories to support the rise of white capital in general and the war effort against Germany in particular. The changes in Africans' relationship to their land had begun long before this, and the objective evidence for this is all around Tekwane. Even now the railway lines reach into their rural village and the children walk through the now "crumbling and eroded land" and gather at the railway lines to wait for the trains, and the half-eaten food that would be tossed out to them. The hillside, once "pretty as a postcard," is soon described as one that "looked like the thin form of a starving girl covered by a thin blanket: you could make out the shape of the insignificant breasts, the meagre belly and the bony knees" (73-74). It is therefore with mixed emotions that Tekwane reminisces about,

> ...the open air of the countryside, the stillness and the songs of the birds also hid the destitution. The food from the fields was beginning to run out, then would come the col-

lection of weeds, if the weather had not dried them up: they would also serve for food. Then came the interminable debts with the White shopkeeper. There was ignorance in the countryside too; in that part of the land one did not see any meetings like the ones which were held in the city. In the cities it was not easy to avoid the movement. The people stirred under the weight of tyranny, then went to meetings in the squares, the halls, houses, to listen to the speakers. (132)

The narrator intrudes here, omnisciently and effectively, to further elucidate Tekwane's ambivbalent but necessary attitude toward the countryside:

Elias had not returned to the countryside after that. He felt that the brown eroded land, the little dwellings on the scrubby hillside held little for him. Besides, his blood had dripped onto the hard grey surface of a city sidewalk, and it was as if it had taken root and held him there. (132-133)

These intellectual images of the thought and attitude of Elias are tightly interwoven with the imagery of the physical, rural environment and, at the same time, move parallel with the major theme of the novel. In other words, Elias' physical movement, from rural to urban, is parallel with the intellectual movement and growth he must experience and the ideological growth of the underground movement. His is an example of "peasant consciousness" benefiting from the now relatively sophisticated urban intellectuals (Ndebele 1994:26).

Elias delights in juggling with the terms and concepts of socio-economic and political theory, and these find their way into his imagery. He juxtaposes the beauty and potential of the rural environment, "the open air...the stillness...the songs of birds" with the "destitution" and political "ignorance" of its population. He then elaborates the comparison to include the exploitation of the White shopkeepers in the countryside and the economic and political tyranny of the urban mulieu. In each instance, though articulated not in political rhetoric but rather in a literary way, Tekwane is expressing one of the basic tensions in contemporary African society: tensions concerning the relative roles of the city and the rural area in determining the relationship of individuals to the society. The tensions between the urban and rural sectors do not stem from the geographical distinction alone. Rather, they are the result of the realization, as Tekwane is clearly aware, that the two situations call for radically different bases of operation in the particular environment. In some sense, this gets at Ndbele's concern with the "disturbing silence in South African literature as far as the peasants, as subjects of artistic attention" (24). Having attended meetings and listened to speakers, having begun to read more and discuss more, Elias has become politically conscious and can no longer accept what is now, to him, an inert, static existence, "the brown eroded land, the little dwellings on the scrubby hillside held little for him" (*In the Fog*, 132).

The pattern established by these examples is that of concurrent images. That is, images of the rural and urban environment that compel the reader to watch their parallel progress while relating them all the time to a common theme. That theme, in this case, is poignantly expressed by Njabulo S. Ndebele as "an attempt at a sincere imaginative perception that sees South African peasant life as having a certain human validity, albeit a problematic one" (1994:26). Rural (like urban) imagery is decisive in determining Tekwane's attitude towards the two environments and his conduct: the role he will play in the liberation movement at this precise historical moment. Ndebele's concerns and queries are especially germane here:

> ...the perception appears to have consolidated within the ranks of the liberation struggle that the decisive element in determining the course of the coming South African future is the workers in the cities. That might be so, and is theoretically understandable. But what of the millions of Africans in the rural areas who, at that very decisive moment, might decide the fate of the hinterland? What of the deliberate peasantisation of urban Africans by the government through Bantustans? The peasant position within the economic and political structures that govern the organic relationship between the urban and rural social formations might be theoretically understandable. But the peasant's actual aspirations, it seems, are a matter that ought not to be taken for granted. (26)

Elias Tekwane, by going to the city, has come to know that what had been was not necessarily what had to be. He sees life in a different light in the city. He rejects—and has to reject—the idea that the rural order is the only order possible. Yet he is grateful for what it does teach in the way of peace and reciprocity and harmony. But because of "the meetings in the squares, halls, houses" and listening to speakers, he joins the movement to change the conditions of African people, rural and urban.

Images of rural and urban life provide the symbols and analogies through which the various phases of Elias' development can be most tellingly expressed. Through Elias' interior life and calculated movement, he evokes a sense of the contradictions within each environment and between each environment—contradictions of class and race—that are presented in images that are precise differentiated, and carefully worked out.

La Guma's use of one of the great and abiding themes of African literature today, the rural/urban contradiction, links up with another equally important theme, and that is the theme of Time:

> To every thing there is a season, and a time to every purpose under the heaven: A time to be born, and a time to die; a time to plant, and a time to pluck up that which is planted; A time to kill, and a time to heal; a time to break down, and a time to build up;... A time to love, and a time to hate; a time of war, and a time of peace. (Ecclesiastes 3:1-8)

The white police know what time it is, and one of them says to Elias "We are at war, and your life really means nothing to us" (174). The leaders of the underground liberation movement also know what time it is; that it is "a time to break down...a time of war"; that it is time for many millions of Tekwanes to move from the countryside to the city; for millions to remain in the hinterland. It is time for radical, fundamental, revolutionary change. As Beukes reflects, "time had become static and the earth lived through a night without change" and nature itself revealed the inertia of the moment: "the thin greyness towards the east remained inscrutable, chill and mocking and insipid as over-watered gruel" (*In the Fog*, 97). This foreboding atmosphere "speaks" to Beukes, and the

events that follow on the morning of the "big strike" convince him
even more of the necessity for revolutionary action:

> ...the people new Time, and in the Township lamps flickered
> into life like fairy lights. Here and there the lights came on
> behind shabby curtains, behind cardboard patches in the
> windows, a length of sacking holding out the cold, and old
> coat stuffed into a hole. The sky weighed down on the
> Township, dark and oppressive, but gradually the night
> surrendered and the dawn crawled in behind a thin mist
> like the smoke of war. (97)

The title, *In the Fog of the Seasons' End*, could easily have come
from this image; as it, metaphorically, speaks of the night of oppression for African people inevitably surrendering to the dawn of
freedom. More specifically, the image relates to the morning the
whole black population of the country had been called on to the
defy the country's law on the carrying of pass-books. Thus, in
addition to the images of the contrasting opulence and poverty of
the city-center, the white wealth and black poverty of the city and
countryside, La Guma adds the image of The Township: youths in
ragged clothes, threadbare shoes, a child sleeping on the floor
"dreaming that she did not have to go to the little one-room school
where she had to sit on the floor all day" (98). This section of the
novel, although set apart from the plot, as an autonomous piece,
where the voice of the omniscient narrator assumes a more dynamic role with a surreal, ethereal tone complementing the events
it describes. The characters in Chapter Nine are, for example, identified not by name, but as The Washerwoman, The Bicycle Messenger, The Child, and the Outlaw—that is, by function or type—
and in this way The Township becomes a "universal" symbol of
African oppression and aspirations (97-105). In this way, the idea
of oppression is both implicit and explicit in the image-type depicted. And aspirations are expressed in the courageous and united
action taken this particular day when the people surrender and destroy their passes.

There were elderly people, and children who had boycotted the
schools that day; workers who had stayed away from the Steel
Town, to show that they were tired of regimentation and chattels,

of bullying police and arrogant foremen, of fines and taxes and having too little money with which to buy food. There were women, singing and swaying in the shade of umbrellas, and young girls giggling under the eyes of youths who strutted in black berets, patched trousers and ragged shirts. (102)

If Alex La Guma were painting a tree, he would undoubtedly show the dirty bark and the yellow leaves. For the artist is not only objective, but must also show that "bullying police and arrogant foremen" and youths in "patched trousers and ragged shirts" are part of the physical as well as moral landscape and that evil minds are as inherent in life as noble ones.

Every element in the above picture of The Township is constructive and informative: elderly people, children, students, workers, managers, and police—all embroidering the theme and expressing an emotion. La Guma has no need to falsify to make romantic, or to sentimentalize to make beautiful. Hence, the images of The Township are related, structurally and thematically, to those of the city-center and to those of the countryside, and even to the Coloured residential area with its "rows of single-story council cottages— all representing a dominant interrelated movement to a supreme conclusion: the entire people must be prepared and convinced it is time for war. Elias Tekwane best expresses such a conclusion as he discusses with Beukes the success of the strategy of mass rallies and demonstrations, a strategy that has outlived its usefulness:

> ...Man, it is becoming quite clear that the Government will not allow the people to organize as before. Yes, they cannot proceed with their plans while allowing the people to prepare to resist. So they will have to outlaw us. Our problem, friends, is going to be that we will have very few people not already known to the police. Mass activity has meant that we have had to expose our cadres. It cannot be helped, because by activity the people's understanding develops. (139)

In other words, the objectively squalid and dehumanizing conditions African people are forced to live in (whether rural or urban), the insulting Pass-Laws, the ubiquitous bullying police, the arrogant foremen, the lack of money or clothing, give rise to the mass demonstrations like that in The Township. The results of this demonstration, narrated with brilliant touches of realism and metaphor, reveal a unity and complementariness between the environment, the people in this environment, and the artist's feelings. Thus, on the day of the strike,

> "There were protests, laughter, mild admonitions...Then for some reason or another, a policeman shot into the noise...Then all the police began to fire, a ragged volley at first...The firing burst out again like a roll of metal-skinned drums," and the result is a massacre (104).
>
> In the open field, in the dusty alleyways where they had tried to flee, the dead and the dying now lay like driftwood.
>
> ...Among the dead was The Washerwoman. She had been shot low down while running away—the femoral arteries in the comfortable thighs had been torn through, so she bled quickly to death, lying heaped on top of her collapsed sunshade by the runningboard of a parked car.
>
> The Child lay on her face and there seemed hardly a mark on her, except when she was turned over and they saw the exit hole the heavy lug made in the meagre chest....
>
> ...The Outlaw...took some time to die...his life bubbling and frothing away through his mouth and nose and the neat line of holes punched through his back and lungs by most of the clip of a sten-gun.
>
> The Bicycle Messenger had died instantly...his flesh burst open, his spine shattered and his splintered ribs thrust into heart and lungs. (104-105)

La Guma certainly has the right idea; for his objective, in this image sequence, seems not so much to give us the means of specific individuals or the date of this particular occurrence, as to tell us of the conditions of humanity in our time. And so the various details in this Township—it too remains nameless, though it is obviously a recreation of the Sharpeville Masacre of 1963—mean nothing to us if they do not express some mood of nature as felt by the artist, a mood that connects him to the environment, the incident, and the people; a mood that becomes a compelling metaphor for summing up this day's events; a mood that begins when "The sun was hot and the sky steely with thunder" and culminates "While the living wandered, some aimlessly and others with purpose, among the dead and dying and wounded, the sky muttered darkly at last and started to shed heavy drops of rain. Thunder clashed along the horizon like a duel of artillery and then the rain began to fall steadily to mingle with the blood" (105). The result is a metaphorically embroidered image that is strikingly appropriate and perfectly adapted to the distinctive mood La Guma wishes to convey. The physical and human dimensions of the image progress in parallel movement: from the day hot with the sun and the demonstrators hot with anger, to a day wet with rain and the demonstrators wet with blood, until blood and rain coagulate into a symbol of death the anonymity intensifying and universalizing the characters and the event.

The idea is the primary thing for an image, and the idea is intertwined with craft and technique in a reciprocal relationship with feeling and theme. The vital idea La Guma is working with in this recreation of the Sharpville Massacre is the movement's need for a new strategy. And for each new idea there must be new invention, new images special to the expression of that idea and no other. And the idea must be valuable, worth the effort of expression; must come of the artist's understanding of life and be a thing he greatly desires to say. Death, therefore, in this image, symbolizes not physical death alone, but the death of an idea, the death of a strategy, a "natural" death that gives rise to something new. For it is on the basis of the events of this day that Elias, Beukes, and the others in the movement decide to go underground, to prepare and convince the people of the necessity for armed struggle: "the Government will not allow the people to organize as before" (96).

In suggesting La Guma's masterly use of imagery, I do not mean that images composed like his are the only ones that should be made, or that motives like his motives should be repeated. Rather, I am pointing out the principles that underlie his selection and execution of a particular image and image pattern, the principles of premeditated selectivity, power of idea, power of intense feeling, and intense respect for the people and the place he's writing about. Besides this principle of motives, there is the principle of technique, that is construction. The construction with words of plot, dialogue, characters, and environments as forms for the expression of ideas.

The good quality of La Guma's images comes from a concerted movement, the selection of certain character types and environments, and the specifying of them with an end in view. To the expression of this end, all of the images and parts of the book must work as an organic whole. All the images and image patterns must be treated as factors in a general, harmonious movement. An environment has got to mean a great deal to an artist, or anyone else, before it can be described, portrayed in any worthwhile way. Everything depends on the attitude of the artist towards his subject. It is because of La Guma's attitude of love and respect for the nouns in his novels that his images of the physical and moral environments of South Africa assume the meaning and impact that they do.

For example, after Beukes is shot in the arm while fleeing from the police, and wanders into an upper-class White suburb, he observes the "Tall gates, high walls...the tall hedge" from behind which floated the sound of dance music, "the crackling barbecue pit, the chatter of voices breaking through the music, 'Rich White folk having themselves a Friday night party," (148), a scene that conveys important symbolism, as the Whites indulge their hedonism within this fortified estate, and the African majority—literally and metaphorically—lies bleeding and hunted without. On the vast lawns of this estate stand two marquee tents. There is a tennis court and swimming pool and colored lights are on, strings of sausages and skewered mutton chops splutter and sizzle in the barbecue pit, and "there's gallons of champagne" (149). Beukes, hiding beneath the wall, wounded, bleeding, overhears snatches of conversation blowing off this scene and his blood and pain mix curiously with it all, as South Africa's two lifestyles coalesce in an apposite image of African pain and White apathy:

> Beukes was carefully drawing off his coat with his good hand. The left sleeve was black with blood.
> "It's that Davey," a girl's voice complained. "Can't keep his awful hands to himself."
> "Don't blame him," a man laughed. "Come on, forget it and let's go and get another drink. There's gallons of champagne."
> "Who wants champagne? Just because his father's got lots

of cash to buy the stuff doesn't mean he can do what he
likes. I'm particular who handles me." (149)

This is one of the most memorable scenes in the novel. It represents both a material as well as an emotional environment. Thus, in
the tight structural development of the image sequence, La Guma
reveals the spirit and not just the material aspects of this environment. The broad symbolic purpose of this image is to underscore
the vacuousness of white bourgeois life and its dependence on
money and conspicuous consumption as a measure of dignity.

La Guma's whole literary effort, in this scene and most others,
is to leave no doubt as to what "the entire people" are fighting
against and what they are fighting for. They are fighting against
the economic injustice of whites who live on massive estates and
drink champagne while blacks live in slums with not enough money
to buy food; they are fighting against the moral damage of a system that degrades blacks and whites alike: "we are not only humbled
as Blacks," Beukes thinks at one point, "but also as workers; our
blackness is only a pretext" (131); they are fighting against the
brutality of a police state, where men are beaten unconscious and
urinated on in police cells; against the humiliation of having to
drop one's trousers to prove one's adulthood; against having to
teach that the Boer War was a holy crusade and that nobody existed in the land before Jan Van Riebeeck; against highly intelli-
gent young men having to work as messenger "boys" for overpaid
and pampered white women with hardly half their ability; against
the eviction of old ladies and the dumping of them on the street;
against summary dismissals from work to make way for white
employees; against the pathetic life of women like Beatie Adams
who spend their lives bringing up the children of too-busy whites;
against the massacre of unarmed innocent men, women, and children protesting dehumanizing pass-laws or the use of Afrikaans;
against widows being compensated, for a while, with two pounds
(about four dollars) a month for their husbands' deaths in mining
accidents, while white widows receive a stipend for life.

It is the political and moral climate of South Africa that gives
rise to these conditions and to the struggle against them. Therefore, throughout the book, one must think of the images of environment and character in their relationship to each other. Images

depicting environments of affluence or poverty are human documents of the lives of the people living in these environments. Adrian Roscoe, examining La Guma's works in *Uhuru's Fire*, writes:

> From pointing out human and economic injustice to attacking the regime by way of ugly pictures of it and suggesting that the victims of oppression ought to band together, there emerges, tiredly and hesitantly, the idea of violence as the only course of action that holds out hope, the only course of action the regime will respect. This development is presented so objectively that the author seems almost to have no part of it. It appears as a tired inevitability. And who, examining current events in Southern Africa, would deny its force? (1977:258)

Human beings, made in the image and likeness of almighty God—their beauty, their dignity, and their nobility—are the inspiration for La Guma's work and the fundamental subsance of his imagery. Any system, therefore, that desecrates, vulgarizes and profanes this beauty, dignity, and nobility—for whatever reason—is, at the very least, inhumane. La Guma's "ugly pictures" of the South African political and social system are a calculated and effective way of attacking that system. For literature, in addition to being a mirror held up to a given society is also a hammer, in that it must also be used to reshape and restructure a society.

It should be observable from the outset that all those things that La Guma and his fellow travelers in South Africa are fighting against are the very things that make for the desecration of human beings. La Guma, however, goes a step farther and particularizes his characters, as well as inanimate objects, in ways that serve as metaphors for the South African situation. This particular technique of La Guma gives rise to some rather unique and interesting metaphors for describing both the physical and moral dimensions of some of his characters. For instance, the Major who questions Elias,

> ...was broad and seemed to be constructed of a series of pink ovals: balding head and fat oval face, fat neck that topped curving shoulders which formed the upper curve of the big oval that was his rotund trunk...and the hands which emerged from the starched cuffs were pink and plump and oval. Only his eyes were small and round and shiny, like two glass beads; small, bright, conscienceless eyes. (3)

Here, La Guma's portrait of the fat, oval, rotund body of the Major becomes an instrument of expression. The obese, gluttonous image of the Major suggests a universal order: one characterized by white hegemony that has grown fat and distorted at the expense of the Colored world. As such, the image of the Major is a form of caricature intended to ridicule and make the target look as ugly, preposterous, hateful, and absurd as possible.

The Major is a stereotype of the garrulous policeman who persuades no one with his oratory, as when he speaks to Elias ("his voice took on a friendly, sympathetic tone, like a doctor advising a patient"), and yet his perception of his position and of his role seems to require this empty performance. The function of the image of the Major is, obviously, to arouse feelings of derision and of indignation; and a similar conclusion must be drawn, somewhat later, when La Guma describes a Police Sergeant as having, "a flabby wrinkled face over hard bone, as if a loose flexible rubber mask had been hastily dropped over a smaller wig stand"(98). By such portraiture, we are encouraged to see the bodies of these men as the physical containers of moral vices (pride and gluttony). La Guma makes certain that the physical deformity is joined with moral decadence, as now the Major goes into a lengthy diatribe about what the government has done for the Africans:

> We have given you nice jobs, houses, education. Education, ja. Take education for instance. We have allowed you people to get education, your own special schools, but you are not satisfied...I have heard that some of your young people even want to learn mathematics... What good is mathematics to you? You see, you people are not the same as we are...You want to be like the Whites. It's impossible. (4)

Thus, the physical and moral portraits of the Major combine to create a balanced picture that holds him up for justifiable ridicule and contempt, while intensifying the emotional reaction of the audience.

Such portrayals are an indication of La Guma's careful management of his images and of how he guides the story into the image then picks the story out of the image for a richer and fuller story than it was before and proceeds with his narrative. La Guma must have wanted just this image of the South African Police, in this particular context; for an image that is not really wanted, and that does nothing in particular to the meaning of the story, or fails to make its effect, is a weakness in the story.

Everywhere we look in La Guma's writings, images of the desecrated and disfigured human body express his sense of the lack of human wholeness. Beukes, for instance, has "a small scar under the left eye, on the cheekbone" (10); Isaac's eyes "bulged a little, giving him a permanent look of permanent surprise" (15); Arthur Bennett "had anxious, harassed eyes that fought to maintain the disguise of bonhomie, but it keeps slipping like a badly-glued moustache in a school play" (20); and the Taxi-driver wears dark green sun-glasses which give the impression of two holes cut out of his face (24); and the old woman evicted from her home has "ropy hair the colour of used, dirty-white knitting wool...(a) brown, clawed face...her hands...were hard and knotted like tangled skeins of brown cord" (29); and Tommy's "kinky" hair "looked like a skull cap" (30); one of the ruffians that accosted Beukes at the fun-fair is described as having a face that looks like "badly-carved mahogany" and another as having "a grimy, pimply face like an unwashed rusty vegetable grater" (35); and nearby, a girl standing with Frances is missing her upper teeth.

The important factor in all these images is the subtle and meticulous way in which the divine element in the human body is desecrated. Such images are undisguised portraits of physical abuse and essential ingredients in the meaning of *In the Fog of the Seasons' End.* La Guma's descriptions of scarred, clawed, pretentious, badly-carved, grimy, bruised human types are metaphors, and should be considered as metaphors for the humiliating imperfections to which all human beings are usually condemned, but which are magnified and exaggerated in the South African situation.

Inanimate objects receive similar treatment and have their equivalents in the human condition. For example, the old deck-chair the evicted woman sat in the middle of the crowd "was worn where it folded around the supporting slats and the thread hung in dirty streamers, like dehydrated entrails" (28). And while in Tommy's apartment, Beukes sponges himself with "a wash-rag that looked and felt like cold grey tripe" and dries himself with "a soiled towel" (59). Later, Tommy "rummaged in a drawer and found knives and forks. They didn't match and one of the forks had a bent prong"; and while eating fish and chips they sip coffee from "chipped cups." Clearly, this physical decay, this desecrated material environment is the objective correlative of the social and moral disintegration of South African society, and of the broken and bruised bodies and lives of too many people. Sections of the city are described as having "the look of an area cleared after a bombing," where "a once well-patronized cinema stood across the way like the leftovers of an earthquake"; a hill that "looked like the thin form of a starving girl covered by a thin blanket"; a unit of segregated housing "with wall peeling like diseased skin...A factory...deserted; a municipal market with stalls empty and shut...a grocery store clamped for safety behind bars and metal grilles, like a manifestation of the moral decay of its customers" (61-62, 73-74, and 164). These images, deeply metaphorical and drawn from different sections of the novel, are used to give an arresting and powerful impression of the conditions in which African people live in South Africa. They are moral reflectors as well, meant to mirror the social and human decay that is South Africa.

It is possible, therefore, to discern certain basic patterns in La Guma's imagery, and describe their thematic and structural role. There are many recurrent images from novel to novel; for example, entrails, skin-disease, rubbish heap, and so forth. There is also the recurrence of the same image, or slight variation on it in different parts of the same novel and in other novels. In *And a Threefold Cord*, for instance, the white character, George Mostert, has a junkyard on the side of his garage where are discarded, entangled, rusty, and broken automobile engines, useless objects. In *In the Fog of the Seasons' End*, the white shop-owner, Wasserman, has a stable behind his house, where, instead of throwing things away for which he no longer has any use, "He threw nothing away" he stowed these odds and ends:

> The stable was the roost of abandoned cartwheels, broken bedsprings, discarded cupboards crushed into splintering polygons of wood, rusty cans, and empty petrol drums, a spade with a broken handle, broken mirrors with leprous faces and an infinity of unidentifiable metal and wooden

contraptions gathering dust and rust. It appeared as if all
the left-overs of several lives had been hastily crammed
into the place. (76)

It is again noticeable that, as we remember the image of Mostert's
junkyard, once La Guma's imagination has been set in motion by
an initial analogy, he is apt to follow it up with different images
centered on the same experience and similar theme. The idea implied by the image is the same in both cases: to wit, the millions of
Africans who are considered expendable, as no longer of use or
value as "items" of labor-property, and are discarded, "endorsed
out" by the apartheid system. This image of Wasserman's stable
is a precise metaphor for the official "homelands" policy of the
South African government. These inanimate objects have their
specific human equivalents of "abandoned...broken...
discarded...crushed...empty...unidentifiable" nameless human beings now discarded and abandoned in the Stinkwaters, Klipgats,
and Limehills being created all over South Africa, areas that represent human "rubbish heaps" of broken communities, broken families, and broken individual lives which is the government's removal
policy. The homelands areas are wretched and desolate places.
The water and waste-disposal facilities are totally inadequate, there
is no industry to support employment, and the land is totally inadequate even for subsistence farming. The inhabitants struggle
against disease on the edge of starvation.

The picture of Wasserman's stable of abandoned and discarded
junk is also the picture of thousands of families uprooted, transported, and then dumped like garbage, some of them in the open
desert—a crime of such magnitude that it often defies belief. Here
the desecration of human lives has been made official policy, in
accordance with the theory of color-race superiority, organized and
made as efficient as the death camps of Adolf Hitler. Father Cosmos Desmond, a catholic priest-in-charge at Maria Ratschitz Mission in the Dundee district of Northern Natal from January 1964
until May 1967, in his book *The Discarded People*, wrote the following:

I have seen the suffering of whole families living in one
tent or a tiny hut, of children sick with typhoid, of their

bodies emaciated with malnutrition and even dying of starvation. I have seen all this in these last few years, in 1968, 1969 and 1970, in the richest most advanced and most rapidly growing economy on the continent of Africa. (1971:1)

It is most fitting, therefore, to conclude with the awareness that the terrifying magnitude of this problem—the forcible removal and resettlement of entire communities as a necessary part of the oppressive regime, and perhaps the greatest atrocity and vulgarization of a social system—is the subject of La Guma's latest novel, *Time of the Butcherbird*.

The main purpose of this study, and it will remain so, is to advance beyond mere individual images and to detect and analyze the predominant patterns and thematic tendencies underlying them. The material discussed here should have provided some idea of the fantastic richness and diversity of La Guma's imagery. It should have also demonstrated the astonishingly high proportion of unique and effective images, which, by their structural and thematic role and the uniqueness of the vision which directed them, capture the reader's imagination and enrich the experience. *In the Fog of the Seasons' End* will long remain aesthetically enjoyable, entertaining, and educational.

Chapter 5

TIME OF THE BUTCHERBIRD: IMAGE AND IDEA

Mother in Wartime

As if it were some noble thing,
She spoke of sons at war,
As if freedom's cause
Were pled anew at some heroic bar,
As if the weapons used today
Killed with great elan,
As if technicolor banners flew
To honor modern man—
Believing everything she read
In the daily news,
(No in-between to choose)
She thought that only
One side won,
Not that both
Might lose.

       —Langston Hughes

Nothing is more powerful than an individual acting out of
his conscience, thus helping to bring the collective conscience to life.

       —Norman Cousins

Like La Guma's previous four novels, *Time of the Butcherbird* is a
microcosmic, slice-of-life view of South Africa. It is the inside
story of the traumatic, psychological, and social effects of perhaps

the most wrenching atrocity of apartheid: the forcible removal and resettlement of entire communities as a necessary part of the oppressive apartheid system. The consequences of resettlement on individuals and the society in general—African, Colored, and European—is the central theme of the work, and concomitant with this theme is that of resistance to this hypocritical policy of "separate development." In the language of Geoffrey Cronje' (1907-1992), "Mixed areas become the dying-places (sterfplekke) of the white race in South Africa and the most fruitful soil [for] bastardization," and such "social disorder and blood-mixing" threaten to create "a single South African mishmash-society" (Coetzee 1996: 172). And God forbid that there be "a single South African...society" according to this Hitlerian logic. The justification for the title of this novel may be found in the dialogue between the grim and vindictive Shilling Murile and the shepherd Madonele:

> "Do you know the butcherbird?" Murile asked.
> "Yes" the shepherd, Madonele, answered "I know the butcherbird. That he is a hunter and smeller-out of sorcerers, because he impales insects." (42)

"The butcherbird," as such, is a metaphor for Shilling Murile in particular and the African and Colored community of South Africa in general: and to complete the metaphor, we would be compelled to say, in this context, that the Europeans of South Africa are the "insects" the butcherbirds impale.

Time of the Butcherbird completes, as if deliberately and organically, the full cycle of Alex La Guma's published novels. After his characters have been hunted and brutalized by police, fired from jobs, watched their children and parents die without medical care, burned to death in shacks unfit for human habitation, murdered their lovers and brothers, thrown into prison for distributing leaflets, pissed on, beaten, tortured, and murdered by security police, it is certainly, unarguably, time for the butcherbird. Yet, there are those who will argue, those who will justifiably question the methods, the tactics, and even the availability of the instruments necessary to "impale the insects." This novel was written while La

Guma was living in exile in London (Abrahams 1991:39). Of the genesis of this work La Guma has said:

> In order to portray as much as possible of the South African scene, the people of the countryside had to be dealt with at some time. The forced removals of people from so-called "black spots" in the "white" areas and the government's attempts to enforce Bantustans form one of the great social tragedies of our country, and a source of both unhappiness and resistance. The peasantry and the country-people generally have been in the midst of important struggles against this aspect of apartheid, and notably since the end of the Second World War. In addition, the brutality and callousness of white landowners towards blacks have been a feature of racism in South Africa. For this reason I had to write *Time of the Butcherbird.* (38)

Because of this nagging question of methods, characters are represented, though not necessarily judged, according to the degree of their particular responses to the machinery of this police state. Thus, the theme of resistance expands and contracts as the novel progresses. This theme, further divided into four competing points of view—the individual, the collective, the violent, and the non-violent—as alternative methods of response, raises the larger question of the morality of armed resistance. In *Reconciliation Through Truth: A Reckoning of Apartheid's Criminal Governance,* Kader and Louise Asmal and Ronald Roberts (1996) note that: "Being part of the resistance was profoundly an act of ethical self-expression. Each participant had individually embarked upon a certain road out of proud and conscious choice" (120). Furthermore, the "scale and nature of human suffering associated with the armed struggle against apartheid can never be equated with the scale and nature of the pain inflicted by apartheid" (41).

La Guma must have wanted these dialectical perspectives to shift the focus of the novel away from the actual act of resettlement to the variety of responses it initiates in individuals and in the collective society. The emphasis, therefore, is not so much on personalities as it is on representative responses to a common situation. His effort seems to be to depict the destructive effects of apartheid on different types of people—thus, all people—and not simply on an atypical, personally vindictive one like Shilling Murile. Even the dedication of the novel—"To The Dispossessed"—lacks the particularity of the previous novels, and suggests the broader, collectivist focus of Butcherbird. The amorphous, nameless mass of people dumped in a nameless bantustan at the beginning of the novel further substantiates this perspective: "people who had been unloaded like odds and ends of furniture...had the look of scare-crows left behind, abandoned in this place" (1). And an anony-mous "hand experimentally dug up some sand and let it trickle away again through horny fingers" (1). It is, therefore, not just that the people are abandoned but also that they are abandoned in a wretched, desolate area that could not even support a subsistence agriculture: "This was no land for ploughing and sowing: it was not even good enough to be buried in" (1).

This image sequence dramatizes the alienation felt by ordinary people when taken out of their living, organic setting and placed by the illogical necessity of racism and capitalism into the sterile wasteland of a so-called homeland. Also, these images immediately establish the widely known and accepted fact that the so-called homelands or bantustan policy is a mockery and a fraud. It is a mockery of the historical rationale on which it supposedly rests: for the so-called home-lands have been located in precisely those areas that were shunned before colonialism by the very people for whom they are now desig-nated. They are sited on land which is almost if not totally useless.

The homelands policy is based on the false historical position that Flotman alludes to in In the Fog of the Seasons' End, i.e., that the land occupied by European people in South Africa today was vacant land. According to this deliberate distortion of history, Africans and Europeans settled in South Africa at the same time, and the two groups occupied then the same lands they presently occupy; therefore, the Europeans are perfectly justified in having the 87% of the land which they found unoccupied when they first came to Southern Africa.

The truth, however, is that the African homelands are but small fragments of African land now carved up into many separate pieces whose boundaries were established by the conquering, desperate European settlers (La Guma, Apartheid, 84). Kobe, one of the minor characters in Butcherbird and an emissary of his uprooted people, understands this intuitively as well as intellectually, as exemplified in his statement to The Commissioner:

> We have been told that we must go from our land, from the
> land of our ancestors. But it is a very difficult thing to
> uproot an old oak of many years. The roots of such a tree
> are very deep. Certainly one can take an axe and cut down
> such a tree, that is easy, but the roots remain and are very
> hard to dig up. So you see, the tree really remains. The tree
> goes on. (12)

Kobe's use of the first person plural, "We have been told that we
must go from our land," reveals the expansive quality of the novel:
it begins as a sort of collectivist novel but gravitates to the fate of
an individual hero, Shilling Murile.

In this manner, the novel becomes an historical document, from
the very beginning answering the historical question of causality,
by telling us how the condition of Africans, in South Africa in
particular, has become what he shows it to be. The reflections of
South African life and history given by La Guma can, perhaps,
best be described as reflections through a prism rather than a mirror, because they are varied and complex rather than
monodimensional and simple. La Guma recognizes and accepts
the pluralism of South Africa. What he does not accept are the
barriers separating these differing peoples. So he writes with the
view of exposing the situation and changing people's ideas about
what is happening while expressing universal ideas that transcend
the legalized separation and compartmentalization of the various
national and cultural groups that make South Africa South Africa.

Kobe's declaration to the Commissioner, a florid, eloquent metaphor, can be seen on at least two levels. First, it is a message of
resistance, of defiance, to wit: "it is very difficult to uproot an old
oak of many years...the roots remain and are hard to dig up"; yet,
on another level, it is a plea to be heard and understood, if not
agreed with. As expected, however, the white Nationalist Government is intractable:

> Now listen for the last time. It says here that you people
> asked the government office to set aside your removal be-
> cause you claim the land you live on has always been
> yours...But now the government has spoken again—the

> government speaks through me. It is written here that I
> should tell you finally that the removal of your people will
> go on as decided long ago. That is all. (12)

This attitude—and legal promulgation—expressed by the European Commissioner is an intellectual image that is firmly attached to the dominant themes of the novel and helps us to better understand its meaning. Such an image enlivens the moral portrait of white South Africa.

In contrast to Kobe (who, it must be remembered, is chosen to speak for "the people") Shilling Murile has long despaired of obtaining a fair and just hearing from the government or, for that matter, from white people in general. As the community discusses and debates what action to take following this rejection by the government, Shilling Murile thinks: "I am finished with Bantu Commissioners now, and with white people" (16). His is a personal decision, if only noted in his emphatic use of the first person singular: "I will do this one thing," he thinks (concentrating on his decision to kill Hannes Meulen, the farmer responsible for his brother's, Timi's, death, and his own ten year imprisonment), "and then I shall be finished with all people" (16).

Shilling Murile represents a contraction, a reduction of La Guma's theme of resistance. Shilling's metaphorical equivalent is nothing so big as a tree, but rather an ant. He watches, fascinated, as an ant crawls "out of the sunlight into the shade of a thorn branch, its jointed body lurching delicately across the powdered soil, leaving no mark or trail behind it, heading for a minute hole in a tiny ridge of earth...He is like me," Shilling contemplates, "that little ant, knowing where he will go, what he will do" (15). This image, comparing Shilling to an ant, is both judgmental and pejorative, but it is also well-suited to the stylistic climate of La Guma's thematic intent: a climate that demands metaphorical comparisons and a theme that favors collective rather than individual rebellion. It is also a marvelously artistic and philosophical picture of the insignificance of the individual in the vast expanse of time and space. The full significance of such imagery, like so much of La Guma's pictorial depictions, will best be appreciated when it is set against the background of the imagery as a whole.

Kobe's image of the tree and its roots, and Shilling's image of the ant and its hole, complement La Guma's dialectical image pattern of selective juxtaposition, of big and small, powerful and powerless, and—most importantly—of the group and the individual. The effect is, then, not the separation of image and meaning but indicative of their fundamental and essential unity. In the simile of the ant, we have the theme of powerlessness and alienation, the oppressive feeling of insignificance combined with another equally important theme—the isolated act of violence and personal vengeance. And as these themes expand, by way of the author's attention to the larger environment (both physical and moral), varied and diverse characterization, and the desecration of human beings and physical objects as a metaphor for the South African situation, this sense of expansiveness, of meaning and theme, is conveyed through a number of poignant, premeditated, and appropriate images.

For instance, Hannes Meulen, a prosperous Boer farmer and prospective parliamentary candidate, is a major character in this work; and in the context of a dialogue with Kasper Steen, (his fiancée Rina's father), they express the central concern of the work in the form of explicit statements:

> "Well, the corporation has accepted the geologist's report. They accept that the land in question must hold certain mineral deposits."...
> "Allemagtig, you did well, boy."
> "As soon as the kaffirs are moved—"
> "We call them Bantu now, boy," Steen said and smiled again. "Things have changed."
> Meulen smiled. "As soon as the Bantu have been Moved, the development of the area will commence. As you know, by request of the people here I myself went to the magistrate to ask that they be moved...."
> "Those black things will move, of course," Steen remarked.
> (61)

Unlike his earlier novels, in *Time of the Butcherbird* there are three distinct ethnic or racial camps—African, Afrikaner, and English; as such, there is no gray area of class to befog the fundamental question of land, the real basis of revolution and independence. The idea conveyed through the above dialogue/image blatantly contradicts the image the ruling National Party of South Africa wishes to project of promoting change, while vigorously pursuing racial separation, the cornerstone of apartheid policy. In fact, over the past 20 years (1964-84), 3.5 million Africans have been forcibly removed and relocated while another two million are under threat of removal (*Africa News* 11 July 1983: 5). La Guma, therefore, in several thematic images, reveals the feelings and cultural ethos that give rise to this conflict over the land and natural resources of South Africa.

Some of the history of this conflict can be noticed in the details of the two photographs that portray a piece of Boer and African history, respectively, in South Africa. The first photograph is observed by Edgar Stopes, the English salesman, as he enters the bar of the Railway Hotel:

> There were pictures on the walls. Above the shelf of bottles and the mirror behind the bar was a big frame of dusty gold-leaf surrounding a blow-up of an old photograph of several men posing together, some standing and others siting near the end of a covered wagon. Most of the men were bearded and all of them wore old fashioned suits and bandoleers draped across their chests, several of them carrying rifles...Edgar Stopes knew that they were members of a commando who had fought in the Boer War. (23)

This photograph evokes memories of Europeans—British and Dutch—fighting, among themselves in the Anglo-Boer War of 1899-1902 for control of African lands, particularly the diamonds in Kimberley (discovered in 1870) and the gold in the Transvaal (discovered in 1886). The Dutch-Boers were obliged to yield to the military might of Britain and by 1902 almost all of South Africa became a British colony. The Dutch-Boer claim to African land is integrally bound up in this and earlier struggles with African people opposed to their expansion. Dissatisfied with the British policy, in regard to the African and so-called Colored peoples, and seeking cheap labor and free lands, the Boers had begun their infamous Great Trek northward in 1834. Successive African leaders opposed this migration. Chaka, Dingaan, and Moshoshoe led armies against the invaders, but their resistance against the superior weapons of the Europeans ended in defeat. In direct contrast

to the photograph hanging in the Railway Hotel is the photograph
hanging on the wall of the hut of the puppet chief, Hlangeni, which
is a reminder of this courageous period in the history of the African people of Southern Africa:

> On the whitewashed wall over the sideboard was a big, faded
> photograph in a chipped gold-leaf frame of a man dressed
> in what looked like an admiral's uniform of the last cen-
> tury. This was Hlangeni's father who had once been re-
> ceived by the then Governor General. There was also a
> smaller picture of Hlangeni as a young man. (85)

This, and the previous photograph/image, shows men in uniform—
Africaners, Englishmen, and Africans—fighting over the land of
South and Southern Africa. The narrative context of Butcherbird
makes it clear, from the musings of Edgar Stopes, that he, an Englishman, feels "he belonged as much as they did" (4)—referring
to the Dutch-Boers. Concerning this English/Boer conflict, La
Guma writing for Moscow's *Literary Gazette* in 1980, says:

> I tried in a small way to present my Boer characters as they
> are within the setting of *Time of the Butcherbird* apart from
> introducing a few urban white people as well. There is also
> the matter of the schism that exists between English-speak-
> ing white people and Afrikaners too, which exists in South
> Africa, although they more often than not united when it
> comes to attitudes towards black folk. (Abrahams 1991:
> 39)

And the statements of Hlangeni's sister, Mma Tau, to her brother,
that the Africans were "Defeated perhaps, but not destroyed" makes
clear that the Anglo-Boer War did not resolve the conflict between
Boer and English and African. Mma Tau goes on to say:

> All this was our land, since the time of our ancestors. In
> that my brother was right. Are not the fields still ours, the
> soil, the hills? All this is our home, in spite of the white
> man's law. (83)

While diametrically opposed to this view is that of the Boer farmer, Hannes Meulen, who, in remembering his father, asserts the Dutch claim to South African land:

> The father loved the land: to him country was not only a geographical entity, an anthem, celebrations of Dingane's Day, the Day of Blood River. For him country was a matter of who owned the flat, dreary red and yellow plains and low, undulating hills, the grass and the water. This was a heritage which had been gained through the sacred blood of their ancestors and the prophetic work of God. It had come to their fathers through the musket and the Bible; they had come into this land like the followers of Joshua. Any other conception was anathema. (57-58)

And a bit later Hannes would say to his fiancée, Rina:

> After all, the foundation and the cement of our people, which is as everlasting as the monument we set up in the capital in honour of our forefathers, that cement and foundation is the ethic of our racial, cultural and religious purity...Afrikaner people is not the work of man, it is the work of God. We shall prevail. (64)

A fundamental element of Afrikaner religion is that separation of races and white supremacy is divinely ordained and that those responsible for the odious apartheid system are responsible only to God. Hannes has merely reiterated the policy of the Dutch Reformed Churches of South Africa, which stipulates strict segregation on racial grounds, "the ethic of our racial, cultural and religious purity." Whether coming from the mouth of a politician, like Hannes Meulen, or a clergyman like the Dominee Visser, another minor character in Butcherbird, the message is the same. For example, in his sermon to the Sunday morning congregation of the small, rural, Dutch community that provides the setting for this novel, the Dominee Visser proclaims:

> Sin came with the mixing of blood as sure as Adam ate of the forbidden apple. Blood pollution and the lowering of

the racial level which goes with it, are the only cause why
old civilizations disappear....

In the purity of our blood also lies the guarantee of our
honourable mission. It is the duty of all of us to unshakeable
keep to our aim, spiritual and earthly, which is to secure for
our children their God-given land and soil on this earth....
(106)

The question of land—intimately intertwined with the principle of
separate development, out of which emerges the inhumane resettlement policy—is the pivotal theme of this work. The Afrikaners,
as observed in the positions taken by Hannes Muelen and the
Dominee Visser, are carefully indoctrinated to believe that they
are engaged in a struggle to protect and preserve what rightly belongs to them. Most importantly, this position very easily translates into the diametrically opposed concepts of whiteness and
blackness, thereby embracing an all-encompassing philosophical
dualism of purity and filthiness, innocence and sin, beauty and
ugliness, good and evil, God and the devil. Such a concept of what
it means to be "Christian" conveys the idea and feeling to white
South Africans of we against they; so to be Christian is to be civilized rather than primitive, European rather than African, white
rather than black. Clifton Crais (1992) in his *The Making of a
Colonial Order: White Supremacy and Black Resistance in the
Western Cape,* 1770-1865, puts the matter this way:

The relations between black and white would soon become projected as the Manichean struggle—between 'good
and evil, superiority and inferiority, civilization and savagery, intelligence and emotion, rationality and intensity,
self and Other, subject and object—that would dominate
every facet of the colonial mentality then emerging in the
world of the Eastern Cape. (Magubane 1996:74)

And Dr. Bernard Magubane, in T*he Making of a Racist State: British Imperialism and the Union of South Africa, 1875-1910,* reminds
us that:

To recall the ideas and gloating of social imperialist is to
remind ourselves that what happened in South Africa in the

latter part of the Victorian era was not the result of moral
lapse, as some apologists of British imperialism have suggested; nor was it the result of a "magnanimous gesture" to
the Afrikaners. These imperial ideas not only lent "scientific proof" to the practice of genocide but they created a
belief that there were higher and lower races, historical and
non-historical peoples, they also cultivated the idea of race
superiority and divine national mission. (1996:82)

The Africans, on the other hand, as represented by Kobe and Mma
Tau, know that their right to South African lands flows from the
right of historical and immemorial possession. As such, their claim
is subject neither to treaty nor to colonial legislation; that is, it is
non-negotiable. In fact, the Afrikaner view, expressed through
Hannes Meulen, that "the land... had come to their fathers through
the musket and the Bible," is not altogether accurate. For example,
Magubane notes that "soon after their defeat, the same imperial
government that had dispossessed the conquered African chiefdoms
and kingdoms gave the Boers their lands" (278).

The English, for their part, lay claim to the supposedly complex and sophisticated economic structures that they have established on the land. It is, therefore, appropriate and most perceptive
of Alex La Guma to choose as his primary characters: the politi-
cian/farmer Hannes Meulen, indicative of the Afrikaner control
of the political apparatus of South Africa (at this time); Edgar
Stopes, the English salesman, indicative of the dominant role of
the English in South Africa's economic institutions; and Shilling
Murile, an African, alienated from his ancestral land and his people.
And even after Nelson Mandela's 1990 release from prison and
subsequent election to President, Njabulo Ndebele observes:

Whites are still in government; they control the army and
the police; they still enjoy what must be one of the highest
standards of living in the world; they still manage the
economy, although they will grudgingly let in competent
blacks; they own practically all the means of production
that matter; they still dominate the privileged universities
and research institutes. Their overall power is still pervasive. (Ndebele 1994:viii)

Then, to further twist the knife, Ndebele adds: "For indeed, to borrow Jay Reddy's quotation in her address, 'the end of apartheid seems to represent for the white minority a defeat in which they have lost nothing'" (156).

The image pattern of *Time of the Butcherbird* strikingly accounts for this pluralistic, intra-national struggle within South Africa, as each national group fights the other two in different ways. Apartheid, the white supremacists' policy of separate development, is nothing more than a strategy for the political dominance of the Afrikaner. Generally, the Afrikaners seem to distrust Africans and fear that an African-English alliance will destroy their hegemony over the political life of South Africa. At the same time, so many privileges and rights go with simply having a white skin that the English will ally themselves with the Afrikaners in the face of African aggression. This can be readily seen in the dialogue between Englishman Edgar Stopes' wife, Masie, and her secret lover, Wally Basson:

> "What about Donny?"
> ....Wally Basson was saying as he offered her a cigarette:
> "The bloody fool is in chooky."
> Maisie took the cigarette and looked at the flame of his gold lighter: "What did you say? Who?"
> "Donny Harris, hey. He's in bloody jail, true as God."
> "Jail? Him? But he was always such a nice and respectable boy."
> "Got himself mixed up with niggers. Coons. The damn fool though [sic] it was a good idea to help the darkies with trade unions or something, true as God...." (*Butcherbird*, 52)

Wally's racist reference to "niggers...Coons...darkies" is indicative of a pervasive attitude and is not just some mental quirk or slip of the tongue. Apart from this, one of the essential ideas revealed by this theme/image is that some Englishmen may well abhor apartheid, yet still feel that the African is inferior to white men; that it is not the apartheid system, the environment, that makes the African inferior in his own land, but nature, his own human nature—or lack thereof—that makes him inferior. This perspective is given

further credence by the Afrikaner Hannes Meulen, who remembering the meetings held in the schoolhouse when the menfolk
gathered to discuss political issues, recounts how the men opposed
the war against Germany, because:

> The Germans stood for unity of the race, of the chosen of
> God. Any war against Germany would uphold ideas of
> miscegenation, of bastardization, of liberal thoughts enter-
> tained by the British and the Jews. Thus the ideas of Hitler
> coincided with those of the men at these meetings. (58).

These intellectual images clearly reveal that Africans must fight
the racism of both the English and the Afrikaners. They must work
as hard to create a wedge between the English-Afrikaner united
front as the Afrikaner does to widen the gap between the English
and the African. It is this triangular conflict, involving the Africans,
the Afrikaners, and the English—and concerning the land (the natural
resources) and the politics and economic structures that are established to control this rich and beautiful country—that provides the
thematic content, as well as the selection of intellectual and pictorial images of the environment and of the characters in *Time of the
Butcherbird.*

Primarily confined to the intellectual level, La Guma's imagery
is decidedly thematic (political and historical) and noticeably varied
in structure; it ranges from brief quips, like that of Edgar Stopes
that "he belonged as much as they did" (referring to the Afrikaners),
to protracted metaphors like Kobe's reference to the deep roots of
an old tree, to major pronouncements of historical, political and religious justification for the system of apartheid—all with the imagistic potential of developing into major symbols in the work.

As with the other works, the main function of the imagery is to
clarify certain political and socio-economic themes. The theme of
resettlement and the Africans' resistance to this heartless practice
revolves around the central issue of the ownership and control of
the land. It is their attitude and feelings about the wealth and beauty
of the land of South Africa that compels Kobe, Edgar Stopes,
Hannes Meulen, and Mma Tau to make the pronouncements that
they make. The triangular conflict between the three national/cul-
tural groups is first and foremost a struggle over control of this rich
physical environment. As Hannes Meulen notes, "the land in ques-

tion must hold certain mineral deposits....As soon as the Bantu have been moved, the development of that area will commence" (61). It is against this background that La Guma's descriptions and recreations of this environment, both animate and inanimate, combine both the objective evidence of his senses and the subjective attitudes and feelings connecting him with this physical landscape. On one particular vivid and memorable occasion, reflected through the consciousness of Shilling Murile, La Guma gives the reader a graphic depiction of the variety and beauty of the physical environment and one African's (his own) feelings for his ancestral homeland:

> It was a country of flat, weary distances scattered with stunted Karoo bush that crumbled underfoot like rotten wood and left small hollows of red earth; a country of basalt and sandstone...of kudu and leopard. The green or brown mamba still slithers here among the pricky-pear cactus and the strewn ironstone, with red spiders that blend into the parched dust from which the scrub and whitethorn sprout as if in defiance of the remorseless sun. The bushbuck or the steenbuck may still be hunted, but this is also the country of the cattle called Afrikander by the white men, although the fat-tailed sheep had grazed on the harsh grass and scrub during the good season...In the good season the rain came quickly, like a gesture from the spirits, bearing down on the camel thorn trees, the milkbushes with their long leaves like thin spearblades, the Stone Age bread trees. Then the rain was gone and it would be the time of the honeybird and the dringo and the wagtail; of thorny aloes, cycads and the common sunflower. (14)

It should be remembered that although the central theme of this novel, the resettlement of Africans, arises from a single (though recurrent and pervasive) experience, the images come from a much wider field—from the total life experiences of the novelist. Contemplating this image, with Shilling Murile as an integral part of it, we are better able to understand Shilling Murile: why he is who and what he is and why he does what he does. The image is not just there for its own sake, but rather to illuminate theme and action. Such images provide a context in which the various phases of Shilling's development can be most tellingly expressed.

Of the passage just cited, it can be noted, among other things, that La Guma's fondness for explicit analogies is also reflected in his frequent use of comparisons that evoke images of touch and sight, for example, "a country...with stunted karoo bush that crumbled underfoot like rotten wood" and "the scrub and whitethorn sprout as if in defiance of the remorseless sun." And sometimes the mere arrangement of a sentence produces the impression of an image, such as "In the good season the rain came quickly, like a gesture from the spirits." The suggestive force of these images work by association and overtones: they help produce a mood of affinity with and nostalgia for the natural environment: they are, also, closely integrated into the overall economy of the novel and play a distinctive part in its total effect.

In addition to broad sweeping images of the rural landscape, there are countless miniature pictures in the incidental imagery, broadening and complicating the reader's vision of the South African landscape, and helping to keep La Guma's style alive. They may be presented directly, as when he reminds us of the urban setting through the vision of Edgar and Maisie:

> They drove away from the dreary district through the traf-
> fic—crowded canyons of the city, the huge granite cliffs
> of office blocks, hotels and apartment houses brilliant with
> neon signs and rolling lights. The pavements were crowded
> and around the theater marquees there were expensive
> people. (37)

To scenes that, although they depict a lifeless, barren wasteland, bestow grandeur, color, and beauty on the rural landscape:

> The sun was dropping nearer to the thin line of brown hills
> to the West and there was a tawny colour to the land, striped
> with blue and mauve; the pale ironstone scattered about
> and the spiny bushes that dotted the landscape all lay in
> their own individual shadows. (19)

Thus, from urban to rural and then to a landscape somewhere in between (like the small Railway town, the central setting for the novel), the reader is transported by images to the internal and private worlds of these contrasting physical environments. And in each case there is a harmonization of landscape and situation; that is, the environment coincides with the situation and with the people involved in that situation. "The huge granite cliffs of office blocks" observed by Edgar and Maisie evoke a sense of hardness and in-difference as opposed to the softer though barren "thin line of brown hills...and the spiny bushes that dotted the landscape (that) lay in their own individual shadows" familiar to Shilling Murile and Kope. Such contrasts form discernable patterns throughout the work and are a mark of La Guma's brilliant image-making style.

Time of the Butcherbird presents distinct images of three spe-cific environments—urban, small-town rural, and the lifeless, bar-ren wasteland—corresponding to the predominant social context of the three major characters in the work—the Englishman Edgar Stopes (urban), the Afrikaner Hannes Meulen (small-town rural), and the African Shilling Murile (landless and homeless). La Guma, as a so-called Colored, is uniquely positioned to elicit such truthful portrayals. For, given the peculiarity and particularity of being a so-called Colored, he is able to convey with a certain affinity and innate insight the specious arguments of the alien Afrikaners and English in South Africa: that they are ordained by God to occupy 87% of South African land and to be master of the indigenous population.

On the other hand, La Guma is African enough to sense and convey the feelings and thoughts of African people towards the land of their fathers and their fathers' fathers. This land where "the bushbuck or the steenbuck may still be hunted," where "In the good season the rain came quickly, like a gesture from the spirits." This land of milkbushes and Stone Age breadtrees, the honeybird, the dringo, the wagtail, and the common sunflower. Thus, La Guma, through images of the magnificent fauna and flora of South Af-rica, imparts also the feelings of the people, particularly the Afri-can people, along with his own feelings of love and nostalgia, that connects them to the total physical environment and not just to the areas of rich soil and mineral deposits.

The objective, historical truth of settled African societies in South-ern Africa centuries before European penetration needs emphasiz-ing, in order to restore the parentage of Southern Africa generally and South Africa in particular to its rightful owners. It is, in fact, precisely in Central and Southern Africa that the achievements of

African people can be measured better than elsewhere on the continent. The Iron Age culture in Southern Africa left marvelous ruins at Zimbabwe and Mapungubwe, Niekerk, Penhalonga, Khani, and elsewhere (Davidson 1959: 211-212). The development and growth of these cities and city-states may be observed from about AD 500 onwards. The distorted account of John Van Reibeck discovering, in 1652, an uninhabited land needs to he laid permanently to rest.

La Guma's images of the rural African environment appear designed to present a picture and sense of what the human and natural environments of South Africa were like in the past—and what they have become—as viewed through the consciousness and historical vision of African people. It also addresses, to some extent, what Njabulo Ndebele sees as a serious vacuum in South African literature: "an attempt at a sincere imaginative perception that sees South African peasant life as having a certain human validity, albeit a problematic one" (1994:25). The following image, for instance, captures the essence of this abnormal development, as Shilling Murile and Madonele, the shepherd, enter their community:

> They came down to where houses had come to rest in the bend in the bank of the dry stream bed. Here there were still leaves on the trees that grew hunched and crookedly patterned against the sky that was turning mauve with twilight; the houses were broken up into groups near the trees to squat in the shade they threw when the sun was high. Some of the houses were of the old circular style with thatched roofs; but in the main they were straight-walled, built as the old huts had crumbled away, some of the walls mud and branch poles, with designs scratched in the plaster when it had still been wet. There were gardens here and there, but the vegetation had dwindled and their walls fallen in places, as if dying plant life had infected the brown clay. In hollow yards outdoor ovens sent up columns of smoke and the children tended them now, nursing the fires while the elders headed towards the open space in front of Hlangeni's house. (41)

The content of this image leaves no doubt that this is a traditional African environment. There is the knowledge and memory of an-

cient rivers represented by "The dry stream bed." There is a delib-
erateness, but also a rather casual acceptance that "the houses
were broken up into groups near the trees to squat in the shade,"
almost as if to ask rhetorically 'where else would the houses go?'
And the design of the houses is distinctly African: "the old circular
style with thatched roofs...with designs scratched into the plaster
when it had still been wet." There is, also, that typical and conti-
nental African orderliness exemplified in the age-grade responsibilities of the children tending the fires "while the elders headed
towards the open space in front of Hlangeni's house" to attend the
obligatory community palaver. The environment and the people
are in harmony: yet, the tone of the image is somber and touched
with the pathos of the abject material condition of a people abnor-
mally petrified in this undeveloped environment. For instance, "the
old huts had crumbled away" and there are only "gardens here and
there" and "the vegetation had dwindled." The image, therefore, in
a very profound sense, is a metaphor, a sort of double entendre—
that is, a still-life portrait with both a literal and a figurative meaning. Whether La Guma intended this or not is really immaterial.
What is significant is that this is one important interpretation a reader
could give to this image.

In direct contrast to the urban and rural environments is the
small Afrikaner town where the major action of the novel takes
place; here,

> ...the town street lay quiet under the last of another swel-
> tering day, hanging out its shadows with relief in front of
> the Railway Hotel: a line of whitewashed houses behind
> burnt hedges: around a speckled car and wagon in front of
> the feed store, heads of mules drooping; from the Boer War
> monument in the dusty square and the face of the old church
> with its red concrete steps. (3)

The idea imbued in this image is one of a people in transition; a
people hesitating between tradition (symbolized by "a wagon" and
"heads of mules drooping") and modernity (symbolized by the
"speckled car"). This kind of juxtaposition of images is a favorite
technique of La Guma's and he uses it to perfection. The completed image is not simply given, but rather evolves as a fundamental pattern in the work as a whole. While fragments may be culled
from the whole to reflect certain internal dynamics on a synchronic

level, the protracted image marks a lucid contrast with the rural African environment, and the pluralistic but predominantly English-Afrikaans urban environment. The full image of this small Afrikaner town comes out incrementally during the course of the novel. One of the most striking images of the town is seen through the consciousness of Hannes Meulen:

> The back street was in darkness. An electric lamp at each end and nothing in between left a sweltering stretch of heavy black. There were few lights on in the windows of the old-fashioned houses which took up one side, and these did not extend into the gravel street. From the back gardens opposite the houses the chorus of cricket sounds clattered in the hot night. Glow-worms trembled against the dark. Agterstraat had been the original street of the little town before the railway had come, the hotel, the shops with their plastic blinds and gaudy displays, the cottages of railway workers, the Bantu Commissioner, the post office, the police station, the garage. Other houses were scattered among the trees but what was now referred to as the Back Street had been the main thorough fare of the old settlement. (56)

Again, there is harmony of environment, character, and situation. Even with no people present in the image—save, of course, the mental presence of Hannes Meulen—there is no question that this is a European, more specifically Afrikaner environment; a fact made more emphatic by the street-name Agterstraat. This is further affirmed by the presence of such minimal material accouterments and more advanced infrastructure as electric lights, a hotel, a post-office, and a police department. Also, by reference to the "cottages of railway workers" and the "Bantu Commissioner," La Guma documents, ever so subtly, very important labor and racial relationships.

La Guma's technique of selective juxtaposition particularizes the reader's focus, making clear distinctions between the material cultures of the three primary national groups. Nowhere is this more apparent than in the images of the housing conditions of the Afrikaners, the English, and the Africans; images that are, again, representative and selective and by no means absolute and inclusive. For example, the house of the Afrikaner woman Rina Steen, Hannes Meulen's betrothed, is described as follows:

> The Steen house had a high stoep reached by stone steps
> at one end, a white gabled front with multipaned windows
> in the façade decorated with plaster moulding and pilas-
> ters. The thatched roof was solid and old Steen had it
> regularly inspected. Lights burned behind the curtains of
> the casement windows and a radio played broadcast music.
> (59)

And when La Guma takes us into the house we find:

> The lounge was off the hallway, full of armchairs, pouffes,
> a big carved sideboard of a past century, a big gilt mirror
> over the cold fireplace, and a chandelier hanging from the
> ceiling which was high on beams. (60)

Neither La Guma nor I want to suggest that all Afrikaners live in
houses like the Steens'. What is useful, however, is to compare
this image—of the home of an Afrikaner elite—to that of an African elite, specifically that of the puppet-chief Hlangeni:

> The house stood a little above the others, on a rise shaded
> by old blue-gum trees, and it had a stoep revetted with
> packed stones that had started to come lose in places. Once
> a wall had surrounded the yard in front of the house, but the
> mud had cracked and crumbled and now there were only
> sections standing, and the yard was gone. (43)

Such images, placed in direct opposition to others equally graphic,
are not accidental, but rather are the result of purposeful, selected,
and premeditated creation by the author. In this instance, La Guma
even takes the same architectural items as elements of comparison, for example: "The Steen house had a high stoep reached by
stone steps," whereas Hlangeni's house "had a stoep revetted with
packed stones that had started to come lose in places." And while
the interior of the Steen house boasted "a chandelier hanging from
the ceiling which was high on beams," in Hlangeni's house, "The
ceiling of hardboard sagged and there were cracks in it" (85).
Njabulo Ndebele, commenting on La Guma's technique, notes:

> La Guma will not leave anything to imagination... no
> interpretation...is necessary: seeing is meaning... What mat-

ters is what is seen. Thinking is secondary to seeing. Subtlety is secondary to obviousness. What is finally left and what is deeply etched in our minds is the spectacular contest between the powerless and the powerful. (1994:46)

Such imagery establishes an obvious pattern based on recognizable class stratification and the consciousness attached to class and race. This pattern is further delineated when we consider the apartment of the pitiful little Englishman, Edgar Stopes:

> The flat was really an outhouse, separate from the main building; perhaps it had once been servants quarters, but now it was cluttered with the odds and ends bachelors accumulated and a modern—looking drinks cabinet with a coffee table scarred with cigarette-burns in front of it…another section was the bed alcove, cramped, untidy, the bed unmade, scattered with soiled clothes, strewn socks. (39)

Here is another example of La Guma's tendency to develop individual images and to complicate the imagistic pattern; to not simply note comparisons, but to enlarge and expand them for a more comprehensive picture of South African reality. Edgar is a poor white. But in the words of Sartre, "colonial privilege is not solely economic…Even the poorest colonizer thought himself to be— and actually was—superior to the colonized" (Memmi 1967:xii). Edgar's apartment is as much a comment on Edgar as it is on the apartment itself. His apathy is, among other things, a consequence of the negative impact of slavery on mediocre whites. Those who, in the words of Lionel Curtis, came to regard manual labor as appropriate only "to a savage and servile race, and would sooner starve than earn their bread by the sweat of their brow" (Magubane 1996:341). This parallel between the physical environment and the people who occupy it is based upon the interplay between the objective physical conditions and the resultant consciousness of the characters.

One of the most important aspects of this kind of comparative imagery is its structural role, the noticeable part it plays in the total effect of the book. This pattern is evident in several persistently recurring images. Those we have noted compare the material conditions (the landscape, the physical dwellings) of the Afrikaner, English, and African communities and is punctuated by critical and informative delineation of the cultural life, including differentiation of the social practices (and even food, which also reflects specific class differences) of the three competing racial and cultural groups. For example, when Oupa Meulen's granddaughter marries, La Guma gives the following picture:

> The hired orchestra has arrived at last, Hendrik Smit en Sy Orkes, and the afternoon resounds with the music, shouts, laughter, whoops. Here is no fiddle and concertina, but trumpet, saxophone, piano-accordian, bass and drums, and their rhythm sends the birds flapping. Besides the old-time vastrap and tickeydraai, there is the rock-and-roll and the cha-cha-cha. The milling guests perspire, empty beer-cans and discarded bottles begin to appear in the big yard. A jukskei contest has started under the trees, yoke-pegs tossed at a target which is a stake on the ground. (70)

An important idea suggested by this image is that the Afrikaners have raised a culture in South Africa that is, for the most part, uniquely their own. And though it represents an amalgam of other cultures, like Afrikaner identity itself, it is distinctive and a source of ethnic or cultural pride. Even the food present at the wedding party—the nappery, rissoles, beef salad, lamb, pumpkin, home-brewed brandy and preserves—is a reflection of their tastes, values, and social position. "It is our kulture" as Hannes Meulen is so fond of saying. Similar esoteric insight can be gleaned from La Guma's description of various fragments of African culture scattered throughout the book. One example is the story Mma Tau tells of the stokfel given for her when she left the city to return to the countryside:

> When I had to leave to return here they gave a stokfel, the people who knew me. Hauw, what a stokfel that was. It lasted all night and the whole of the next day. A crowd came, people coming and going all the time—I lived in a local township. Each time anybody wished to partake in the stokfel he or she paid something. For instance when one wished someone to dance, he put something in the

> plate; there was a band and they did not play until those
> had contributed. Or if somebody wanted to drink, or relate
> some anecdote or story, or tell a joke, each event required a
> coin or two...Hauw, there was singing and dancing and
> speeches, you know how an indaba can go on for time
> without end. (82)

Africans too have their cultural ethos and values to defend and
maintain. We don't really have to know definitively what a stokfel
or an indaba is in order to grasp the essential meaning of these
images. We know, from the context, that La Guma is giving us a
glimpse of a popular African celebration that has survived the transition from the countryside to the city. When compared with the
image of the Meulens' wedding party, a couple of significant social and economic differences emerge.

The Meulens, for example, had hired an orchestra and the drinks
and food were provided by the hosts. At the stokfel, on the other
hand, the band would not play, and people could not dance or get a
drink, or relate a story, or even tell a joke until they had put a coin
or two in the plate. Obviously, this is done in order to help defray
the costs of putting on the stokfel. Even though the spirit of the
stokfel does not suggest coercion or graft of any sort, the fact that
it had to be conducted in this manner is indicative of a culture of
poverty; and a people uprooted but doggedly determined to perpetuate, in unison, certain aspects of their traditional culture in the
face of adversity and limited financial means.

In addition, the food at the stokfel is further indicative of the
economic and material differences separating Africans and Europeans in South Africa. For example, instead of the rissoles, beef
salad, lamb, and pumpkin of the Meulens' wedding party, Mma
Tau contemplates coming home to "fried dough, the watery tripe,
sour porridge, the slabs of yesterday's bread, the patchwork children behind the fences, the smell of smoke in the dusty yards"
(88). Malnutrition, poverty, and the tenacious will of the African
people to resist and survive stand poised against the racism, oppression, greed, and affluence of the Europeans as vital themes
and images of the physical and moral environment in *Time of the
Butcherbird*; images that are deliberately composed, summed-up,
and re-emphasized until they are firmly rooted in the reader's con-

sciousness. It is precisely this process of arranging, patterning images in the mind and feelings of the audience that allow the images to actually grow, develop, and live in the consciousness of the reader. In like manner, the characters in this novel produce dynamic impressions and are developed over the course of their main action in the work and are not presented as whole, complete individuals, identifiable by simply naming them. A complete picture of each character is the result of the assimilation of different impressions and perspectives, a sort of chain of representations. The images of the major characters—Edgar Stopes, Shilling Murile, and Hannes Meulen—are separated, juxtaposed with others, and reassembled to evoke a more complete and rounded portrait of the initial image. The complete image is, therefore, the work of both author and audience. In *Time of the Butcherbird*, the movement of the major characters can be seen as a kind of parallel, linear, movement that converges at the point of Shilling's gruesome murder of Hannes Meulen and Edgar Stopes. This movement can be illustrated as follows:

> Edgar Stopes—
> Shilling Murile—   =MURDER
> Hannes Meulen—

What this illustration attempts to suggest is that the images of the major characters are intimately related, intertwined with each other, and that there is a dominant movement among them to a supreme, catastrophic conclusion.

Each of these characters expresses a philosophy of life that compels them, unwittingly, to this inevitable disaster. Edgar's motto is "In God we trust and all others cash" (34). A traveling salesman, Edgar must travel into the Afrikaner communities to sell his wares: plastic combs, drag chains, electric light bulbs, hairpins, greeting cards, cough-drops, and a veritable miscellany of trivia. Through Edgar Stopes, La Guma shows the inveterate and cancerous effects of the philosophy of individualism—born of capitalism. The method he uses is, primarily, that of the intellectual image; although, as has been noted, certain images of the physical environment in which Edgar lives depict (and are a comment on) the impact of his attitude on the immediate world around him—for example, his apartment. Edgar's individualism, an echo of that of Shilling after the murder of his brother, Timi, must be an important subject for La Guma, and one that he definitely wants to say something about. On several occasions and in various ways, Edgar promulgates his philosophy of life:

> "You got to get after the gravy, everybody for himself and
> the devil take the bugger at the back. That's life." (38)

And at another time, in another way, he expresses the same view to Maisie, his eventual wife:

> "...there's no need to be poor. Are you poor, am I poor?
> No, because we got initiative, hey. We got brains. Look
> after number one that's what I say. If it wasn't for people
> like us, why the country would never be civilised." (39)

This man, Edgar Stopes, seems, by virtue of La Guma's narrative method, to exist primarily in the superficial world of his senses, defined largely by what he sees and what he smells and what he hears. In this sensory world, people are merely objects among other objects; like the paraphernalia he panders, and the "nigger doll hanging by its neck above the middle of the (car) windscreen" (2). And the Afrikaners fare no better than the Africans as objects of his derision, as he thinks of them as "bloody farmboys, a lot of bloody backward Dutchmen as dumb as the sheep they raise" (24).

When Edgar first meets Maisie, his eventual wife, his offer to take the whole family to an evening at the lounge is, to him "an investment in the future," because "Maisie looked a bit of a good thing" (35). And his thoughts of Maisie are constantly focused on the external: her hips, her breasts, her lips, and her hair, never on the inner person—her character or personality or intelligence. Edgar's "you got to look out for number one" is contagious, and Maisie, in an ironic twist, is soon a practicing convert of this philosophy. During Edgar's selling trips, she takes up with another man, Wally Basson, who—from the same individualistic perspective as Edgar's—wants Maisie to become a prostitute:

"Now look here. Me and you, we like the good life, isn't it?
The shows, clubs, trips?"
"Naturally."
"But it costs, hey. So we got to speculate to accumulate,
there isn't no other way."
"Oh, I reckon not."
"There, you see? You got it. You got understanding, baby,
true as God." He smoothed out a fold in his news-paper.
"The way I see it, I mean the way I been looking at it is like
this. There's a lot of guts with cash go to those places we
go to. Right? Rich jokers. So maybe some of them want
some extra fun." (54)

Maisie is, to say the least, shocked: "Her voice froze into gritty
ice." Maisie's intent was, of course, to use Wally, but now the
tables have turned. Whenever her husband, Edgar, is away there
are the plush cinemas, the cocktail lounges, discotheques, gam-
bling casinos in Swaziland, and her abiding fantasy of being like
one of the American film stars she idolizes—Alice Faye, June
Allyson, Greer Garson, Lana Turner, Rhonda Fleming, Olivia De
Havilland; and the men around her, particularly Edgar and Wally,
she envisions and compares to Tony Curtis, Robert Mitchum, Audie
Murphy, Van Johnson, Brian Donlevy, Cary Grant, Errol Flynn,
John Wayne, Clint Eastwood, Robert Redford, Boris Karloff, and
James Bond. La Guma's citing of these American film stars, primarily through the interior monologue of Maisie, serves at least
three distinct functions. First, it exposes the deep penetration of
American cultural values into the consciousness and culture of
South Africa, black and white. Second, the names, themselves,
provide an historical context (the 1970s—excluding flashbacks that
are a significant dimension of Maisie's romantic nostalgia) for the
major action of the novel. Third, Maisie's preoccupation with film
stars enables La Guma to demonstrate the superficiality and artifi-
ciality of the make-believe world in which she is immersed. Contemplating the triangular relationship between Edgar, Maisie, and
Wally, one is struck by the rather simple yet terrifying logic it reveals. Edgar, for instance, sells things; Maisie also sells things—
at the family store; and Wally also wants to sell something—Maisie.
Edgar uses Maisie as his personal plaything; in fact, she gets pregnant during their courtship. And, due to the encouragement of her

mother—who, more or less, sells Maisie to Edgar because, to her, "That young man got go...He'll get places"—Maisie ends up selling herself to Edgar, to get ahead, materially, financially, to "get places." Then there is Wally, who uses her for his own sexual needs and then wants to sell her as a prostitute. At the same time, Maisie is using Wally to satisfy her infantile fantasies of Hollywood stardom, and what's even more selfish and callous (but certainly consistent with the "look out for number one philosophy"), wishes Edgar would die so that she can collect the four thousand rands in life insurance.

> It struck her that she had seen in some film that an insurance company paid double if the insured died in some uncommon accident. Two times two thousand pounds, roughly speaking. Here Jesus, girl, you can set out on your own with that much; no useless loudmouthed Edgar, no old bag of a stingy mother, and you wouldn't need Wally Basson to depend on for a flash life. With eight thousand rand, who need Wally bloody Basson? Independence. You got to look after number one, that's what old Edgar always was on about, wasn't he? (55)

The cancerous philosophy of "looking out for number one" is infectious, and Maisie is now a carrier and believer of this morally degenerating idea. She even begins contemplating a way to kill Edgar: she has a little pistol from the gun club and "Maybe she could pretend she couldn't handle it properly and Edgar could show her and it could go off, accidental like" (55).

Maisie and Edgar are united by their rabid individualism and, ironically, by their contempt for each other. She wishes him dead and contemplates his murder; while he thinks of her as a "second-rate chorus girl who believed she was a star and should be out front under the lights" (9)—so, he is always happy to be away from her during his travels as a salesman. They also share their contempt for Africans, evidenced by their constant references to niggers, coons, and kaffirs. The irony is further complicated by the fact that Maisie is an Afrikaner, and Edgar expresses nothing but contempt for Afrikaners every opportunity he gets. In their company, "he, Edgar Stopes, was the stranger, the outsider...Christ, one would think a man was a bloody nigger, them and their bloody ox-wagons and ploughs" (24). And upon meeting Hannes Meulen and hearing him comment on the importance of unity among South African whites, Edgar thinks, "bit of a pompous ass, if you ask me. English and Afrikaans people unite—but did he bother to speak a bit of English?" (29)

Where Maisie and Edgar are concerned, however, the economic motive takes precedence over the considerations of nationality and ethnicity. Their relationship has been reduced to a mere money relation. Here again, La Guma's careful and meticulous selection of characters, and their attendant attitudes and actions, provides critical insights into the intrinsic and complex nature of South African race relations. The images of Edgar and Maisie help to clarify much of this complexity while, concomitantly, demonstrating the political and cultural hegemony of the Afrikaners: an hegemony vehemently resented by the English and Africans alike. The musings and behavior of Edgar make this deep-felt resentment perfectly clear:

> ...in the countryside he was like a foreigner and he had learnt that he would make no headway with these people unless he submitted to their narrow arrogance... why in hell couldn't a man talk his own language instead of having to struggle with their mumbo-jumbo? After all he belonged as much as they did, and above all he was doing them a service. Yet in order to maintain goodwill, to obtain the orders of plastic combs, drag chains, electric light bulbs, he had to surrender his identity, become a bad imitation of one of these bloody Dutchmen. (4)

Of course it never occurs to Edgar, representative of a rather pervasive, universal European attitude, that Africans also ask the question, "Why in hell Afrikaans? Why in hell couldn't a man talk his own language?"—that Africans too must weigh the benefits of surrendering their identity to become bad imitations of the bloody Dutch or English, before they can expect to receive respect as human beings. For Africans also realize that the right to be treated equally and with respect is not an earned right, it is a right to which the mere fact of one's humanity entitles one.

Through Edgar and Maisie, Alex La Guma continues his effort to demonstrate the inhumanity of the myth of white supremacy through the myopic shallowness of the lives of the characters. As such, the malignant Western ideology of "look out for number one" has personal and national consequences of serious socio-political significance. In *Time of the Butcherbird*, all those who adopt this ideology fail. The national consequences of the "look out for number one" philosophy are emphatically expressed when Hannes Meulen says to Edgar Stopes:

> Yes, it is needful to keep in touch with the country folk, Mr. Stopes. You are lucky in that your affairs bring you among us. I am really talking of contact between the English-speaking people and the Afrikaans. In these times it is necessary that we stand together. (28)

Here, the "number one" is thought of as all white people, and Edgar agrees "one hundred per cent." Hannes goes on to say:

> ...parties need not divide us, what must be uppermost in our minds must be the survival of our united people... we must forget old wounds and think of the common good. I am talking about our way of life, everything which our People have done to make this a hospitable and proud country. (28)

These intellectual images of character speak directly to the attempt of Afrikaners and the English to create a false unity predicated solely on color. They also express a typical and ubiquitous attitude of colonizers that categorically denies the innate equality between all human beings; that "Africans would do what they were told, and their countries would be 'developed' for them" (Davidson 1992:41); and "their extraordinary assumption that the key to Civilization is in their hands" (Baldwin 1985:80-81). So there is a dominant movement among these and similar images, revealing European attitudes towards each other and toward Africans; attitudes that cause the death of Timi, Hannes Meulen, and Edgar Stopes.

The Germans, as Hannes remembers, also stood for unity of the race, of the chosen people of God. However, being aware of the disastrous consequences of this kind of thinking does not deter Hannes, or his kith and kin. Thus, when he speaks of "the common good" his narrow vision does not allow him to see humanity, but only "the common good" of Europeans. Hannes is utterly convinced that the wealth and material comfort of the Afrikaner people is founded on and cemented by their racial, cultural, and religious purity (64) and unrelated to the slavery and labor of African people.

Hannes Meulen, like his father before him, believes in the philosophy and opinions of Adolf Hitler. The Afrikaner people as a whole, at least as they are represented in *Time of the Butcherbird*, opposed war with Germany because the Germans stood for unity and purity of white people. It was clearly understood by Hitler, if by no one else, that the Hebrew people, the original Jewish people, came from Africa; that is, out of ancient Ethiopia. Hannes Meulen accepts the myopic vision and narrow-mindedness of his predecessors and his contemporary kith and kin throughout Europe and America, and thus offers himself as his peoples' candidate in the election for parliament—the Volksraad. Hannes' acceptance of this leadership position for the Afrikaner people means that he will be measured, or judged, effective or ineffective, acceptable or unacceptable, based on his ability to maintain the apartheid, racist (white supremacist) mythic ideology and the color and class structure it demands.

Therefore, more important than the physical portraits of Hannes are the various moral, intellectual portraits we get of him—the content of his character, rather than the color of his skin (Dr. Martin Luther King). We know, for example, that he is forty years old, smokes a pipe, golfs, is a candidate for Parliament, is engaged to be married to Rina Steen, and, perhaps, more importantly from the perspective of the central focus of the novel on the question of land and separate development, he is heir to his father's farm, the source of the Meulen family wealth:

> The farm was a going concern, except of course for the present drought, but there had been droughts before: his sister had been married off years ago and was happily settled; he himself had made strides. He had joined the national party after graduation, the nearest thing to what his father had upheld, and he was a prospective Member of Parliament for his constituency. Marriage to the girl he cared for and a public future lay ahead of him. (58-59)

From this portrait, the reader gets a more rounded image of Hannes Meulen, the measure of his success as a politician, and an assessment of him as simply another man who comes from a normal family. A man who has the normal hopes and dreams of any man, and whose hamartia, like Macbeth's, is his political and economic ambition. The measure of his success is also predicated upon his ability to keep or put the *niggers* or *kaffirs* in their place. Hannes accepts this burden of racism (white supremacy) and says to Kasper Steen:

> "As soon as the Bantu have been moved, the development of that area will commence. As you know, by request of the people here I myself went to the magistrate to ask that they be moved...."
> "Those black things will move, of course," Steen remarked. (61)

This image of Hannes and Kasper in dialogue is certainly meant to serve a social function. That is, it describes the social or collective attitude of the Afrikaner people, as understood by La Guma, towards African people: as opposed to, or in addition to, just Hannes' and Kasper's individual or personal attitudes. This attitude is identical to the German attitude toward the Jews of Nazi Germany. Dehumanizing each person, "the Bantu...Those black things," robbing them of their individuality, by rendering each, to the Afrikaner eye, but another body in an undifferentiated mass, is but the first step towards fashioning their "subhumans" (Goldhagen 1996:176). We know, for example, that Dr. Hendrik Verwoerd, the primary architect of apartheid, studied at universities in Hamburg, Leipzig and Berlin in Germany, obtained his doctorate in psychology in 1924 and titled his thesis *The Blunting of the Emotions*, which is precisely what he proceeded to accomplish in South Africa. It is, therefore, easy to see the similarity of the homelands policy in South Africa and the camp system in Germany, and with similar results:

> By denying the camp system's population adequate nutrition, indeed by subjecting many to starvation, by forcing them to perform backbreaking labor for unmanageably long

hours, by providing them with grossly inadequate clothing
and shelter, not to mention medical care, and by perpetrating steady violence on their bodies and minds, the Germans succeeded in making many of the camp system's inhabitants take on the appearance...and behavioral attributes
of the "subhumans" that the Germans imagined them to be.
(Goldhagen 176)

Oppression does indeed justify itself through oppression. As Jean-
Paul Sartre states so very clearly: "the oppressors produce and
maintain by force the evils that render the oppressed, in their eyes,
more and more like what they would have to be like to deserve
their fate" (Memmi 1967: xxvi). The material conditions in which
African people are confined confirms in the Afrikaner mind—and
in the universal white mind—how devoid of dignity, how far removed from being humans worthy of respect and full moral consideration are Africans and other people of color (176). These observations can be illustrated vividly in the image sequence leading
to the death of Timi, Shilling Murile's brother, a central though not
major character in the work, and a pivotal event. During the wedding festivities of Oupa Meulen's granddaughter, one of the African serving-women has sneaked out two bottles of brandy to share
with her coworkers. The men get intoxicated and some fall asleep
"sprawled against the walls and stretched out in the scattered hay,
among the bales of lucerne grass, limp and ragged, like fallen scare-
crows" (71). Among the drunk and fallen are Shilling and his
brother, Timi. As they stagger homeward, they pass a sheep kraal,
and in their inebriated stupor open the kraal gate and wander drunkenly among the sheep exhorting them to dance: "Dance, dance, my
sheep, everybody dance" (72). Soon the sheep break through the
open gate and trot out into the open field. They go one way and
the brothers, giggling and staggering drunkenly, go another. When
Hannes and his farm-foreman, Opperman, discover the wandering
sheep—a compelling metaphor for the African masses—and the
two drunk brothers responsible for "freeing" them, Hannes is beside himself with anger, and says to Opperman: "Well, man, tie up
those baboons. Fasten them to the posts. They'll be all right here
till morning" (74). Shilling, seeking a reprieve, says to Hannes,

"Baas, you know me. This is a bad thing to do, boss. Why, you know me, I carried the buck which you shot, I cleaned your guns, you know me."

"Know you shit," Meulen said with contempt. "Since when do I know a kaffir? One kaffir looks just like another as it concerns me." (74-75)

Anger and a lack of any sense of the human value of the two Africans combine to make Opperman vicious, and he binds the two brothers to a fence-post with wire—so tight that it cut into their flesh, restricting even the flow of blood. Timi, we learn earlier, "had always been a little weak in the chest," and the wire inhibiting his blood circulation is simply too much for him to take, and during the night he dies.

The next morning, when Hannes and Opperman discover that Timi is dead, and think that the two of them will be blamed for his death, Hannes, consistent with his insensitive and racist character remarks, "Dammit... these kaffirs are always causing trouble" (76). As previously noted, La Guma is quite fond of juxtaposing images; particularly those indicative of class and race (color) differences. Thus, we have the contrasting image sequences depicting the consciousness and material condition of Edgar Stopes and Maisie, juxtaposed with images depicting Hannes and Rina. Perhaps the most interesting aspect of this image-patterning is the realization that the white South African lower class, typified by Edgar and Maisie, share the same racist consciousness in relation to Africans. The reader is left with the valid impression that South African society is permeated, from bottom to top, with the dehumanizing values of white supremacy (racism). Even the judicial process aids and abets this system of oppression. The District Court decided that, as far as Timi's death is concerned,

...there had been provocation. Meneer Meulen had not intended the death of this Bantu, but he should have acted with more thought...Meneer Meulen was a well-liked and well-known figure in the local community and should have known better. The judge had no alternative but to render a severe reprimand and a stiff fine. (77)

It is amazing how much the circumstances of life in South Africa resemble those of the slave-holding southern United States of two hundred years ago. The Peculiar Institution, while never reluctant to protect and maximize property rights (Shilling, for example, is charged with sheep-stealing) produced judges and legislators who were reluctant to recognize that Africans in America had, in their own right, any basic human rights. The above event, for example, echoes Mark Twain's *Huckleberry Finn*, in a parody of white attitudes of the 19th century where concerning a particular incident, he writes:

> "Good gracious. Anybody hurt?"
> "No'm. Killed a nigger."
> "Well, it's lucky because sometimes people do get hurt."
> (Higginbotham 1978:7)

Similarly, judges in South Africa, today, so it appears from La Guma's eye-witness report, fear that any judicial protection of Africans would encourage challenges to the legitimacy of the de-humanized status of Africans as property and wage slaves; as "a species apart from white humans, the difference justifying separate and different treatment" (Higginbotham 7). South Africa seems to have borrowed from their white American cousins and jurisprudence the notion that the power of the white South Africans must be absolute and unquestioned, to make the submission of black South Africans perfect.

It is, therefore, of primary significance to the structural and thematic design of *Time of the Butcherbird*, that the climax, the denouement—Shilling Murile's shotgun murder of the lower-class Englishman, Edgar Stopes, and the upper class Afrikaner, Hannes Meulen—would be simultaneous. Shilling's target is, specifically, Hannes, whom he holds personally accountable for his brother Timi's death; however, when it comes to the precise moment of active revenge, he sees only white faces. In the same manner that Edgar and Hannes deny the individuality of Shilling and other Africans ("One kaffir looks just like another as it concerns me" Hannes had said), now Shilling too, his vision distorted by rage and personal "look out for number one" vengeance, looses sight of his primary target and kills both Edgar and Hannes. The fantastic irony implied by this imagistic and thematic development is politically instructive and profound.

Edgar Stopes saw the sunlight irregularly obscured by the
face and form of the black man who Meulen saw but did not
recognize.

Hannes Meulen did not recognize his own latest model
automatic shotgun either, but wondered for a second why
the black man had it because that wasn't allowed; behind
him Edgar Stopes saw the look of anger, then the flash and
heard the blast, and the next thing there was a slither and a
heavy thump together with a wet slap across his cheek,
which was made by one of Hannes Meulen's ears as his
head was blown off, and the whitewash of the passage-wall
was suddenly decorated with a blossom petalled with blood
and brains and pieces of bone and fragments of teeth like
pomegranate pips.

Edgar Stopes, still holding his catalogue and order-book,
knowing something was wrong, stared open-mouthed back
at the single eye of the shotgun that was leaking foul-smell-
ing vapour, and somewhere he could hear a nerve-torment-
ing, birdlike shrieking while his bowels turned helpless and
his mind cried out to somebody called Maisie, but the sound
of the tortured bird was the only Sound he heard as the next
blast killed him. (110)

It is not Shilling's intention to kill Edgar Stopes; he just happens to
be in the wrong place at the wrong time. Yet, La Guma, by design-
ing this scene in this way, is able to make several insightful statements concerning the vulgarity of homicide, the meaning of innocence, and the blinding effects of rage and racial hatred. La Guma
makes this image as horrifying and repulsive as possible, without
losing its quality of realism and aesthetic sense. The alliteration of
B's—blossom, blood, brains, and bone—tends to indicate the acti-
vation of the author's poetic sense in deference to and engendered
by this highly emotionally charged event.

The "accidental" murder of Edgar Stopes makes it clear that
the effects of racial (color) hatred, by blacks or whites, is blinding
and leaves no room for individual distinctions. We remember Shilling saying "I am finished with white people" (without distinction,
without exception) and Hannes saying "Since when do I know a
kaffir? One kaffir looks just like another as it concerns me," and
suddenly Shilling's premeditated murder of Hannes and accidental
murder of Edgar makes sense. The individualism and selfishness
of these three men has profound meaning and implications for the

larger South African context. It suggests that in the throes of revolutionary violence of the African majority, and the counter-revolutionary violence of the European minority, there is no distinction of persons, no individuality, no innocence: Africans are on one side and Europeans on the other. And what stands between them is a wall (a wall of dust, to use La Guma's metaphor) of racism, bigotry, greed, and ignorance. La Guma's metaphor of dust is masterful, because it suggests that "the wall" is not solid or insurmountable, but it does contaminate, obfuscate, irritate, and often blind. *Time of the Butcherbird* is told, predominantly, through the distorted perceptions of these three narrators, whose interaction with the other characters in the story weaves a complex tapestry of the anguished soul of South Africa. As with much of La Guma's writing, it does not matter whose version of South African history is true; in fact, there can be no true version of the perspectives presented, given the subjectivity of the points of view. What is significant to each of La Guma's characters—and, indeed, to ourselves—is the search for an understanding of reality each of us undertakes as we engage his works. And what we discover in *Butcherbird* is that the composite vision produced by Shilling Murile, Edgar Stopes, and Hannes Meulen is true to the racial history of South Africa.

The murder of Hannes and Edgar is thematically and aesthetically necessary to the meaning of the work. Their deaths, in effect, mark the end of the story. But it is not the end of the social reality the novel reflects. For it is knowledge of the social reality that provides the key to Shilling's behavior.

For Shilling, the critical point, the turning point is reached much earlier in the novel, that is, when his brother, Timi, died coughing in the cold, windy South African night—a Christ-like figure lashed to a fence-post with wire cutting into his flesh. And La Guma extends this Christ-like metaphor with the *risen* Shilling Murile who can think of nothing but vindicating his brother's unnecessary death. Up until the night of the *crucifixion*, Timi and Shilling had had a *normal* South African childhood; that is, a family and community environment that provided the security and succor necessary for healthy psychological growth; and it is the disruption and displacement of this environment that is responsible for Shilling's psychic and behavioral alienation from his people. The shepherd, Madonele, understands this, intuitively, and tries to comfort Shilling in his vindictive nostalgia:

> "It was a bad thing that the white man did to you and to your brother. Badder still was what he did to your brother...."
> "Since your brother is gone, does that mean there is no home, no family, people? We are all your brothers. I recall you and your brother. You were boys who had zest and always did things together. You cared for the animals together and what men are meant to do in the village. I remember when you went through the rites of manhood. You stayed away a long time and others had to be sent to find you."
> "We had found a leopard's tracks and followed it," the other said. "Now I do not wish to talk of those times." (18-19)

Shilling does not want to hear any arguments that will deter him from his single-minded goal of vindicating Timi's death: "I am finished with white people," Shilling exclaims. And in so saying, he expresses a blanket, generalized condemnation of all white people, and not just those immediately responsible for his brother's death—Hannes Meulen and Opperman. In his own inarticulate way, Shilling knows that the root cause of his brother's death and the displacement of his people is systemic and not some mental quirk on the part of a couple of misguided individuals.

We observe, therefore, in Shilling, Edgar, and Hannes a similar, if not identical point of view, despite La Guma's delineation of them in terms of race, class, and personal ambition. There is, for example, no motivation based on love of country (i.e., inclusive of all who live there), and no interest in the welfare of anyone outside their own immediate family. For Hannes and Edgar the "look out for number one" philosophy is part of their cultural ethos, a part of their habitual thought pattern. For Shilling, however, this attitude of mind is foreign to his culture, a culture whose essence is predicated on the axiom "I am because we are," and the shepherd, Madonele, encourages Shilling to remember himself as part of this tradition. Shilling will have none of it, and tells Madonele, "Now I do not wish to talk of those times." He wants to admit nothing that will obscure his singular vision of revenge. Thus, Shilling's behavior, at the heart of the action, is not in keeping with either his essential nature or the values of his society, but is in direct contrast with its most basic philosophy—"I am because we are."

Mma Tau, sister of the puppet-chief Hlangeni, sensing Shilling's motives of personal vengeance, tries to redirect his thinking back to the collective, and in dialogue with him brings out the essential nature of the struggle to be waged and the selfish, narrow-minded pitfall of personal revenge:

> "Listen to me, they say revenge is sweet. Is that it, the sweetness of revenge?"
>
> "What is it to you? It is a debt," Shilling Murile told her. "Somebody owes a debt."
>
> "Certainly," Mma-Tau said. "There are many debts to be collected. It is not for me to stand in your way if you wish to collect your debt, but hear this. A whole people is starting to think of collecting a collective debt, the time for collecting this debt is drawing on. All over the country people are feeling it. You have been away for years so you do not know how the porridge is boiling in the pot. In relation to that, your debt, though important to you, become of small significance."
>
> "It is my thing," Shilling Murile said morosely. "Wasn't my brother killed?"
>
> "Who is denying that? You are entitled to justice."
>
> "I have been eight years in the white man's prison."
>
> "Of course, man. But our people go to prison every day. Are not our leaders in prison? We are all in prison, the whole country is a prison. Our people die all the time, of starvation, diseases, of murder, of shooting and hanging."
>
> "Why are you telling me this?"
>
> "You can be of use to us. You have hatred, the desire to find justice. But do not be satisfied with your personal achievement of justice, if you find it. It is a small thing when compared with the people's need for justice. As I have said, a man with your desire for vengeance belongs with the people."
>
> Shilling Murile scowled at her. "I have no need of People. This is my thing, and afterwards I'll go my way." (80)

Shilling does not trust fate or the unknown "whole people *starting to think* of collecting a collective debt"; he trusts only a known quantity, himself, to put his vengeance into action. In short, he has no faith, which requires imagination. He has succumbed to the "look out for number one" Western *Weltanschauung* and that, in a word, is his hamartia, and his tragedy.

The isolation and alienation of Shilling Murile, which is concomitantly a punishment and sort of tragic dignity or honor—in the sense that he is an individual acting out of his own conscience—takes place by stages and by deliberate choice. It begins when Timi is "accidentally" murdered and reaches its height in the final action when he murders Hannes Meulen and Edgar Stopes.

The nature of Shilling's alienation and the self-destructive, single-minded, vindictive state of mind it induces is such that it can be adequately expressed only in metaphorical terms, particularly that of an ant, of which Shilling thinks: "He has somewhere to go and he knows that he is going there. He is like me, that little ant, knowing where he will go, what he will do" (15). Shilling's metaphorical equivalent is the ant, just as the metaphorical equivalent of "the people" is that of sheep. In fact, these images—of the ant and the sheep—would appear incidental or even superfluous were it not for the metaphorical value they convey.

For example, Mandonele cares for a herd of sheep that are emaciated and dying for lack of water and food. Throughout the novel, there are references to the sheep: "bleating in protest" (17), ambling "wearily along the stream bed," heading "slowly towards a kraal" (21); and most revealing of all is the attitude of Hannes Meulen and the white establishment—when resettlement is imminent—that lumps the people and the sheep together without the slightest distinction. So Hannes is able to say to Kasper Steen, "some of the trucks have taken sheep over to where there is more water, and I have promised two lorries to the Commissioner to transport the kaffirs tomorrow" (63). This image pattern makes it possible to interpret Shilling's and Timi's drunken act of releasing the sheep as a metaphor for Shilling's murder of Hannes and Edgar; that is, bringing the collective conscience to life. Without taking this too far, it should be remembered that it is Shilling's murder of these to white men that has the potential of bringing this conscience to life.

Pursuing this metaphor a bit further, we find that after his hei-
nous crime, Shilling makes his way back toward the village and
again, as in the beginning, he runs into Mandonele and they exchange words: "You and your sheep," Shilling says to him, to which
Mandonele replies, "So it is you... You came far and even ahead of
me"; to which Shilling answers, "I'm not slowed down by sheep"
(117). This seems a very important comment in light of the fact
that he has just killed two white men. And Sartre, in his Preface to
Fanon's *The Wretched of the Earth* quickens our understanding of
this event when he writes:

> When the peasant takes a gun in his hands, the old myths
> grow dim and the prohibitions are one by one forgotten.
> The rebel's weapon is the proof of his humanity. For in the
> first days of revolt you must kill: to shoot a European is to
> kill two birds with one stone, to destroy an oppressor and
> the man he oppresses at the same time: there remain a dead
> man, and a free man; the survivor, for the first time, feels a
> national soil under his foot. (1981:18-19)

Shilling, therefore, remains a tragic but heroic figure. If anything,
he seems to improve as the result of his crime. As the novel is
ending, we notice that Shilling is throwing off his alienation and
isolation and is on his way to becoming absorbed again into his
community—but, insisting until the end on his individuality. Evidence of this can be obtained from the dialogue that takes place
between Shilling and Mandonele, after the former has murdered
Hannes and Edgar, and the two men are sitting drinking water from
a bottle:

> The shepherd replaced the cork and asked, his eyes Low-
> ered: "Tell me, did you do what you came to do?"
>   "I do not wish to talk about such things now. Say that
> my brother Timi rests peacefully."....
>   "They will come after you."
>   "How? Do they know me?"
>   "Hmmm! Then you must join with us, the villagers, and
> be lost among us. But they will be coming after the villag-
> ers too. The woman said they would send police and even
> flying machines." (117)

Again, strategically interrupting their exchange is the metaphor that has pursued Shilling throughout the novel, as another ant "circled a blade of cracked grass and went out of sight down a crease in the sand" (118).

Shilling is not a monster, though in some catalogue he might be listed as one because of the repulsiveness of his deed. But his deed is only the wishes and fears of the average, undistinguished African translated into action; which is why the shepherd, Mandonele, can suggest that he lose himself among the villagers. This offer and Shilling's "improved" attitude is even more explicit after he shows the shotgun to Mandonele, who asks "Will you keep it?" To which Shilling replies, "Why not? We might find out what can be done with it." And Mandonele, excited by hearing this plural pronoun from Shilling for the first time is quick to add: "You said we. Are you coming with our people?" And Shilling, clinging to his individuality, quips with wry humor, "Let us say I am coming with you, old man...Remember, you have my tobacco" (118). That is the tobacco Shilling had given to Mandonele upon first meeting him in the countryside in the early pages of the novel.

It seems that only the courageous, outspoken, and perceptive Mma Tau is able to see the situation whole, and says to her people: "We are still a people. With laws and guns and money he [the white man] knows nothing of people, does not sense the dignity of people. This inability to see mystifies him, baffles him, for he cannot understand it, and he is defeated because in him there is no heart, no dignity" (46). Then, given La Guma's intransigent Marxism, she adds:

> "They exist in a false happiness of guns and laws, they exist with false laughter, for the laughter is not really theirs. Do they know the meaning of their laws and their false happiness and their undignified laughter? The meaning is this: that men are of two kinds, the poor who toil and create the riches of the earth: and the rich who do not toil but devour it. The meaning is this: that the people demand their share of the fruits of the earth, and their rulers, of whom the white man is a lackey, a servant, refuse them a fair portion. And it is this: that the people insist, the rulers deprive them of work, drive them from their homes, and if they still resist, send their lackeys to shoot them down with guns." (47)

Mma Tau's *analysis* is correct—up to a point. It is correct when it recognizes that the average white person is a "lackey" and "servant" of larger interests, such as transnational corporations and organizations like the Trilateral Commission. However, it is deficient in failing to clearly admit that the lackeys' rulers, European and American capitalism, are also white; that they are at the same time the cause and effect of their malaise. It is, perhaps, wise to remember the admonition of Frantz Fanon, who in inserting the color factor into the colonial equation observed, "You are rich because you are white and you are white because you are rich."

Between the two positions (Shilling's and Mma Tau's) however, Mma Tau has the more correct theory (i.e., the need for organization and collective resistance), but the wrong practice. She still conceives of power as numbers per se, and marching on the capital to protest the pass laws she says, "I was one of those who marched to the capital to protest. Thousands of women, and it gave a sense of power. One learned the power of numbers" (81). Her theoretical position that the "whole people is starting to think of collecting a collective debt" (80) is in direct contrast to Shilling's "a thing of my own" (49). Shilling has the wrong theory; yet, where the masses of African people are concerned, and considering the depth and duration of African suffering, his practice—given the revolutionary principles subsumed under the Marxist theory La Guma adhears to—is more correct.

Finally, we want to consider that peculiar use of imagery that distinguishes La Guma's image-making technique and style and provides the most recognizable symbolism in his works; and that is the desecration of physical bodies as a metaphor for the South African white supremacist system. In *Time of the Butcherbird*, the image that conveys the idea of desecration is the image of dust.

The image of the dust is ubiquitous in this novel; especially when it is recognized that the overall barrenness of the imagistic style is an appropriate response to the actual barrenness of the environment in which the predominant actions in the novel take place.

In the very first paragraph of the story, there are no fewer than six specific references to dust: it "hung over the plain and smudged the blistering afternoon sun"; it "hung in the sky"; it "settled slowly on the metal of the [water] tank and on the surface of the brackish water it contained" and "on the rough cubist mounds of folded and piled tents dumped there by officialdom" and "on the sullen faces of the people who had been unloaded like the odds and ends of furniture...settling on the unkempt and travel-creased clothes, so that they had the look of scarecrows left behind, abandoned in this place." La Guma succeeds in making perfectly clear, from the outset, that the area set aside by the white South African government for the resettlement of Africans is a desolate wasteland unfit for human habitation. Thus, having been dumped like useless furniture in their new homeland, La Guma writes:

> The people stood in the afternoon burn of the molten-metal sun, the scorching air turning the sweat and dust to plaster on their faces. They shuffled in the dust...An infant wailed ...a child complained, someone spat out the dust and hummed the opening bars of a song. (1)

Somehow, some people could still manage to sing in this wretched and deserted land—aware, it seems, of why the caged bird sings. It is an environment where everything is permeated by or literally turns to dust: "This was no land for ploughing and sowing," one of the nameless refugees laments, "it was not even good enough to be buried in" (1).

As such, from the very beginning, a series of images helps to emphasize the idea that the dust, along with the humid and oppressive physical landscape of the South African veldt, is going to be an important factor in the story in both physical and moral terms. The impact of the environment on psychological and emotional states is inherent and inseparable from the repetitive image of dust; its effects play a distinctive part in the structure and atmosphere of the novel.

The dust, like the myth of white superiority, distorts and disfigures, "turning the sweat and dust to plaster on their faces"; it strangles and chokes ("someone spat out dust"); and perhaps most importantly, it obscures and taints the consciousness and vision of those like Edgar Stopes, who looks out "across the dusty landscape.... In front of the dust-powdered windscreen" to the "scorched countryside" (2).

Several images portray the obfuscating and debilitating effects of the dust: "the town's only service station displayed its petrol pumps and dusty flags." Upon entering the small town, Edgar notices "the Boer War monument in the dusty square." Then a man comes out of the store and begins to sweep the sidewalk, when suddenly "a boy on a bicycle raised the wake of red dust, unnecessarily," and "A man in untidy khaki and felt hat…climbed into his dusty car." And as Kobe and Hlangeni left the Commissioner's office "Kobe…put a finger to one nostril and blew his nose in the dust," and the boy came by on his bicycle again "spraying them with red dust…. They slapped dust from their clothes" and "They set out across the square raising little spurts of dust that settled back in the footprints made by their old and cracked shoes." And as Shilling makes his way across the veldt, on his way back home after eight years in prison, "the red dust rose from underfoot and got into his nostrils and between his lips, but he was use to fine dust, dust was nothing—there were other more important things about which a man should think."

By the recurrent use of the image of dust, together with the step-by-step development of the rendezvous of Shilling, Hannes, and Edgar, La Guma gives the reader a sense of continuity and gives the dust imagery structural and thematic consistency and depth. Character and atmosphere therefore condition the reader to this climactic convergence.

The abundant use of a particular image to convey thematic ideas appears to be an habitual mode of expression for La Guma. We see it in the image of nausea in *A Walk in the Night*: and in the image of the rain in *And a Threefold Cord*: and in the image of the wind in *The Stone Country*. Evidence of such a technique or stylistic habit may be useful in understanding the author's works.

Except, perhaps, to the student of imagery, such images would not be conspicuous at all. They are tightly woven into the pattern of the story and do not attract unnecessary attention. The story moves so fast that most readers have little time to pause and consider such fine points of style. They are, however, of particular interest if only because of the exceptionally close integration of the images into the narrative.

In *Butcherbird* nothing remains untouched and in some way defiled or distorted by the ubiquitous dust. In Maisie's father's store, "the stacked products gathered dust"; and in the African village, of Mma Tau, Hlangeni, and their people, "dust drifted like a fog and clung to the German-print dresses of the older women, powdered the coats of the dogs twitching in the shadows, and settled in new layers on the rusty roofs."

Like racism, the dust corrodes, taints, and vulgarizes everyone and everything it touches; it is, indeed, a fitting analogy for the myth of white superiority and systems derive and predicated on this myth. To the reader, therefore, the dust is not simply dust, which would undoubtedly be a topographical fact of the humid South African veldt, but conveys overtones of meaning which are multidimensional, transcendent, and implicit in the meaning of the story. In other words, La Guma has taken what is specific and objective in his environment and has imbued and combined it with what is transcendent and universal in expression.

Viewed from this perspective, the imagery of dust, as it desecrates physical bodies, imparts a deeper intellectual meaning by its pattern of interlocking images. It is, therefore, a shaping principle (helping to organize the movement and episodes in the work) as well as a containing principle holding the work together.

Dust—minute particles, small and light and easily raised and carried in a cloud by the wind—is analogous to the minute, small, light, and otherwise insignificant ideas that undergird the universal white supremacy myth. Such irritating ideas, like dust, become influential when consolidated and carried in a consciousness by racist rhetoric—like that of the Dutch Reform Church. The Dominee Visser is carrier of such rhetoric, as when he speaks to his flock:

> The heathen around us have blighted us since the times of our forefathers who delivered this country into our hands. The victors sinned against keeping the blood pure. Sin came with the mixing of blood as sure as Adam ate of the forbidden apple. Blood pollution and the lowering of the racial level which goes with it, are the only cause why old civilizations disappear. The causes are not lost wars, but the lost power of resistance which ensures the purity of the blood. (106)

Here the image is intellectual and auditory. This is not a symbolic statement but the expression of a Christian Church minister, standing just for itself. The small, minute minds that disseminate such ideas are like the wind that carries the *dust*. And these are, as La Guma describes them, "fundamentally a simple people and took what he said for granted" (107). *Dust,* therefore, a recurrent symbol of the desecration of physical bodies, also stands for the desecration of human consciousness and human values, as articulated by the Dominee Visser.

If a writer continually draws upon certain types of natural elements (like rain, wind, dust) and certain qualities in them (like their capriciousness, indifference, force or desecrating effects) and certain conditions of life (like the poor, the abused, the imprisoned, the dispossessed, the courageous) for his illustrations, then we are justified in arguing that these qualities and these aspects especially interest him and appeal to him as elements with human and social equivalents.

In addition to our discovery of recurrent images and modes of thought, and imagistic patterns that have a way of repeating themselves, we have also noted the relationship of La Guma's earlier work to his more recent work. *Time of the Butcherbird,* for instance, is an expansion of La Guma's short story "Coffee for the Road," with all of the thematic and structural and character elaboration and expansiveness demanded of the novel form.

In "Coffee for the Road," one quickly notices that the nameless protagonist, an Indian woman who is travelling with her two young children, Zaida and Ray, has been replaced in the novel by the travelling English salesman, Edgar Stopes. And if we are not alerted by the car that "hurtled along the asphalt road, its tyres roaring along the black surface," ("Coffee for the Road," 85) and a similar image of Edgar Stopes driving along as "The tyres rumbled on the asphalt surface of the secondary road at low speed," we are confident of the imagistic affinity of the two works when we read:

> The car passed the sheds of a railway siding, with the sheep milling in corrals, then lurched over the crossing and bounced back on to the roadway. A Coloured man went by on a bicycle, and they drove slowly past the nondescript brown front of the Railway Hotel, a line of stores, and beyond a burnt hedge a group of white men with red, sun-skinned, wind-honed faces sat drinking at tables in front of another hotel with an imitation Dutch-colonial façade. There was other traffic parked along the dusty, gravel street of the little town: powdered cars and battered pick-up trucks, a wagon in front of a feed store. An old Coloured man swept

the pavement in front of a shop, his reed broom making a
hissing sound, like gas escaping in spurts. ("Coffee," 88)

Here the familiar images from *Time of the Butcherbird*—of sheep,
the Railway Hotel, a small town, a line of stores, dust, a Coloured
man sweeping the pavement, a bicycle rider—are all present, incu-
bating in the short story until brought to life in the following way
in the novel:

> Ahead of him the town street lay quiet under the last of
> another sweltering day, hanging out its shadows with relief
> in front of the Railway Hotel; a line of white-washed houses
> behind burnt hedges; around a speckled car and a wagon in
> front of the feed store, heads of mules drooping; from the
> Boer War monument in the dusty square and the face of the
> old church with its red concrete steps. The sun was begin-
> ning to take shape now above the flat crest of the hill with
> its white-washed boulders, slowly contracting into a disc
> of quivering red, like heated roundshot. An old coloured
> man came out of the feed store and commenced to sweep
> the sidewalk with a reed broom, and from the direction of
> the square a boy on a bicycle raised the wake of red dust,
> unnecessarily ringing his way along the otherwise deserted
> street. (*Butcherbird*, 3)

Though similar in length, the latter image has greater density and
is more complex in structure and content. Instead of "another hotel with an imitation Dutch-colonial façade," La Guma substitutes
"the Boer War monument in the dusty square and the face of the
old church with its red concrete steps." Also, the image from the
novel creates a more vivid and sensual awareness of the pervasive
atmosphere of heat by direct statement and creative allusions that
suggest this rather torrid environment. There is, for example, the
repetitive use of the color red: "red concrete steps," and the sun is
"a disc of quivering red," and "a boy on a bicycle raise the wake of
red dust." Then there are the direct and indirect references to the
heat—e.g., "another sweltering day" and "burnt hedges" and "heads
of mules drooping"—which suggest the kind of lethargy associated
with heat. And the sun is compared to "heated roundshot," while
reference to "the otherwise deserted street" may be a final re-

minder, in this image, that this is an Afrikaner town and, like most white people, they must take refuge, unable to enjoy the healing rays of the sun.

In the short story, it is the Indian woman protagonist who is the outsider; who, upon entering a small shop to get coffee for herself and her insistent children, is told by the white woman behind the counter, "A bedammed coolie girl in here!...*Coolies, Kaffirs and Hottentots* outside" (90). And her reaction foreshadows the more premeditated action of Shilling Murile. Unlike Shilling, however, her reaction is impulsive and spontaneous as she throws her flask at the white woman behind the counter, striking her forehead and causing a bleeding gash. The story ends with the woman being caught by a police roadblock and asked to follow a police car back to the small town, as the children continue to demand, "I wish we had some coffee." Also, like Timi lashed to fence-posts with wire in Christ-like imagery, "Coffee on the Road" reminds us of "the heavily pregnant Mary being turned away from every inn until the baby Jesus was born in a simple manger" (Ndebele 1994:44).

Thematically and imagistically the two works are quite alike. And even though the protagonist in one is Indian and female and in the other is English and male, both stories are about human relationships in South Africa, and about the violent consequences of racial hatred, albeit in a small, rural, closed Afrikaner town. Above all, such comparative observations are intended to illuminate the sometimes mysterious and magical process of artistic creation, while helping us recognize the consistency of La Guma's thematic interests and his image-making technique and style as peculiar to him and to no other. No matter how much he may have embellished and embroidered his material by imaginative additions, both short story and novel, ultimately, give the effect of essential truth about life as it is lived by the various cultures and people of South Africa. Alex La Guma seems always to have taken a serious view of his obligations to truth of human nature, and the moral and material environment that conditions and shapes that nature.

The primary focus of this study has been to show that the main body of his images fall into four principal areas: those that reveal theme; those that depict the environment; those that distinguish character; and those that reveal the desecration of physical bodies, including human beings, as a metaphor for the South African situation.

BIBLIOGRAPHY

A. Primary Sources: Works by or about Alex La Guma

I. Books

La Guma, Alex. *A Walk in the Night.* Ibadan, Nigeria: Mbari Publications, 1962.

___. *A Walk in the Night and Other Stories.* Evanston: Northwestern University Press, 1967.

___. *And a Threefold Cord.* Berlin: Seven Seas Press, 1964.

___. *And a Threefold Cord.* London: Kliptown Books Ltd, 1988.

___. *The Stone Country.* London: Heinemann, 1967.

___, ed. *Apartheid: A Collection of Writings on South African Racism* by South Africans. New York: International Publishers, 1971.

___. *In the Fog of the Seasons' End.* London: Heinemann, 1972.

___. *A Soviet Journey.* Moscow: Progress Publishers, 1978.

___. *Time of the Butcherbird.* London: Heinemann, 1979.

II. Short Stories

La Guma, Alex. "A Glass of Wine." *Black Orpheus: An Anthology of African and Afro-American Prose*, ed., Ullii Beier. Nigeria: Longmans, 1964.

___. "Coffee for the Road." *Modern African Stories*, eds., Ellis Ayitey Komey and Ezekiel Mphahlele. London: Faber and Faber, 1964.

___. "A Matter of Taste." *Modern African Stories*, ed., Charles R. Larson. London: Collins, 1971.

___. "Out of Darkness," "Slipper Satin," "A Glass of Wine," and "Nocturn." *Quartet: New Voices From South Africa*, ed., Richard Rive. London: Heinemann, 1965.

___. "On a Wedding Day." *Memories of Home*, ed., Cecil Abrahams. Trenton: Africa World Press, 1991.

III. Newspaper Articles by La Guma

La Guma, Alex. "Up My Alley." A weekly column by La Guma in the *Cape Town Weekly, New Age.* 2 May 1957 to 28 June 1962.
___. "A Pick and a Shovel." 30 August 1956, p. 3, cols. 2-5.
___. "Law of the Jungle Rules in Jail." 4 October 1956, p.5, cols. 1-4.
___. "A Day at Court." 1 November 1956, p. 3, cols. 1-3.
___. "Don't Sneeze - The Walls May Fall Down." 4 December 1956, p. 5, cols.2-6.
___. "They All Have Their Troubles, But Nobody Complains." 24 January 1957, p.3, cols. 2-4.
___. "Triple Wedding of Treason Accused." 7 February 1957, p.5, cols. 3-5.
___. "People's Leaders Expect Every Democrat To Do His Duty." 31 January 1957, p. 4, cols. 2-4.
___. "Christian National Education For The Coloured People." 13 June 1957, p. 5 cols. 2-5.
___. "Treason Accused Still Need Your Help." 12 September 1957, p. 6, cols. 3-5.

IV. Journal Articles by La Guma

La Guma, Alex. "From The Dicussion." *The Writer in Modern Africa.* ed., Per Wastberg. New York: Africana Publishing Corp., 1969.
___. "African Culture and National Liberation." *Journal of the New African Literature and the Arts* 8 July 1969.
___. "Literature and Life." *Afro-Asian Writings* 1, 4 (1970).
___. "The Condition of Culture in South Africa." *Presence Africaine* 80 (1971).
___. "Address by Lotus Award Winner." *Afro-Asian Writings* 10 (1971).
___. "Alex La Guma: An Interview with Robert Serumaga." Recorded: London, October 1966. *African Writers Talking,* eds., Cosmo Pieterse and Dennis Duerden. New York: Africana Publishing Corp., 1972.
___. "On Short Stories." *Afro-Asian Writings* 17 (1973).
___. "Sounds of a Cowhide Drum by Oswald Joseph Mtshali." *Afro-Asian Writings* 21 (1974).
___. "South African Writing Under Apartheid." *Afro-Asian Writings* 23 (1975).
___. "Culture and Liberation." Sechaba 10, 4 (1976).

V. New Age Editorials About La Guma and Related Subjects

"Shots Fired At New Age Reporter—Night Attempt to Murder Alex La Guma." Editorial. 15 May 1958, p. 1, cols. 1—5.

"Police Follow Up Clues In La Guma Shooting." Editorial. 22 May 1958, p.3, col. 1.

"No 'New Deal' For The Coloureds." Editorial. 22 May 1958, p. 5, cols. 2-5.

"Coloured Mass Meeting Backs African Demands." Editorial. 13 April 1961, p. 3, cols. 1-2.

"Death of Mr. Jimmy La Guma." Editorial. 3 August 1961, p. 2, cols. 4-5.

"A Tribute To Jimmy La Guma." Editorial. 24 August 1961, p. 3, cols. 1-2.

"Jimmy La Guma Memorial Fund." Editorial. 29 March 1962, p. 8, cols. 1-2.

"Non-White Salaries Cut By 30%: Discrimination At Fort Hare." Editorial. 14 June 1962, p.6, cols.1-2.

"Locked Out Of Houses—Families Scattered By Rent Ejectments." Editorial. 14 June 1962, p. 6, cols. 4-5.

"Prohibited." [Editorial] New Age 28 June 1962, p.2.

VI. Reviews and Journal Articles About La Guma

Asein, Samuel O. "The Revolutionary Vision in Alex La Guma's Novels." *Black Images: A Critical Quarterly on Black Culture* 3, 2 (1974).

Bunting, Brian. Foreword to *And a Threefold Cord*, by Alex La Guma. Berlin: Seven Seas Press, 1964.

___. Preface to *And a Threefold Cord*, by Alex La Guma. London: Kliptown Books, 1988.

Chennells, Anothony. "Alex La Guma and the South African Political Novel." *Mambo Review of Contemporary African Literature* (Salisbury), 1 November 1974.

Coetzee, J.M. "Alex La Guma and the Responsibilities of the South African Writer." *Journal of the New African Literature and the Arts* 9 (1971).

___. "Man's Fate in the Novels of Alex La Guma." *Studies in Black Literature* 5,
1 (1974).

Kibera, Leonard. "A Critical Appreciation of Alex La Guma's *In the Fog of the Seasons' End.*" Busara 8 (1976).

Kunene, Daniel. "Ideas Under Arrest: Censorship in South Africa." n.d.

Lewis, Rupert. *Rev. of In the Fog of the Seasons' End*. Black World 24, 4 (1975).

Lindfords, Bernth. "Form and Technique in the Novels of Richard Rive and Alex La Guma." *Journal of the New African Literature and the Arts* 2 (1966).

Mphahlele, Ezekiel. "Tribute to Alex La Guma." Sechaba 5, 2 (1971).

Nkosi, Lewis. "Alex La Guma - The Man and His Work." *South Africa: Information And Analysis* (Paris) 59 (January 1968).

Obuke, J. Okpure. "The Structure of Commitment: A Study of Alex La Guma." Ba Shiru 5, 1 (1973).

Rabkin, David. "La Guma and Reality in South Africa." *Journal of Commonwealth Literature* 8, 1 (1973).

Wanjala, Chris L. "The Face of Injustice: Alex La Guma's Fiction." *Standpoints on African Literature—A Critical Anthology*. East African Literature Bureau, 1973.

Whitman, Scarlet. "A Story of Resistance." *Rev. of Time of the Butcherbird. African Communist* 77 (1979).

B. Secondary Sources
I. Books Dealing with the Life and Career of La Guma

Abrahams, Cecil. *Memories of Home: The Writings of Alex La Guma*. Trenton: Africa World Press, 1991.

Cartey, Wilfred. *Whispers from a Continent: The Literature of Contemporary Black Africa*. New York: Random House, 1969.

Dathorne, O. R. *African Literature in the Twentieth Century*. Minneapolis: University of Minnesota Press, 1975.

February. Vernon, A. *Mind Your Colour: The "Coloured" Stereotype in South African Literature*. London: Kegan Paul International, Ltd., 1981.

Gakwandi, Shatto Arthur. *The Novel and Contemporary Experience in Africa*. London: Heinemann, 1980.

Heywood, Christopher, ed. *Aspects of South African Literature*. London: Heinemann, 1976.

Moore, Gerald. *The Chosen Tongue: English Writing in the Tropical World*. New York: Harper & Row, 1969.

___. *Twelve African Writers*. Bloomington: Indiana University Press, 1980.

Ndebele, Njabulo. *South African Literature and Culture: Rediscovery of the Ordinary*.Manchester: Manchester University Press, 1994.

Nkosi, Lewis. *Tasks and Masks: Themes and Styles of African Literature*. London: Longman, 1981.

Odendaal, Andre and Roger Field, eds. *Liberation Chabalala: The World of Alex La Guma*. Bellville, South Africa: Mayibuye Books, 1993.

Pieterse, Cosmo and Donald Munro, eds. *Protest and Conflict in African Literature*. New York: Africana Publishing Corp., 1969.

Roscoe, Adrian. *Uhuru's Fire: African Literature East to South*. London: Cambridge University Press, 1977.

II. Other Books

Abrahams, Peter. *Mine Boy*. New York: Collier Books, 1970.

___. *Tell Freedom*. New York: Collier Books, 1970.

___. *A Wreath for Udomo*. Collier Books, 1971.

___. *This Island Now*. Collier Books, 1971.

Achebe, Chinua. *Morning Yet on Creation Day*. London: Heinemann, 1975.

African National Congress (ANC). *The Reconstruction and Development Program*. Johannesburg: ANC, 1994.

Aidoo, Ama Ata. Introduction to *The Beautyful Ones Are Not Yet Born*, by Ayi Kwei Armah. Boston: Houghton Mifflin, 1968.

Allen, Don Cameron. *Image and Meaning: Metaphoric Traditions in Renaissance Poetry*. Baltimore: The John Hopkins Press, 1960.

Altick, Richard D. The Art of Literary Research. New York: W.W. Norton & Co., Inc., 1963.

Armah, Ayi Kwei. *The Beautyful Ones Are Not Yet Born*. Boston: Houghton Mifflin, 1968.

___. *Two Thousand Seasons*. Nairobi: East African Publishing House, 1973.

Asante, Molefi and Abu Abarry, eds. *African Intellectual Heritage: A Book of Sources*. Philadelphia: Temple University Press, 1996.

Asmal, Kader with Louise Asmal and Ronald Suresh Roberts. *Reconciliation Through Truth: A Reckoning of Apartheid's Criminal Governance*. Bellville, South Africa: Mayibuye Books, 1996.

Barker, Francis. *Solzhenitsyn: Politics and Form*. New York: Barnes & Noble, 1977.

Baldwin, James. *The Fire Next Time*. New York: Vintage International, 1962.

___. *The Evidence of Things Not Seen*. New York: Henry Holt & Co., 1985.

Barnett, Ursula A. Ezekiel Mphahlele. Boston: Twayne Publishers, 1976.

Beach, Joseph Warren. *The Technique of Thomas Hardy*. New York: Russell & Russell, 1962.

Berzon, Judith R. *Neither White Nor Black: The Mulatto Character in American Fiction*. New York: New York University Press, 1978.

Biko, Steve. *I Write What I Like: A Selection of His Writings*, ed., Aelred Stubs, C.R. New York: Harper & Row, 1978.

Boggs, James. Racism and the Class Struggle. *New York: Monthly Review*, 1970.

Booth, Wayne C. *The Rhetoric of Fiction*. Chicago: University of Chicago Press, 1961.

Breytenbach, Breyten. *A Season in Paradise: The First Part of the Acclaimed Personal Chronicle of South Africa*. New York: Harcourt Brace, 1980.

___. *The True Confessions of an Albino Terrorist: The Second Part of the Acclaimed Personal Chronicle of South Africa*. New York: Harcourt Brace, 1983.

Brooks, Jean R. *Thomas Hardy: The Poetic Structure*. Ithaca: Cornell University Press, 1971.

Burg, David and George Feifer. Solzhenitsyn. New York: Stein and Day, 1972.

Carmichael, Stokely and Charles V. Hamilton. *Black Power: The Politics of Liberation in America*. New York: Vintage Books, 1967.

Cary, Joyce. *Art and Reality: Ways of the Creative Process*. New York: Harper Brothers, Publishers, 1958.

Cell, John W. *The Highest Stage of White Supremacy: The Origins of Segregation in South Africa and the American South*. New York: Cambridge University Press, 1982.

Chesnutt, Charles W. *The House Behind the Cedars*. New York: Collier Books, 1971.

Chinweizu, Onwuchekwa Jemie and Ihechukwu Madubuike. *Toward the Decolonization of African Literature: African Fiction and Poetry and Their Critics*. Volume 1. Washington, D.C.: Howard University Press, 1983.

Coetzee, J.M. *Life and Times of Michael K*. New York: Penguin, 1983.

___. *Giving Offense: Essays on Censorship*. Chicago: University of Chicago Press, 1996.

Cook, David. *African Literature A Critical View*. London: Longman, 1977.

Cox, Oliver Cromwell. *Caste, Class & Race: A Study in Social Dynamics*. New York: Monthly Review Press, 1959; Rpt. *Modern Reader Paperback*, 1970.

Craig, David, ed. *Marxists on Literature*. Baltimore: Penguin Books, 1975.

Bibliography

Crais, Clifton. *The Making of a Colonial Order: White Supremacy and Black Resistance in the Western Cape, 1770-1865*. Johannesburg: Witwatersrand University Press, 1992. Quoted in Bernard Magubane, *The Making of a Racist State:British Imperialism and the Union of South Africa, 1875-1910* (Trenton: Africa World Press, 1994), 74.

Dangor, Achmat. *The Z Town Trilogy*. Johannesburg: Ravan Press, 1990.

Davis, Angela. *Women Race & Class*. New York: Vintage Books, 1983.

___. *Blues Legacies and Black Feminism*. New York: Pantheon Books, 1998.

Davis, Charles T. *Black is the Color of the Cosmos: Essays on Afro-American Literature and Culture, 1942-1981*. Washington,D.C.: Howard University Press, 1982.

Davidson, Basil. *The Lost Cities of Africa*. Boston: Little Brown, 1959, rpt., 1970.

___. *Africa in History: Themes and Outlines*. New York: The Macmillan Co., 1968.

___. *The Black Man's Burden: Africa and the Curse of the Nation-State*. New York: Random House, 1992.

Degler, Carl N. *Neither Black Nor White: Slavery and Race Relations in Brazil and The United States*. New York: Macmillan, 1971.

De Kiewiet, C.W. *A History of South Africa: Social & Economic*. London: Oxford University Press, 1968.

Dell, Floyd. *Upton Sinclair: A Study in Social Protest*. New York: AMS Press, 1927.

Desmond, Cosmas. *The Discarded People: An Account of African Resettlement in South Africa*. Baltimore: Penguin Books, 1971.

Deutschmann, David, ed. *Changing the History of Africa: Angola and Namibia*. Melbourne: Ocean Press, 1989.

Devisse, Jean. *The Image of the Black in Western Art: From the Early Christian Era to the Age of Discovery*. New York: William Morrow, 1979.

Du Bois, W.E.B. *The Souls of Black Folk*. Chicago: A.C. McClurg & Co., 1903.

___. *The World and Africa*. New York: International Publishers, 1965.

___. "Karl Marx and the Negro." *The Crisis* 40, 3 (March 1933).

Eagleton, Terry. *Criticism and Ideology "A Study in Marxist Literary Theory."* Atlantic Highlands: Humanities Press, 1976.

Edel, Leon. *The Modern Psychological Novel*. New York: Grosset & Dunlap, 1964.

Egbert, Donald Drew. *Social Radicalism and the Arts: Western Europe. A Cultural History from the French Revolution to 1968*. New York: Alfred Knopf, 1970.

Egejuru, Phanuel Akubueze. *Black Writers: White Audience. A Critical Approach to African Literature.* Hicksvill, New York: Exposition Press, 1978.

Ehrmann, Jacques. *Structuralism.* Garden City, New York: Anchor Books, 1970.

Ericson, Edward E., Jr. *Solzhenitsyn: The Moral Vision.* Grand Rapids: William B. Eerdmans Publishing Company, 1980.

Fabre, Michel. *The Unfinished Quest of Richard Wright.* Trans. Isabel Barzun. New York: William Morrow & Co., Inc., 1973.

Fanon, Frantz. *Black Skin White Masks: The Experience of a Black Man in a White World.* New York: Grove Press, Inc., 1967.

___. *The Wretched of the Earth.* Trans. Constance Farrington. New York: Grove Press, Inc., 1981.

February, Vernon A. *Mind Your Colour: The "Coloured" Stereotype in South African Literature.* London: Kegan Paul International, Ltd., 1981.

Fisher, Ernst. *Art Against Ideology.* New York: George Braziller, 1969.

Foster, E.M. *Aspects of the Novel.* New York: Harcourt, Brace & World, Inc., 1954.

Franklin, John Hope, ed. *Color and Race.* Boston: Houghton Mifflin, 1968.

___. *The Color Line: Legacy for the Twenty-First Century.* Columbia, Mo.: University of Missouri Press, 1993.

Fraser, Robert. *The Novels of Ayi Kwei Armah: A Study in Polemical Fiction.* London: Heinemann, 1980.

Frazier, E. Franklin. *Race and Culture Contacts in the Modern World.* New York: Alfred Knopf, 1957.

___. *The Black Bourgeoisie.* Glencoe: Free Press, 1957.

Fredrickson, George M. *White Supremacy: A Comparative Study in American & South African History.* New York: Oxford University Press, 1981.

Gakwandi, Shatto Arthur. *The Novel and Contemporary Experience in Africa.* London: Heinemann, 1980.

Gayle, Addison Jr. *The Black Aesthetic.* New York: Doubleday, 1971.

Gerhart, Gail M. *Black Power in South Africa: The Evolution of an Ideology.* Berkeley: University of California Press, 1978.

___, and Thomas Karis. *From Protest to Challenge.* 4 vols. Standford, Calif.: Hoover Institution Press, 1977.

Gibson, Richard. *African Liberation Movements: Contemporary Struggles Against White Minority Rule.* London: Oxford University Press, 1972.

Goldhagen, Daniel J. *Hitler's Willing Executioners: Ordinary Germans and the Holocaust.* New York: Alfred A. Knopf, 1996.

Gordimer, Nadine. *Crimes of Conscience*. London: Heinemann, 1991.

Grace, William J. *Response to Literature*. New York: McGraw Hill, 1965.

Grier, William H. and Price Cobbs. *Black Rage*. New York: Basic Books, 1968.

Grimsditch, Herbert B. *Character and Environment in the Novels of Thomas Hardy*. New York: Russell & Russell, 1962.

Gross, Seymour L. and John Edward Hardy, eds. *Images of the Negro in American Literature*. Chicago: University of Chicago Press, 1966.

Hachten, William A. *Muffled Drums: The News Media in Africa*. Ames: The Iowa State University Press, 1971.

Harvey, W.J. *Character and the Novel*. Ithaca: Cornell University Press, 1965.

Hemenway, Robert, ed. *The Black Novelist*. Columbus: Charles E. Merrill, 1970.

Hersey, John, ed. Ralph Ellison: *A Collection of Critical Essays*. Englewood Cliffs: Prentice-Hall, 1974.

Heywood, Christopher, ed. *Perspectives on African Literature*. New York: Africana Publishing Corp., 1971.

___, ed. *Aspects of South African Literature*. London: Heinemann, 1976.

Higginbotham, Leon A. Jr. *In the Matter of Color: Race and the American Legal Process*. New York: Oxford University Press, 1978.

Hirsch, E.D. Jr. *Validity in Interpretation*. New Haven: Yale University Press, 1967.

Howe, Irving. *Politics and the Novel*. New York: Meridian Books, 1957.

Jahn, Janheinz. *Neo-African Literature: A History of Black Writing*. New York: Grove Press, 1968.

James, Henry. *The Art of the Novel: Critical Prefaces*. New York: Charles Scribner's Sons, 1962.

Jameson, Fredric. *Marxism and Form: Twentieth Century Dialectical Theories of Literature*. Princeton: Princeton University Press, 1974.

Jones, LeRoi. *Blues People: Negro Music in White America*. Westport, Conn.: Greenwood Press, 1963.

___. *The Autobiography of LeRoi Jones/Amiri Baraka*. New York: Freundlich Books, 1984.

Jordan, A.C. *Tales from Southern Africa*. Berkeley: University of California Press, 1973.

Jordan, Winthrop D. *White Over Black: Historical Origins of Racism in the United States*. New York: Oxford University Press, 1974.

Kane, Cheikh Hamidou. *Ambiguous Adventure*. New York: Heinemann, 1972.

Karenga, Ron M. *Essays on Struggle: Position and Analysis*. San Diego: Kawaida Publications, 1978.

Kearns, Francis E., ed. *The Black Experience: An Anthology of American Literature for the 1970's*. New York: The Viking Press, 1970.

Killiam, G.D. ed. *African Writers on African Writing*. Evanston: Northwestern University Press, 1970.

King, Adele. *The Writings of Camara Laye*. London: Heinemann, n.d.

Kunene, Daniel. *Heroic Poetry of the Basotho*. London: Oxford University Press, 1971.

___. *Pirates Have Become Our Kings*. Nairobi: East African Publishing House, 1978.

___. *A Seed Must Seem to Die*. Johannesburg: Ravan Press, 1981.

___. Trans. Chaka. London: Heinemann, 1981.

___. *Thomas Mofolo and the Emergence of Written Sesotho Prose*. Johannesburg: Ravan Press, 1989.

Kunene, Mazisi. Zulu Poems. New York: Africana, 1970.

___. *Emperor Shaka the Great: A Zulu Epic*. London: Heinemann, 1979.

Lamb, David. *The Africans*. New York: Random House, 1982.

Laurence, Margaret. *Long Drums and Canons: Nigerian Dramatists and Novelists*. New York: Frederic A. Praeger, 1969.

Lessing, Doris. *Prisons We Choose to Live Inside*. New York: Harper & Row, 1987.

Lewis, C. Day. *The Poetic Image*. London: Jonathan Cape, 1946; Rpt. Fair Lawn: Essential Books, 1958.

Lubbock, Percy. *The Craft of Fiction*. New York: Peter Smith, 1947.

Lukacs, Georg. *The Historical Novel*. Trans. Hannah and Stanley Mitchell. Boston: Beacon Press, 1963.

___. *Writer & Critic*. Trans. Arthur D. Kahn. New York: Grosset & Dunlap, 1974.

___. *The Theory of the Novel: A Historico-Philosophical Essay on the Forms of Great Epic Literature*. Trans. Anna Bostock. Cambridge: The MIT Press, 1975.

Magona, Sindiwe. *To My Children's Children*. New York: Interlink Books, 1990.

___. *Living Loving, and Lying Awake at Night*. New York: Interlink Books, 1991.

___. *Forced to Grow*. New York: Interlink Books, 1992.

Magubane, Bernard M. *The Making of a Racist State: British Imperialism and the Union of South Africa, 1875-1910*. Trenton: Africa World Press, 1996.

___. *The Ties That Bind: African American Consciousness of Africa*. Trenton: Africa World Press, 1994.

Bibliography

Mandela, Nelson. *Long Walk to Freedom: The Autobiography.* New York: Little, Brown and Co., 1994.

Matshoba, Mtutuzeli. *Call Me Not A Man.* Johannesburg: Ravan Press, 1979.

Memmi, Albert. *The Colonizer and the Colonized.* Boston: Beacon Press, 1967.

Modisane, Bloke. *Blame Me on History.* New York: E.P. Dutton & Co., 1963.

Moore, Gerald. *The Chosen Tongue: English Writing in the Tropical World.* New York: Harper & Row, 1969.

___. *Twelve African Writers.* Bloomington: Indiana University Press, 1980.

Morrison, Toni. *The Bluest Eye.* New York: Plume, 1994.

Mphahlele, Ezekiel. *Down Second Avenue.* Garden City: Doubleday & Co., 1971.

___. *Voices in the Whirlwind and Other Essays.* New York: Hill and Wang, 1972.

Mutiso, G-C. M. *Socio-Political Thought in African Literature*: Weusi? New York:Barnes & Noble, 1974.

Ngara, Emanuel. *Stylistic Criticism and the African Novel: A Study of the Language, Art and Content of African Fiction.* London: Heinemann, 1982.

Nkosi, Lewis. *Tasks and Masks: Themes and Styles of African Literature.* London: Longman, 1981.

Nkrumah, Kwame. *Class Struggle in Africa.* New York: International Publishers, 1970.

Obiechina, Emmanuel. *Language and Theme: Essays on African Literature.* Washington, D.C.: Howard University Press, 1990.

O'Meally, Robert G. *The Craft of Ralph Ellison.* Cambridge: Harvard University Press, 1980.

Padmore, George. *Pan-Africanism or Communism.* New York: Doubleday, 1971.

Palmer, Eustace. *The Growth of the African Novel.* London: Heinemann, 1979.

Patterson-Mudavanha, David. *The Constitution: An Ex-Slave Interpretation.* Diss. Berkeley: University of California, 1978.

Pieterse, Cosmo and Dennis Duerden, eds. African Writers Talking. New York: Africana Publishing Co., 1972.

Pinion, F.B. *Thomas Hardy: Art and Thought.* Totowa, N.J.: Rowman and Littlefield, 1977.

Redd, Teresa, ed. *Revelations: An Anthology of Expository Essays By and About Blacks.* Needham Heights, Mass: Simon & Schuster, 1997.

Rive, Richard. *Emergency*. London: Collier-Macmillan, Ltd., 1970.

___. Emergency Continued. Cape Town: David Philip, 1990.

___. "Buckingham Palace," District Six. Cape Town: David Philip, 1986.

Robinson, Cedric J. *Black Marxism: The Making of the Black Radical Tradition*. London: Zed Press, 1983.

Robinson, Randall. *Defending the Spirit: A Black Life in America*. New York: Dutton, 1998.

Rodney, Walter. *How Europe Underdeveloped Africa*. Washington, D.C.: Howard University Press, 1981.

___. "Toward the Sixth Pan African Congress: Aspects of the International Class Struggle in Africa, the Caribbean, and America." In *African Intellectual Tradition*, eds. Asante, Molefi and Abu Abarry. Philadelphia: Temple University Press, 1996.

Rosen, Robert C. *John Dos Passos: Politics and the Writer*. Lincoln: University of Nebraska Press, 1981.

Ross, Robert, ed. *Racism and Colonialism: Essays on Ideology and Social Structure*. Leiden: Martinus Nijhoff, 1982.

Russell, Kathy, Midge Wilson and Ronald Hall. *The Color Complex: The Politics of Skin Color Among African Americans*. New York: Harcourt, Brace, Jovanovich, 1992.

Said, Edward W. *Culture and Imperialism*. New York: Alfred Knopf, 1993.

Sartre, Jean-Paul. *What is Literature?* Trans. Bernard Frechtman. New York: Harper & Row, 1965.

Scholes, Robert. *Structuralism in Literature*. New Haven: Yale University Press, 1976a.

___ and Robert Kellogg. *The Nature of Narrative*. London: Oxford University Press, 1976b.

Sepamla, Sipho. *The Soweto I Love*. London: Rex Collings, 1977.

Setchkarev, Vsevolod. *Gogol: His Life and Works*. Trans. Robert Kramer. New York: New York University Press, 1965.

Shore, Herbert L. and Megchelina Shore-Bos. *Come Back Africa: Fourteen Short Stories from South Africa*. New York: International Publishers, 1970.

Simmons, Ernest J. *Introduction to Russian Realism*. Bloomington: Indiana University Press, 1965.

Spurgeon, Caroline F.E. *Shakespeare's Imagery and What it Tells Us*. Boston: Beacon Press, 1958.

Stern, J.P. *On Realism*. Boston: Routledge & Kegan Paul, 1973.

Swingewood, Allen. *The Novel and Revolution*. New York: Barnes & Noble, 1975.

Tocqueville, Alexis De. *Democracy in America*. New York: Doubleday, 1969.

Trotsky, Leon. *Literature and Revolution*. Ann Arbor: The University of Michigan Press, 1975.

Turkington, Kate. *Chinua Achebe: Things Fall Apart*. London: Edward Arnold, 1977.

Tutu, Desmond. *The Rainbow People of God: The Making of a Peaceful Revolution*. New York: Doubleday, 1994.

Twain, Mark. *The Adventures of Huckleberry Finn*. New York: Harper & Brothers, 1884.

Twine, France Winddance. *Racism in a Racial Democracy: The Maintenance of White Supremacy in Brazil*. New Brunswick, New Jersey: Rutgers University Press, 1998.

Ullman, Stephen. *The Image in the Modern French Novel*. Cambridge: Cambridge University Press, 1960.

U.S. Congr. Subcommittee on Africa of the Committee on Foreign Affairs. Hearings. 92nd. Congr., 1st Sess. Part 2. Washington, D.C.: GPO, 1972.

U.S. Congr. *Report of Special Study Missions to Africa. The Faces of Africa: Diversity and Progress: Repression and Struggle*. 92nd. Cong., 2nd Sess. Washington, D.C.: GPO, 1972.

Wagner, Kathrin. *Rereading Nadine Gordimer*. Johannesburg: Witwatersrand University Press, 1994.

Wastberg, Per, ed. *The Writer in Modern Africa*. New York: Africana Publishing Corporation, 1969.

Wa Thiongo, Ngugi. *Homecoming: Essays on African and Caribbean Literature, Culture and Politics*. London: Heinemann, 1975.

___. *Writers in Politics*. London: Heinemann, 1981.

___. *Moving the Centre: The Struggle for Cultural Freedoms*. Portsmouth, NH., 1993.

Watt, Ian. *The Rise of the Novel*. Berkeley: University of California Press, 1962.

Wellek, Rene and Austin Warren. *Theory of Literature*. New York: Harcourt, Brace & World, Inc., 1970.

Welsing, Francis. *The Isis Papers: The Keys to the Colors*. Chicago: Third World Press, 1991.

Williams, Chancellor. *The Destruction of Black Civilization: Great Issues of a Race From 4500 BC to 2000 AD*. Chicago: Third World Press, 1976.

Wilson, Monica and Leonard Thompson. *The Oxford History of South Africa*. 2 vols. London: Oxford University Press, 1971.

Winter, Gordon. *Inside BOSS.* New York: Penguin Books, 1981.

Wolf, Naomi. *The Beauty Myth: How Images of Beauty are used Against Women.* New York: Doubleday, 1991.

Woods, Donald. *Biko.* New York: Paddington Press, 1978.

III. Other Articles

Achebe, Chinua. "Thoughts on the African Novel." Dalhousie Review 53 (1974): 631-37.

___. "What Do African Intellectuals Read?" *Times Literary Supplement,* 12 May 1972, p. 547.

Asein, Samuel O. "The Impact of the New World on Modern African Literature." Comparative Literature Studies 14 (1977): 74-93.

Awoonor, Kofi. "Tradition and Continuity in African Literature." *Dalhousie Review* 53 (1974): 665-71.

___. "Nationalism: Masks and Consciousness." Books Abroad 45 (1971): 207-11.

Bishop, Rand. "African Critics and the Western Literary Tradition." Ba Shiru 8, 1 (1977): 65-75.

___. "On Identifying a Standard of African Literary Criticism: Characterization in the Novel." *Journal of the New African Literature and the Arts* 11/12 (1971): 1-18.

Brandford, William. "Literature Across Cultures." English Studies in Africa 13 (1970): 37-49.

Breytenbach, Breyten. 1971 "Vulture Culture: The Alienation of White South Africa." In *Apartheid: A Collection of Writings on South African Racism by South Africans,* edited by Alex La Guma. New York: International Publishers.

Burness, Donald. "Six Responses to Apartheid." Presence Africaine 76 (1970): 82-95.

Dorsinville, Max. "Levels of Ambiguity in the African Novel." *Canadian Journal of African Studies* 5 (1971): 213-25.

Duodu, Cameron. "The Literary Critic and Social Realities." Legon Observer 4, vi (1969): 24-26.

Dzeagu, S.A. "The Criticism of Modern African Literature." Universitas 3, iii (1974): 134-140.

Gerard, Albert. "Preservation of Tradition in African Creative Writing." *Research in African Literature* 1 (1970): 35-39.

Gordimer, Nadine. "One Man Living Through It." Classic 2, 1 (1966): 11-16.

___. "South Africa: Towards a Desk Drawer Literature." Classic 2, iv (1968): 64-74.

___. "How Not to Know the African." Contrast 15 (1967): 44-49.

___. "Politics: A Dirtier Word Than Sex!" Solidarity 3, xi (1968): 69-71.

Henderson, Lennel J. *Rev. of The Black Experience: Analysis and Synthesis*, by Charles Young, ed. In The Black Scholar 39 (1963): 57.

hooks, bell. 1997. "Straightening Our Hair." In *Revelations*, edited by Teresa Redd. Needham Heights, Mass.: Simon & Schuster.

Irele, Abiola. "A New Mood in the African Novel." West Africa, 20 September 1969, pp. 1113-15.

Ismail, Ezzedine. "Afro-Asian Literature: Its Nature and the Role it Plays Against Imperialist Aggression, Racial Discrimination and Zionism." *Lotus: Afro-Asian Writings* 20 (1974): 41-60.

Izevbaye, Dan S. "The State of Criticism in African Literature." *African Literature Today* 7 (1975): 1-19.

Jahn, Janheinz. "Freedom in Exile: On the Mobility of African Writers." *Pan-African Journal* 4, iv (1971): 473-76.

Kunene, Daniel P. "The Crusading Writer, His Modes, Themes and Styles." *African Perspectives* 1 (1977): 99-112.

___. "Deculturation: The African Writer's Response." *Africa Today* 15, iv (1968): 19-24.

Kunene, Mazisi. "Revolutionary Challenges and Cultural Perspectives." *Journal of the New African Literature and the Arts* 7/8 (1969-70): 93-98.

Larson, Charles R. "African-Afro-American Literary Relations: Basic Parallels." *Negro Digest* 19, ii (1969): 35-42.

___. "Whither the African Novel?" College Language Association Journal 13 (1969): 144-52.

___. "Patterns of African Fiction." Dissertation Abstracts International 31 (1971): 3508A.

Lewis, Primila. "Politics and the Novel: An Appreciation of A Wreath for Udomo and This Island Now by Peter Abrahams." Zuka 2 (1968): 41-47.

Maclennan, Dan. "The South African Short Story." English Studies in Africa 13 (1970): 105-123.

Malcolm X. 1996. "Message to the Grassroots." In African Intellectual History. Asante, Molefi and Abu Abarry, eds. Philadelphia: Temple University Press.

Nwoga, Donatus I. "Humanitarianism and Criticism of African Literature, 1770-1810." Research in African Literature 3 (1972): 171-179.

___. "Shadows of Christian Civilization: The Image of the Educated African in African Literature." *Presence Africaine* 79 (1971): 34-50.

___. "The Limitations of Universal Literary Criteria." *Ufahamu* 4, I (1973):10-33.

Obumselu, Ben. "African Eden: Cultural Nationalism in the African Novel." Ibadan Studies in English 2 (1970): 131-155.

Oculi, Okello. "Applied Literature and Social Imagination in Africa." *East African Journal* 7, viii (1970): 7-20.

Okpaku, Joseph. "The Artist and Politics: The Dynamics of Contemporary African Society." *Journal of the New African Literature and the Arts* 7/8 (1969): 49-55.

Onoge, Omafume F. "The Crisis of Consciousness in Modern African Literature: A Survey." *Canadian Journal of African Studies* 8 (1974): 385-410.

Oyugi, Edward. "Critical Literature and Revolutionary Moratorium." Joliso 1, ii (1973): 41-44.

Partridge, A.C. "The Novel of Social Purpose in South Africa." *South African P.E.A. Year Book 1956-1957.* Johannesburg: International P.E.N. Club, p.64.

Povey, John. "African Literature's Widening Range." *Africa Report* 14, v-vi (1969): 67-69.

Sands, Raymond. "The South African Novel: Some Observations." *English Studies in Africa 13 (1970): 89-104.*

Sepamla, Sipho. "The Black Writer in South Africa Today: Problems and Dilemmas." *New Classic* 3 (1976): 18-26.

Shelton, Austin J. "Critical Criteria for the Study of African Literature." *Literature East and West* 12, I (1968): 1-21.

Tanna, Laura. "African Literature and Its Western Critics." Abbia 27-28 (1974): 53-63.

Tucker, Martin. "Color and Guilt." *Africa Today* 12, ii (1965): 13-14.

Uka, Kalu. "From Commitment to Essence: A View of African Writing." Muse 8 (1976): 42-52.

Wauthier, Claude. "No Ebony Tower for African Writers." Optima 18 (1968): 194-200.

INDEX

Abrahams, Cecil 127
African Nationalism 152
African nationalism
    93, 120, 121, 132, 152
Afrikaner 15, 231, 234, 236-238,
    241, 243-245, 247, 249, 252,
    255, 257, 260, 273
Armah, Ayi Kwei 36
Asein, Samuel Omo 47
Asmal, Louise 227
Aidoo, Ama Ata 26

Baldwin, James 36, 123, 149
Bantustan 53, 196, 228
Berzon, Judith 14
Biko, Steven 30
Black Consciousness 116-117, 125
Boggs, James 115-116
Booth, Wyane 20
Breytenbach, Breyten 53
Bunting, Brian 46-47

Capitalism 5, 37, 88, 94, 97-99,
    156, 162-163, 228, 249, 267
Cartey, Wilfred 68-69, 74, 80, 83
Cary, Joyce 25
Chinweizu, Onwuchekwa Jemie
    14, 22
Color consciousness 95-96, 98,
    100-101
Colorism 19, 21-22, 44, 178
Communism 4, 97-98, 132-
    133, 151
Crais, Clifton 235
Crosby, Bing 82

Davidson, Basil 242, 254
Davis, Angela 149
Debs, Eugene 160
Desmond, Cosmos 223
DeToquville 127
Devisse, Jean 99
Dingaan 232
District Six 4-5, 10-12, 14-15, 19-
    21, 29, 32-33, 54, 128-129,
    207
Drake, St. Clair 22
DuBois, W.E.B. 91, 93, 132
Dutch Reform Church 270

Fanon, Frantz 92, 151, 175, 267
February, Basil 178
February, Vernon 51, 56-57, 110,
    188

Gerhart, Gail M. 149
Gibson, Richard 151
Goldhagen, Daniel J. 10
Gordimer, Nadine 14
Grimsditch, Herbert 53

Hamidou, Cheikh Kane 36
Hamlet 38
Holocaust 173
hooks, bell 109
Howe, Irving 132
Hughes, Langston 27, 225

Ideology 18, 40, 91, 97-98, 108,
    134, 151-152, 162, 169, 174,
    194, 254-255

Jordan, Winthrop 94

Karenga, Maulana 150
Kellogg, Robert 13
Kunene, Daniel 21, 32, 34-35, 45
Kunene, Mazisi 177

Lukacs, Georg 18
Lumumba, Patrice 132

Magubane, Bernard 235
Malcolm X 94, 121
Mandela, Nelson 179
Marx, Karl 97
Memmi, Albert 96, 174
Middle Ages 99
Modisane, Bloke 147
Moore, Gerald 139, 146
Mulatto 14, 91, 105-106, 111, 115, 124, 149
Multiracial 90, 108, 132, 151
Myth of white supremacy 47, 49, 53, 71, 89, 126, 128, 134, 147, 158, 164, 173, 253

Nationalism 93, 97-98, 120, 132, 152, 187
Ndebele, Njabulo 43, 179, 236, 242, 245
Negritude 110
Nkosi, Lewis 6, 40, 97, 131, 178
Nkrumah, Kwame 132
Nyerere, Julius 132

Pan-African Congress (PAC) 152, 180
Padmore, George 132
Pass laws 195, 267
Passes 85, 126, 177-178, 213

Rabkin, David 75
Reconstruction and Developent Programme (RDP) 43
Rive, Richard 15
Roberts, Ronald 227
Rodney, Walter 93, 133

Sartre 204, 246, 257, 265
Scholes, Robert 13
separate development 101, 125, 226, 235, 237, 255
Snowden, Frank M., Jr. 99
Suppression of Communism Act 4

Toure, Sekou 132

Verwoerd, Hendrik 256

white supremacy myth 270
Williams, Chancellor 98, 112
Winters, Gordon 181
Wolf, Naomi 108
Wright, Richard 1

Zedong, Mao 189